What They Say about Us

"One organization with a long record of success
in helping people find jobs is The Five O'Clock Club."
FORTUNE

"Many managers left to fend for themselves are turning to the camaraderie
O'Clock Club]. Members share tips and advice, and hear experts."
The Wall Street Jou

"If you have been out of work for some time . . . consider The Five O'Clock Club."
The New York Times

"Wendleton has reinvented the historic gentlemen's fraternal oasis and built it into a chain of strategy clubs for job seekers."
The Philadelphia Inquirer

"Organizations such as The Five O'Clock Club are building . . . an extended professional family."
Jessica Lipnack, author, *Professional Teams*

"[The Five O'Clock Club] will ask not what you do, but 'What do you want to do?' . . . [And] don't expect to get any great happy hour drink specials at this joint. The seminars are all business."
The Washington Times

"The Five O'Clock Club's proven philosophy is that job hunting is a learned skill like any other. The Five O'Clock Club becomes the engine that drives [your] search."
Black Enterprise

"Job hunting is a science at The Five O'Clock Club. [Members] find the discipline, direction and much-needed support that keeps a job search on track."
Modern Maturity

"Wendleton tells you how to beat the odds—even in an economy where pink slips are more common than perks. Her savvy and practical guide[s] are chockablock with sample résumés, cover letters, worksheets, negotiating tips, networking suggestions and inspirational quotes from such far-flung achievers as Abraham Lincoln, Malcolm Forbes, and Lily Tomlin."
Working Woman

What Job Hunters Say

"During the time I was looking for a job, I kept Kate's books by my bed. I read a little every night, a little every morning. Her common-sense advice, methodical approach, and hints for keeping the spirits up were extremely useful."
Harold Levine, coordinator, Yale Alumni Career Resource Network

"I've just been going over the books with my daughter, who is 23 and finally starting to think she ought to have a career. She won't listen to anything I say, but you she believes."
Newspaper columnist

"Thank you, Kate, for all your help. I ended up with four offers and at least 15 compliments in two months. Thanks!"
President and CEO, large banking organization

"I have doubled my salary during the past five years by using The Five O'Clock Club techniques. Now I earn what I deserve. I think everyone needs The Five O'Clock Club."
M. S., attorney, entertainment industry

"I dragged myself to my first meeting, totally demoralized. Ten weeks later, I chose from among job offers and started a new life. Bless You!"
Senior editor, not-for-profit

"I'm an artistic person, and I don't think about business. Kate provided the disciplined business approach so I could practice my art. After adopting her system, I landed a role on Broadway in Hamlet."
Bruce Faulk, actor

"I've referred at least a dozen people to The Five O'Clock Club since I was there. The Club was a major factor in getting my dream job, which I am now in."
B. R., research head

"My Five O'Clock Club coach was a God-Send!!! She is truly one of the most dynamic and qualified people I've ever met. Without her understanding and guidance, I wouldn't have made the steps I've made toward my goals."
Operating room nurse

"The Five O'Clock Club has been a fantastic experience for my job search. I couldn't have done it without you. Keep up the good work."
Former restaurant owner, who found his dream job with
an organization that advises small businesses

What Human Resources Executives Say about
The Five O'Clock Club Outplacement

"**This thing works.** *I saw a structured, yet nurturing, environment where individuals searching for jobs positioned themselves for success. I saw 'accountability' in a nonintimidating environment. I was struck by the support and willingness to encourage those who had just started the process by the group members who had been there for a while.*"

Employee relations officer, financial services organization

"**Wow! I was immediately struck by the electric atmosphere** *and people's commitment to following the program. Job hunters reported on where they were in their searches and what they had accomplished the previous week. The overall environment fosters sharing and mutual learning.*"

Head of human resources, major law firm

"*The Five O'Clock Club program is* **far more effective** *than conventional outplacement. Excellent materials, effective coaching and nanosecond responsiveness combine to get people focused on the central tasks of the job search. Selecting The Five O'Clock Club Outplacement Program was one of my best decisions this year.*"

Sr. vice president, human resources, manufacturing company

"**You have made me look like a real genius** *in recommending The Five O'Clock Club [to our divisions around the country]!*"

Sr. vice president, human resources, major publishing firm

Go to our website
www.fiveoclockclub.com
Join our mailing list and receive FREE periodic
emailings on job search or career development.

The Five O'Clock Club®

FInd your personal path in job search and career success

Mastering the Job Interview
and Winning
the Money Game

KATE WENDLETON

CENGAGE
Learning®

Professional • Technical • Reference

Australia • Canada • Mexico • Singapore • Spain • United Kingdom • United States

CENGAGE Learning

Professional • Technical • Reference

Mastering the Job Interview and Winning the Money Game
Kate Wendleton

Vice President, Career Education SBU: Dawn Gerrain
Director of Editorial: Sherry Gomoll
Publisher and General Manager,
Cengage Learning PTR: Stacy L. Hiquet
Associate Director of Marketing: Sarah Panella
Manager of Editorial Services: Heather Talbot
Senior Marketing Manager: Mark Hughes
Acquisitions Editors: Martine Edwards and Mitzi Koontz
Developmental Editor: Kristen Shenfield
Editorial Assistant: Jennifer Anderson
Director of Production: Wendy A. Troeger
Production Manager: J.P. Henkel
Production Editor: Rebecca Goldthwaite
Technology Project Manager: Sandy Charette
Director of Marketing: Wendy E. Mapstone
Channel Manager: Gerard McAvey
Marketing Coordinator: Erica Conley
Cover Design: TDB Publishing Services
Text Design: Bookwrights

All images © Cengage Learning unless otherwise noted.
Cartoons courtesy © Jerry King of Cartoons, Inc.
For product information and technology assistance, contact us at Cengage Learning Customer & Sales Support, 1-800-354-9706
For permission to use material from this text or product, submit all requests online at cengage.com/permissions
Further permissions questions can be emailed to permissionrequest@cengage.com

Cengage Learning PTR
20 Channel Center Street
Boston, MA 02210
USA

Cengage Learning is a leading provider of customized learning solutions with office locations around the globe, including Singapore, the United Kingdom, Australia, Mexico, Brazil, and Japan. Locate your local office at: **international.cengage.com/region**

Cengage Learning products are represented in Canada by Nelson Education, Ltd.

For your lifelong learning solutions, visit **cengageptr.com**
Visit our corporate website at **cengage.com** For your lifelong learning solutions, visit **cengageptr.com**
Visit our corporate website at **cengage.com**

For information, please contact: The Five O'Clock Club®
300 East 40th Street
New York, New York 10016 www.fiveoclockclub.com

Library of Congress Cataloging-in-Publication Data
Mastering the Job Interview and Winning the Money Game/ Kate Wendleton.
p. cm.
"The Five O'Clock Club."
Includes index.
ISBN 978-1-285-75349-2

2013937126

NOTICE TO THE READER

Publisher does not warrant or guarantee any of the products described herein or perform any independent analysis in connection with any of the product information contained herein. Publisher does not assume, and expressly disclaims, any obligation to obtain and include information other than that provided to it by the manufacturer.

The reader is expressly warned to consider and adopt all safety precautions that might be indicated by the activities herein and to avoid all potential hazards. By following the instructions contained herein, the reader willingly assumes all risks in connection with such instructions.

The Publisher makes no representation or warranties of any kind, including but not limited to the warranties of fitness for particular purpose or merchantability, nor are any such representations implied with respect to the material set forth here in, and the publisher takes no responsibility with respect to such material. The publisher shall not be liable for any special, consequential, or exemplary damages resulting, in whole or part, from the readers' use of, or reliance upon, this material.

The authors and Cengage Learning affirm that the Web site URLs referenced herein were accurate at the time of printing. However, due to the fluid nature of the Internet, we cannot guarantee their accuracy for the life of the edition. The authors and Thomson Delmar Learning affirm that the Web site URLs referenced herein were accurate at the time of printing. However, due to the fluid nature of the Internet, we cannot guarantee their accuracy for the life of the edition.

Perhaps the truth lies in what most of the world outside the modern
West has always believed, namely that there are
practices of life, good in themselves, that are inherently fulfilling.

Perhaps work that is intrinsically rewarding
is better for human beings than work
that is only extrinsically rewarded.

Perhaps enduring commitment to those we love
and civic friendship toward our fellow citizens
are preferable to restless competition
and anxious self-defense.

Perhaps common worship,
in which we express our gratitude and wonder
in the face of the mystery of being itself,
is the most important thing of all.

If so, we will have to change our lives
and begin to remember
what we have been happier to forget.

Robert N. Bellah, Richard Madsen, William Sullivan,
Ann Swindler, and Steven Tipton, *Habits of the Heart*

Preface

Dear Member or Prospective Member of The Five O'Clock Club:

I am very happy to bring you this book.

When I started The Five O'Clock Club in Philadelphia in 1978, professionals and managers who were job hunting came to my apartment every Thursday evening. Career coaches from corporations and consulting firms taught us their job-hunting techniques, and I will be forever grateful to those experts who helped us get started. We were able to compare their approaches. We experimented. We tried various job-hunting techniques and reported our results back to the group.

At The Five O'Clock Club, it was not enough for us to learn about job hunting. We wanted to learn about the job *hiring* process. What happens when your résumé crosses the desk of a hiring manager? How effective are direct-mail campaigns? Why does one person find a job quickly, while someone else takes longer—even though both work hard and are equally well qualified?

This book series answers those questions. We found that there is no one job-hunting technique that works. Job-hunting formulas hold true in the aggregate but may not for a specific situation. The techniques that work depend, to a large extent, on the industry in which you are interested, on the kind of job you want to have within that industry, and on your own style and personality.

This book gives you guidelines, but it also gives you flexibility in deciding which job-hunting approach is right for you. When you understand what is happening and why, you can be in a better position to plan your own job-hunting campaign, and not rely so much on chance or on what a specific expert tells you.

Job hunting can be thought of as a project—much like any project you might handle in your regular job. Most of the approaches in this book are businesslike rather than intensely psychological. Thinking of job hunting in a business type of way allows you to use the problem-solving skills you might use at work.

This book series is organized for busy people like you. Skip to the part you need. If you already know what you want in your next job, go directly to our book *Shortcut Your Job Search: Get Meetings That Get You The Job* to learn the most powerful, up-to-date techniques available today for getting interviews. If you have an interview coming up, this book, *Mastering the Job Interview and Winning the Money Game*, will give you the latest ideas for getting what you want, including how to assess the interview and turn it into a job offer.

I feel duty-bound to address the issue of career planning. Most people are interested in job-hunting techniques but don't want to give much thought to what they should do with their *lives*. So read *Targeting a Great Career* to make sure your job targets are correct. Most job hunters think it was the smartest thing they did in their searches. Make the wise decision to spend the time it takes to give your life some direction and a real sense of satisfaction.

These books are the result of over 25 years of continual research into how successful job hunters land the best jobs at the best pay. Together, these books provide the most detailed explanation of the search process:

1. *Targeting a Great Career* tells you where to look for a job. It is a relatively painless way to think about the career-planning process. It also contains an extensive overview of the entire Five O'Clock Club approach to job search.

2. *Packaging Yourself: The Targeted Résumé* is quite simply the best résumé book on the market. It uses the résumés of real people and tells you their stories. It refers to over 100 industries and professions.

3. *Shortcut Your Job Search: Get Meetings That Get You the Job* tells you how to get job leads—part-time or full-time, freelance or consulting. It also contains worksheets, which you may copy for your own use. In addition, it contains the most comprehensive job-search bibliography around.

4. This book tells you The Five O'Clock Club way to interview, get the offer, and negotiate.

In addition to interviewing, following up, and negotiating, this book covers the overview of the job-search process. That way, you are not forced to refer to the other books when you are in the middle of this one.

Finally, in each book you will find a lot of inspirational writing. I have needed it myself often enough, as have the many unemployed and unhappy working people with whom I have worked. The techniques by themselves are worthless without the right frame of mind. I hope the quotations will inspire you as they have inspired me and my fellow job hunters.

Thank you for supporting The Five O'Clock Club through your purchase of this book. Because of people like you, we can keep the program going so we'll be there when you need us. Our goal is, and always has been, to provide the best and most affordable career advice. And—with you as our partner—we will continue to do this.

Cheers, God bless, and good luck!

Kate Wendleton
New York City, 2013
www.fiveoclockclub.com

Contents

PART FOUR **Turning Job Interviews into Offers: The Brainiest Part of the Job-Search Process**

PART FIVE **The Five O'Clock Club Approach to Salary Negotiation: A Four-Step Strategy**

PART SIX **Keeping It Going after You've Gotten the Job You Want**

PART SEVEN What Is The Five O'Clock Club? "Where Professional Success Gets Personal Attention"

Introduction

People can be divided into three groups:
those who make things happen,
those who watch things happen—
and those who wonder, What happened?

ANONYMOUS

We've all heard too many painful stories: out of work for over a year... networking, mailings, search firms, ads—but can't get a job or even an assignment. Lots and lots of interviews but...

At The Five O'Clock Club, we get impressive results. The average professional, manager, or executive who attends on a regular basis gets a job within 10 to 15 weeks. (Many had been looking for a year or more.) That's because they used the principles taught in this book series. As you will see, these techniques work at all levels—and for all types of people. They have even been used successfully by actors and actresses and at least one orchestra conductor. Whatever your field, this book will give you the inside track.

When job hunters find jobs, they report to the group. Last week, a man reported that he had been unemployed for three years. His wife had a good job, he spent time with his kids, and he found a few temporary assignments, but he was essentially unemployed and was trying very hard to get a job. After only four Five O'Clock Club sessions, he found a great one.

The week before, a woman spoke who had been unemployed for a year and a half; she had come to six sessions. Her first session had been a full year earlier, and she had decided to search on her own. After a year, she came back, attended five more sessions, and got a great job.

The week before that, a man who had been unemployed for six months before joining The Five O'Clock Club found a great job. In his four months with the Club, the group had helped him see how he was coming across in interviews (very stiff and preachy) and how to expand his job targets. Some people take longer because they are at the beginning of their search or because they have not searched in many years and need to learn this new skill.

Many job hunters think they have to lower their salary expectations because they are unemployed or have been job searching for a long time. You may have to lower your salary expectations for other reasons, but none of these three people did. Their unemployment did not affect their salary negotiations. In this book you will learn how to negotiate properly and increase your chances of getting what you deserve—whether you are employed or not.

The Five O'Clock Club techniques in this book work whether a job hunter is employed or unemployed. Most job hunters try to get interviews and then try to do well in them. They are skipping two important parts of the process and are therefore probably not doing the two remaining parts very well. At The Five O'Clock Club, we consider all four parts to be important. They are:

- **Assessment**: Deciding what you want results in better job targets (see our book *Targeting a Great Career*). Assessment also results in better résumés (see our book *Packaging Yourself: The Targeted Résumé*).
- **Campaign Preparation**: Planning your

campaign results in lots and lots of interviews in each job target (see our book *Shortcut Your Job Search: Get Meetings That Get You the Job*).

- **Interviewing**: Interviews result in an assessment of the company's needs.
- **Interview Follow-Up**: Follow-up after the interview results in job offers.

As you can see, job hunters who think that interviews lead to offers have skipped a step. Interviews lead to a better understanding of what the company wants. What you do after the interview leads to an offer.

Here are a few quick stories to get you started.

CASE STUDY Phil
Expanded his job-hunting targets—and went through the brick wall to get the job.

Phil had been earning hundreds of thousands of dollars a year as a senior executive in a large publishing company. When I met him, he had been job searching for a year, focusing on 24 publishing and health-care companies in his geographic area. Given his level, his search was obviously not going to work: his target was too small. He needed to look into other industries and other geographic areas.

In addition, Phil needed a new attitude. He expected people to recognize his credentials and simply hire him—something that had always happened in the past. Now he needed to go through the brick wall to get a job.

Phil found a job within three weeks after our meeting. He answered an ad in the paper for a job—not in publishing or health care—in another state. (It doesn't matter how you get the interview: through a search firm, an ad, networking, or direct contact.) He was called in for two interviews and then received a rejection letter: The company had decided against him.

But this time Phil wanted to fight for the job. He wrote to the president of the company and said there had obviously been a big mistake. The company reconsidered and hired him.

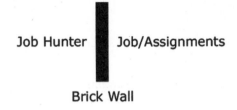

Job Hunter | Job/Assignments

Brick Wall

You have to be willing to go through the brick wall to get the jobs.

CASE STUDY Steelworkers
Who gets hired?

A colleague of mine, Aaron Nierenberg, tells of a coach who did a workshop for steelworkers a few years back when many of them were losing jobs. They were not of a mind to do résumés (many of them didn't even speak English), so the coach concentrated on the most important part of the search process—follow-up.

The coach asked, "How many of you have already contacted companies about getting a job?" Sixteen hands went up. "Your homework for tomorrow," he said, "is to *recontact* those companies and report back here." The next day, four workers had gotten jobs.

The explanation for this is simple. Look at it from the hiring manager's point of view. The steel industry was laying off thousands of workers, who went to other steel mills looking for work. Hundreds of workers went to the hiring managers and said, "Have you got any work?" How could a manager easily decide which workers to hire? But when a worker said, "I was here last week looking for work. Do you have anything now?" the manager then knew whom to select.

Much of the selection process is a self-selection process: the *job hunter* decides which companies he or she wants to work for and behaves very differently toward those companies than toward others in which he or she is not interested.

Job hunters put most of their effort into getting interviews and doing brilliantly well in those interviews. Then they stop. Five O'Clock Club job hunters keep going and turn more interviews into offers. Don't follow up with a silly thank you note. Instead, *influence* the person. This book will give you a process for analyzing the interview so you can decide what to do next.

People are always blaming their circumstances for what they are. I don't believe in circumstances. The people who get on in this world are the people who get up and look for the circumstances they want, and if they can't find them, make them.

GEORGE BERNARD SHAW, *MRS. WARREN'S PROFESSION*

See People Two Levels Higher Than You Are

Norman had been searching for a job for over a year. He did what he had been told: He networked. By now he had met with almost 250 people! Yet he could not find a job. The problem: He was meeting with people at his own level. When he started meeting with higher-level people (through direct contact), he started seeing results. Within two months, he found a great job.

Most job hunters network incorrectly. In our book *Shortcut Your Job Search*, we tell you exactly how to network so you can get the most out of it. We also cover the other techniques for getting interviews: through search firms, answering ads, and directly contacting companies.

Take the Long View

The next job you take will not be your last. Where will you go after that one? When deciding between two or more possibilities, select the one that positions you best for the long term.

Christine is a good example. She had three job offers—which is what we like people to have.

Two offers paid $10,000 more than the third one. Which job should she take?

Christine selected the one that positioned her best for the long term—which happened to be the lower-paying job. She is now as happy as a person can be, getting tremendous experience and meeting lots of important people. After a few years, she could easily leave (if she wants) and get much more money than she ever would have gotten had she taken one of the other two positions.

Julio is a portfolio manager with strong connections to South America. He had five job offers and wondered which one he should take. I couldn't help him until I knew his long-term plans. Otherwise, his decision would be based strictly on the money or the kind of people at each company. We spent 10 minutes working on his Fifteen- and Forty-Year Visions, which are covered in *Targeting a Great Career*. It turned out that he imagined himself working out of his house 5 to 10 years down the road. Then, the decision-making process became easy. Only two of the companies would eventually allow him to work from home. He selected one of them. Had he selected one of the others, he would have had a problem in a few years.

Targeting a Great Career helps you think about *your* long-term vision. Your next job is simply a step. You can plan that step and the ones after that. Job hunters are not powerless. They can do a lot to influence the hiring process and their own long-term careers.

Understanding How the Job-Hunting Market Works

Knowing why things work the way they do will give you flexibility and control over your job hunt. Knowing how the hiring system works will help you understand why things go right and why they go wrong—why certain things work and others don't. Then you can modify the system to fit your own needs, temperament, and the workings of the job market you are interested in.

It is overly simplistic to say that only one job-hunting system works. The job-selection process is more complicated than that. Employers can do what they want. You need to understand the process from their point of view. Then you can plan your own job hunt, in your own industry. You will learn how to compete in this market.

Always remember, the best jobs don't necessarily go to the most qualified people, but to the people who are the best job hunters. You'll increase your chances of finding the job you want by using a methodical job-hunting approach.

The Five O'Clock Club Coaching Approach

Our approach is methodical. Our coaches are the best. Five O'Clock Club coaches are full-time career coaches. Each one has met with hundreds of job hunters. Often we can pinpoint what is wrong with a person's search and turn it around. In this book, you will get that same information. Like our Five O'Clock Club job hunters, you will learn the techniques and hear the stories of other people so you can job hunt more effectively.

How The Five O'Clock Club Works

The Five O'Clock Club provides both individual and group career coaching, including individual coaching in person or by phone. On request, club members are matched up with Five O'Clock Club career coaches who we think are appropriate for them.

The weekly small-group strategy sessions are critical to a person's job-search success. Generally, half the people who attend are employed (and perhaps unhappy); half are unemployed. Members are from various industries and professions—usually difficult situations, or they wouldn't need us. The basic format is the same: The small group of 5 or 6 job hunters *who are in the same salary range* meet with the coach every week for an hour. They will spend a few minutes discussing the job-search topic of the week, which they will have heard before the small-group meeting. These techniques are presented in this book and in our audio lectures.

These small-group strategy-planning sessions are crucial to a person's job-search success. For each person in the group, they will assess how this person can move his or her search along. How can he get more interviews in his target market or turn those interviews into offers? Job hunters learn from the coach and from the strategies other job hunters are pursuing. They get feedback on their own searches and critique the searches of others. They aim to get 6 to 10 contacts in the works and have 3 job offers.

Those who stick with the process find that it works. That process is presented in this book series.

It is other people's experience that makes the older man wiser than the younger man.

Yoruba Proverb

PART ONE

The Changing Job-Hunting Process

AND CONTROLLING YOUR JOB-SEARCH CAMPAIGN

An Overview of the Job-Search Process

If you only care enough for a result you will almost certainly obtain it. If you wish to be rich, you will be rich; if you wish to be learned, you will be learned; if you wish to be good, you will be good.

HENRY HOLT (WILLIAM JAMES, *TALKS TO TEACHERS ON PSYCHOLOGY*, 1907)

The following chart outlines each part of the process. It's best to do every part, however quickly you may do it. Experienced job hunters pay attention to the details and do not skip a step.

The first part of the process is assessment (or evaluation). You evaluate yourself by doing the exercises in *Targeting a Great Career*, and you evaluate your prospects by doing some preliminary research in the library or by talking to people.

Sometimes it's best if a man just spends a moment or two thinking. It is one of the toughest things he will ever do, and that's probably why so few bother to do it.

ALONZO HERNDON, BORN A SLAVE; DIED A MILLIONAIRE; FOUNDER, ATLANTA LIFE INSURANCE COMPANY

<u>Assessment consists of the following exercises</u>:
- The Seven Stories Exercise
- Interests
- Values
- Satisfiers and Dissatisfiers
- Your Fifteen- and Forty-Year Visions

If you are working privately with a career coach, he or she may ask you to do a few additional exercises, such as a personality test.

<u>Assessment results in</u>
- a listing of all the targets you think are worth exploring
- a résumé that makes you look appropriate to your first target (and may work with other targets as well)

Research will help you figure out which of your targets
- are a good fit for you
- offer some hope in terms of being a good market

You can't have too many targets—as long as you rank them. Then, *for each one*, conduct a campaign to get interviews in that target area.

The circumstances that surround a man's life are not important. How that man responds to those circumstances is important. His response is the ultimate determining factor between success and failure.

BOOKER T. WASHINGTON

Step I: Campaign Preparation

1. Conduct research to develop a list of all the companies in your first target. Find out the names of people you should contact in the appropriate departments in each of those companies. This is called your Targeting Map.

2. Develop your cover letter (paragraph 1 is the opening; paragraph 2 is a summary about yourself appropriate for this target; paragraph 3 contains your bulleted accomplishments ("You may be interested in some of the things I've done"); paragraph 4 is the close. (Lots of sample letters are in this book.)

3. Develop your plan for getting l**ots of interviews in this target**. You have four basic choices:

- networking
- direct contact
- search firms
- ads

You will read lots about each of these methods in the *Shortcut Your Job Search* book.

Step II: Interviewing

Most people think interviews result in job offers. But there are usually a few intervening steps before a final offer is made. Interviews should result in getting and giving information.

Did you learn the issues important to each person with whom you met? What did they think were your strongest positives? Where are they in the hiring process? How many other people are they considering? How do you compare with those people? Why might they be reluctant to bring you on board, compared with the other candidates? How can you overcome the decision-makers' objections?

This is one of the most important and yet most overlooked parts of the job-search process. It is covered in extensive detail in this book.

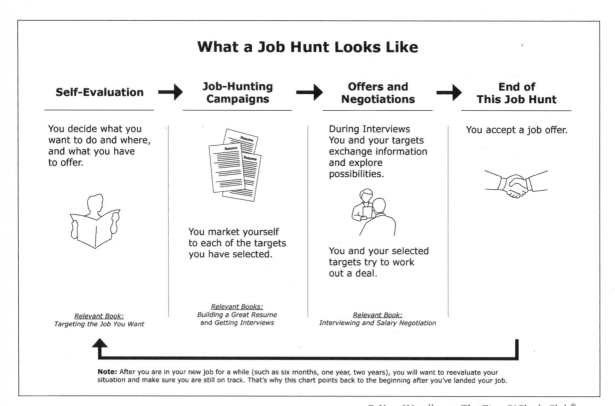

What a Job Hunt Looks Like

Self-Evaluation → **Job-Hunting Campaigns** → **Offers and Negotiations** → **End of This Job Hunt**

You decide what you want to do and where, and what you have to offer.

You market yourself to each of the targets you have selected.

During Interviews You and your targets exchange information and explore possibilities.

You and your selected targets try to work out a deal.

You accept a job offer.

Relevant Book:
Targeting the Job You Want

Relevant Books:
Building a Great Resume and Getting Interviews

Relevant Book:
Interviewing and Salary Negotiation

Note: After you are in your new job for a while (such as six months, one year, two years), you will want to reevaluate your situation and make sure you are still on track. That's why this chart points back to the beginning after you've landed your job.

© Kate Wendleton, The Five O'Clock Club®

Step III: Follow-Up

Now that you have analyzed the interview, you can figure out how to follow up with each person with whom you interviewed. Aim to be following up with 6 to 10 companies. Five job possibilities will fall away through no fault of your own.

What's more, with 6 to 10 things going, you increase your chances of having 3 good offers to choose from. You would be surprised: Even in a tight market, job hunters are able to develop multiple offers.

Develop Your Unique Résumé

Read all of the case studies in *Packaging Yourself: The Targeted Résumé*. You will learn a powerful new way of thinking about how to position yourself for the kinds of jobs you want. Each résumé in that book is for a unique person aiming at a specific target. Seeing how other people position themselves will help you think about what you want a prospective employer to know about you.

Now, it is best to go back to the first part of the process, assessment. In *Targeting a Great Career*, you will read actual case studies that will show you how real people benefited from doing the assessment, including the Forty-Year Vision.

However, if your targets are already defined, just keep reading.

Everyone should learn to do one thing supremely well because he likes it, and one thing supremely well because he detests it.

B. W. M. YOUNG, HEADMASTER, CHARTERHOUSE SCHOOL

Life never leaves you stranded. If life hands you a problem, it also hands you the ability to overcome that problem. Are you ever tempted to blame the world for your failures and shortcomings? If so, I suggest you pause and reconsider. Does the problem lie with the world, or with you? Dare to dream.

DENNIS KIMBRO, *THINK AND GROW RICH: A BLACK CHOICE*

Current List of Active Stage-1 Contacts

Networking Contacts With Whom You Want To Keep in Touch

The Beginning of a Search

Measure the effectiveness of your search by listing the number of people with whom you are currently in contact on an ongoing basis, either by phone or mail, who are in a position to hire you or recommend that you be hired. The rule of thumb: If you are seriously job hunting, **you should have 6 to 10 active contacts going at one time. At the beginning of your search, these will simply be networking contacts with whom you want to keep in touch**. You are unlikely to get an offer at this stage. You are gathering information to find out how things work—getting your feet wet. You look like an outsider and outsiders are rarely given a break. Keep adding names to your list because certain people will become inappropriate. Cross their names off. You should probably have some contact once a month with the people who remain on your list.

Because you have already developed targets for your search, please note below the target area for each contact or note it is serendipitous and does not fit in with any of your organized targets. This will help you see the progress you are making in each target area.

Name of Contact	Company	Position	Date of Last Contact	Targeted Date of Next Contact	Target Area
1.					
2.					
3.					
4.					
5.					
6.					
7.					
8.					
9.					
10.					
11.					
12.					
13.					
14.					
15.					
16.					
17.					
18.					
19.					
20.					

Current List of Active Stage-2 Contacts

The Right People at the Right Levels in the Right Companies

The Middle of a Search

The nature of your "6 to 10 things in the works" changes over time. Instead of simply finding networking contacts to get your search started, you meet people who are closer to what you want.

Getting a job offer is not the way to test the quality of your campaign. A real test is when people say they'd want you—but not now. Do some people say: **"Boy, I wish I had an opening. I'd sure like to have someone like you here"?** Then you are interviewing well with the right people. All you need now are luck and timing to help you contact (and recontact) the right people when they also have a need.

If people are not saying they want you, find out why not. If you think you are in the right targets talking to people at the right level and are not early on in your search, you need feedback. Ask: "If you had an opening, would you consider hiring someone like me?" Find out what is wrong.

Become an insider—a competent person who can prove he or she has somehow already done what the interviewer needs. *Prove* you can do the job and that the interviewer is *not* taking a chance on you.

You still need 6 to 10 contacts at this level whom you will recontact later. Keep adding names to your list because certain people will become inappropriate. Cross their names off. You should probably have some contact once a month with the people who remain on your list.

Name of Contact	Company	Position	Date of Last Contact	Targeted Date of Next Contact	Target Area
1.					
2.					
3.					
4.					
5.					
6.					
7.					
8.					
9.					
10.					
11.					
12.					
13.					
14.					
15.					
16.					
17.					
18.					
19.					
20.					

Current List of Active Stage-3 Contacts

Moving Along Toward Actual Jobs or the Possibility of Creating a Job

The Final Stages of a Search

In this stage, you **uncover 6 to 10 actual jobs (or the possibility of creating a job) to move along**. These job possibilities could come from any of your target areas or from serendipitous leads. Find a lot of people who would hire you if they could. If you have only one lead that could turn into an offer, you are likely to try to close too soon. Get more leads. You will be more attractive to the manager, will interview better, and will not lose momentum if your best lead falls apart. A good number of your job possibilities will fall away through no fault of your own (such as job freezes or major changes in the job requirements).

To get more leads, notice which targets are working and which are not. Make additional contacts in the targets that seem to be working or develop new targets. **Recontact just about everyone you met earlier in your search.** You want to develop more offers.

Aim for three concurrent offers: This is the stage of your search when you want them. When an offer comes during Stage 1 or Stage 2, you probably have not had a chance to develop momentum so you can get a number of offers. When choosing among offers, **select the job that positions you best for the long term.**

Name of Contact	Company	Position	Date of Last Contact	Targeted Date of Next Contact	Target Area
1.					
2.					
3.					
4.					
5.					
6.					
7.					
8.					
9.					
10.					
11.					
12.					
13.					
14.					
15.					
16.					
17.					
18.					
19.					
20.					

Stuck in Your Search? What to Do Next

Drive thy business, or it will drive thee.

BENJAMIN FRANKLIN

How to Measure the Effectiveness of Your Search

Most job hunters say, "I'll know my search was good when I get a job." That's not a very good way to measure your search. You need to be able to tell as you go along whether you are heading in the right direction. There are a number of hints you can pick up along the way.

What Stage Are You In?

As you go along, the basic measurement tool to use in your search is this: Do you have 6 to 10 things in the works? That is, are you talking to 6 to 10 people on an ongoing basis who are in a position to hire you or recommend that you be hired?

The world is moving so fast these days that the man who says it can't be done is generally interrupted by someone doing it.

HARRY EMERSON FOSDICK

The quality of your contacts varies with where you are in your search.

- In the beginning of your search, you will speak to as many people as possible in your target market—regardless of the organization for which they work. At this stage, you simply want market information. If you plan to stay in touch with them on an ongoing basis, they are Stage-1 contacts. To have any momentum going in the beginning of your search, keep in touch with 6 to 10 people on an ongoing basis (every few months).

    Over time, you will talk to more and more people who are Stage-1 contacts—perhaps 60 to 100 people during the course of your search. Some of those contacts will bubble up and become Stage-2 contacts.

- Stage-2 contacts are people who are the right people at the right level in the right jobs in the right organizations in your targeted areas. They are senior to you, perhaps future hiring managers. Your goal is to have contact with 6 to 10 of the right people on an ongoing basis. Then you have a full Stage-2 search going: You are in the middle of your search.

    However, you will rarely get a good job offer at Stage 2. You aren't even talking to these people about real jobs at this point. You just want the right people to know you and remember you. And if one later happens to have a job opening, you still need to go after 6 to 10 other job possibilities, because 5 will fall away through no fault of your own. If you do get an offer at Stage 2, you won't have many others with which to compare it. Keep in touch with your current Stage-1 contacts (using networking follow-ups), and develop additional Stage-1 contacts so more will bubble up to Stage 2. Some of those will bubble up to Stage 3 (real job possibilities)—and then you're really cooking.

- You are in a full Stage-3 search when you are talking to 6 to 10 people on an ongoing basis who actually have a job opening or who have the possibility of creating a job for you. Then you have a number of opportunities that you can move along (using *job* follow-ups), and are in the best possible position to get the right job for you: the one that positions you best for the long term and the one that pays you what you are worth.

If you have 6 to 10 possibilities in Stage 3, you have the chance of getting 3 offers. Remember, these do not have to be ideal jobs—some may even be disgusting. But an offer is an offer and makes you more desirable in the market. You don't have to want to work at each of these places, but at least you will have a fallback position and can honestly say, if appropriate, "I have a number of job offers, but there's no place I'd rather work than yours." With a number of offers in hand, you are less likely to be taken advantage of by a prospective employer who thinks you are desperate.

The Five O'Clock Club®

The Stages of Your Job Search

Most job hunters say, "I'll know my job search was good if I get a job." That's not a very good way to measure your search. You need to be able to tell **as you go along** if you have a good search. This is the test: Do you have six to ten things in the works? That is, are you talking on an ongoing basis to six to ten people who are in a position to hire you or recommend that you be hired? Which stage are *you* in? Start at the bottom of this page.

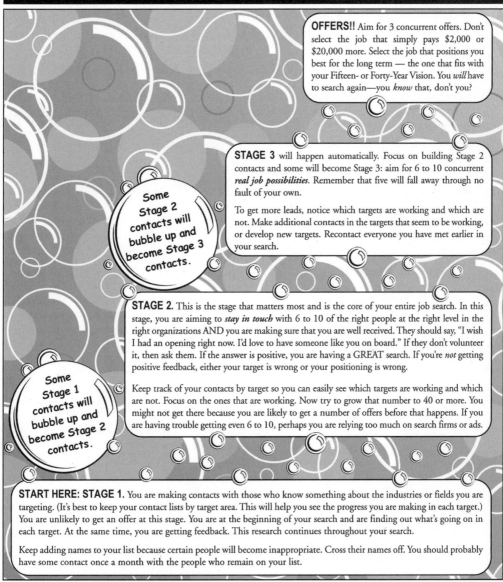

OFFERS!! Aim for 3 concurrent offers. Don't select the job that simply pays $2,000 or $20,000 more. Select the job that positions you best for the long term — the one that fits with your Fifteen- or Forty-Year Vision. You *will* have to search again—you *know* that, don't you?

STAGE 3 will happen automatically. Focus on building Stage 2 contacts and some will become Stage 3: aim for 6 to 10 concurrent *real job possibilities*. Remember that five will fall away through no fault of your own.

To get more leads, notice which targets are working and which are not. Make additional contacts in the targets that seem to be working, or develop new targets. Recontact everyone you have met earlier in your search.

Some Stage 2 contacts will bubble up and become Stage 3 contacts.

STAGE 2. This is the stage that matters most and is the core of your entire job search. In this stage, you are aiming to *stay in touch* with 6 to 10 of the right people at the right level in the right organizations AND you are making sure that you are well received. They should say, "I wish I had an opening right now. I'd love to have someone like you on board." If they don't volunteer it, then ask them. If the answer is positive, you are having a GREAT search. If you're *not* getting positive feedback, either your target is wrong or your positioning is wrong.

Keep track of your contacts by target so you can easily see which targets are working and which are not. Focus on the ones that are working. Now try to grow that number to 40 or more. You might not get there because you are likely to get a number of offers before that happens. If you are having trouble getting even 6 to 10, perhaps you are relying too much on search firms or ads.

Some Stage 1 contacts will bubble up and become Stage 2 contacts.

START HERE: STAGE 1. You are making contacts with those who know something about the industries or fields you are targeting. (It's best to keep your contact lists by target area. This will help you see the progress you are making in each target.) You are unlikely to get an offer at this stage. You are at the beginning of your search and are finding out what's going on in each target. At the same time, you are getting feedback. This research continues throughout your search.

Keep adding names to your list because certain people will become inappropriate. Cross their names off. You should probably have some contact once a month with the people who remain on your list.

How's Your Search Going?

When I ask you how your search is going, I don't want to hear that a prospective employer really likes you. That's not a good measure of how well your search is going, because one prospect could easily fall away: They may decide to hire no one or they may decide they want an accounting person instead of a marketing person. A lot can happen that is beyond your control.

Instead I expect you to tell me how many things you have in the works. You would say, for example, "My search is going great. I have five Stage-1 contacts in the works. I'm just getting started."

Or you might say, "I have nine Stage-2 contacts and three contacts in Stage 3." If you are expert at this, you may even add: "I want more Stage-3 contacts, so my goal is to get 30 more in Stage 2. Right now, I'm digging up lots of new contacts and keeping the other ones going. With my Stage-2 contacts, I'm generally doing networking follow-ups and with my Stage-3 contacts, I'm generally doing job follow-ups."

That kind of talk is music to my ears.

It usually takes very little effort to get a few more things "in the works." Simply recontact your network, network into someone you haven't met with yet, directly contact someone, talk to a search firm, answer an ad. You will soon have more activity in your search.

I know God will not give me anything I can't handle. I just wish He didn't trust me so much.

Mother Teresa

What Job Hunters Do Wrong

In addition to looking at the *stage* of your overall search, it is also helpful to look at what can go wrong in each *step* of your campaigns. Some job hunters err in their overall search approach or attitude. Then things can go wrong in the assessment step or in the other parts of your campaigns (the planning, interviewing, or follow-up steps). We'll examine each of these to determine what you may be doing wrong, if anything.

Procrastination is the fear of success. People procrastinate because they are afraid of the success that they know will result if they move ahead now. Because success is heavy, carries a responsibility with it, it is much easier to procrastinate and live on the "someday I'll" philosophy.

Denis Waitley

The Overall Search: What Can Go Wrong?

Here are some problems that are general to the entire search:

- **Not spending enough time** on your search. If you are unemployed, you should be spending 35 hours a week on your search. If you are employed, spend 15 hours a week to get some momentum going. If you spend only two or three hours a week on your job search, you may complain that you have been searching forever, when actually you have not even begun. If you are employed, you can do most of your work in the evenings and on weekends—researching, writing cover letters and follow-up letters. You can even schedule your meetings in the evenings or early mornings.

- **Not having enough fun.** Some job hunters—especially those who are unemployed—say they will start having fun after they get a job. But your search may take many months and you are more likely to come across as desperate if you are not allowing yourself to have some fun. Having fun will make you seem like a more normal person in your meetings and you'll feel better about yourself. The Five O'Clock Club formula is that you *must* have at least three hours of fun a week.

- **Not having 6 to 10 things in the works.** See the beginning of this chapter about Stages 1, 2, and 3 of your search.
- **Talking to people who are at the wrong level.** At the beginning of your search, talk to peers just to gather information to decide whether a prospective target is worth a full campaign. When you have selected a few good targets, talk to those who are at a higher level.
- **Trying to bypass the system.** Some job hunters feel they don't have time for this and simply want to go on job interviews (usually through search firms or answering ads). Others want to skip the assessment process (see our book *Targeting a Great Career*) or don't even do the Seven Stories Exercise. Their campaigns are weaker because they have no foundation.

  At least touch on every step in the process. You will have a quicker and more productive search.
- **Lowering your salary expectations just because you have been unemployed a while.** Even those who have been unemployed a year or two land jobs at market rates. They get what they are worth in the market because they have followed the system. At The Five O'Clock Club, half the people who attend are employed; half are unemployed. Many of those who are unemployed have been out of work for a year or two. Usually, they have been doing something wrong in their searches, and the coach and their group can help them figure out what it is. When they get a job (which they almost certainly will if they stick with the system), they usually wind up getting something appropriate at an appropriate salary level.
- Sometimes, if people really need money, we suggest they take something inappropriate to earn some money and continue to search while they are working.

The world is moving so fast these days that the man who says it can't be done is generally interrupted by someone doing it.

Harry Emerson Fosdick

- **Getting discouraged.** Half the battle is controlling your emotions. Jack had been unemployed one-and-a-half years when he joined us. He seemed very agitated—almost angry— which happens when a person has been working at a job search for so long. I told him I was afraid he might come across that way during meetings. He assured me (with irritation in his voice) that he was completely pleasant during meetings but was simply letting his hair down in the group.

  In career coaching, we have nothing to go on but the way the person acts in the group: The way you are in the group probably bears some resemblance to the way you are in the interview. We would recognize you as being the same person. Anyway, it's all we have to go on, so we have to point out to you what we see.

  The next week, Jack still seemed angry. I asked the group what they thought and of course they could see it too. It was easier for him to hear it from his peers, and, because he was a mature person, Jack listened to them.

  The third week, Jack laughingly announced that he had had a lobotomy and was a completely different person. He said he had changed his attitude and that his meetings reflected this change.

  The fourth week he announced that he had had another lobotomy because he felt he still had room for improvement. He was a noticeably different person and did not seem at all like someone who had been out of work a long time. Every day Jack read the books we use at The Five O'Clock Club and provided very good insights to the other job hunters in our small group.

By the fifth week, Jack was almost acting like a co-coach in the group. He had made great strides in his own search (with three Stage-3 contacts and lots of contacts in Stage 2) and was able to astutely analyze the problems others were having. He was a wonderful contributor.

By the seventh week, Jack was close to a number of offers and in the eighth week, Jack proudly addressed the group and reported on his successful search. We were sorry to see him go.

By the way, Jack did not have to take a pay cut or a job that was beneath him. His prolonged search did not affect his salary negotiation.

Do what you need to do to keep your spirits up. Don't ask yourself if you feel like searching. Of course you don't. Just do it anyway. And act as if you enjoy it.

- **Not having support.** Looking for a job is a lonely business. You may want to "buddy" with another job hunter. You can call each other every morning to talk about what you are each going to do that day and to review what you each accomplished the day before. You could also join free emotional-support groups at places of worship. You may find you need such help in addition to the job-search strategy you get at The Five O'Clock Club. Or you may find you would like to see a coach privately to help you with specifics having to do with your search, such as your résumé, a review of your search, salary negotiation, or the follow-up to a very important job interview. Get the help you need.
- **Inflating in your own mind the time you have actually been searching**. You may feel as though you've been searching forever. But if you are searching only three hours a week, you have not yet begun. If at the end of a year, you finally start to put in the required 15 to 35 hours a week, you have just really started

to search. Then when people ask how long you have been searching, the correct answer is "a few weeks." It's good to be honest with yourself about how long you have actually been searching.

During the Assessment Step: What Can Go Wrong?

In the Assessment Step you use our book, *Targeting a Great Career* to go through the exercises (Seven Stories, Values, Forty-Year Vision, and so on) and select job targets (industries or companies of a certain size, the position you would like in each target, and the geographic area).

If you are not sure what you should do with your life, assessment is a time to explore—perhaps with the help of a career coach. What can go wrong in that step?

- **Selecting 1 or 2 targets too quickly.** Rather than exploring, a job hunter may pick a target, go after it, find out it doesn't work, and then not know what to do next. Instead, brainstorm as many targets as you can at the beginning of your search, rank them, and go after them in a methodical way.
- **Not being specific in selecting a target.** Some job hunters say, "I just want a job. I don't care what it is." You may not care, but the hiring team wants someone who cares about their specific industry and organization. In the beginning of your search, you want to explore and stay calm while you are doing your research to find out what the likely targets are for you. If you don't have targets defined (such as "being a Web developer in a medium-sized organization in the Albuquerque area"), then you are still exploring and that's okay. But it is not an organized search. And even when your search is organized and targeted, you will

still have plenty of room for serendipitous leads.

- **Not doing the right research.** Read the chapter on research, including the bibliography at the back of *Shortcut Your Search: Get Meetings That Get You The Job.* Research is critical throughout your search and separates those who follow The Five O'Clock Club method from other job hunters. Instead of just *doing* research, why not learn to enjoy it and make it part of your life?

  The better your research, the richer your targets will become—well defined rather than superficial—and the more knowledgeable you will sound to prospective employers. In addition, you will save a lot of time as you discover where the markets are and which ones are the best fit for you.

- **Not ranking your targets.** Some job hunters go after everything at once. For a more organized search, overlap your targets, but still conduct a condensed search focusing on each target and keeping them separate in your mind.

  Take a look at the chart below, which shows a campaign aimed at each target (Target 1, Target 2, and Target 3). Yet the targets overlap to speed up the search.

Next, let's look at what can go wrong in the various steps of the campaign aimed at each target.

Life moves on, whether we act as cowards or heroes. Life has no other discipline to impose, if we would but realize it, than to accept life unquestioningly. Everything we shut our eyes to, everything we run away from, everything we deny, denigrate or despise, serves to defeat us in the end. What seems nasty, painful, evil, can become a source of beauty, joy, and strength, if faced with an open mind. Every moment is a golden one for him who has the vision to recognize it as such.

HENRY MILLER

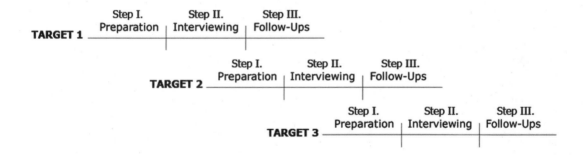

During the Preparation Step: What Can Go Wrong?

- **Relying on only one technique for getting meetings.** Consider using all four techniques for getting meetings: networking, direct contact, search firms, and ads (in print and online). Even in fields where people like to talk to people, such as sales or human resources, though networking is easier, it is not thorough. It is a scattered approach.

  Make a list of all the organizations in your target area—say, 120.

  ✓ Perhaps network into 20 of them;

✓ Do a targeted mailing into 20—it's just like networking: use a letter with a follow-up phone call. Remember that you want to see this person whether or not he or she has a job opening;

✓ Talk to search firms (if appropriate); and

✓ Answer ads.

✓ Do a direct-mail campaign (no follow-up phone call) to the remaining 80 organizations—just to be thorough so all the organizations in your target area know that you exist and are looking.

- **Contacting the wrong person.** The human resources person is the wrong one unless you want a job in human resources. The right person is one or two levels higher than you are in the department or division in which you want to work. If you are very senior and want to work for the president, the right person for you to contact is the president or perhaps someone on the board. If you want to be the president, the right person is someone on the board, or whoever may influence the selection of the president.

- **Being positioned improperly.** If you are not positioned properly, you will not be able to get meetings. Write out your Two-Minute Pitch. In your small group, be sure to practice your pitch. Try role-playing. Tell the group who they are pretending to be, and ask them to critique you. You want to make sure you have your pitch down pat. Write it out.

- **Using skimpy cover letters**. We use a four-paragraph approach that is thorough. Most job hunters write paragraphs one and four and skip the meat.

- **Having a weak or inappropriate résumé.** If your résumé doesn't speak for you in your absence and tell them exactly who you are, your level, and what you bring to the party, develop one that

helps you. We have a whole book on this topic—along with case studies of real live people.

- **Skipping the research step to develop a good list of target organizations**. If you have a good list, you will get more out of every one of your networking contacts. Show your list of prospective organizations to your contacts, ask them what they think of the organizations on the list, who they suggest you should contact at the good organizations, and ask, "May I use your name?"

The thing always happens that you believe in; and the belief in a thing makes it happen.

Frank Lloyd Wright

If you want a quality, act as if you already had it. Try the "as if" technique.

William James

During the Interviewing Step: What Can Go Wrong?

- **Trying to close too soon.** When a company is interested in you, you may have the tendency, like most job hunters, to focus on that one possibility and hope you get an offer. Because everything depends on that one possibility, chances are that you will do something wrong—trying to force them to decide before they are ready.

    Instead, get other things going while you keep an eye on the company you are already interested in. Ease the pressure on yourself and that company. Get your 6 to 10 things in the works and you'll have a balanced search.

- **Being seen as an outsider**. It's okay to be

an outsider when it's early in your search. However, to get offers, you must be seen as an insider. When you are an insider, higher-level networking contacts say, "I really wish I had an opening because I would love to have someone like you on board." You are being well received, and this person counts as a Stage-2 contact. Keep in touch with him or her. Find lots more. It's only a matter of time until you get a job if the target you picked is a good one, if you contact more and more people who say the same thing, and if you keep in touch with those you already met.

- **Not using the worksheets.** Fill out What I Have/Want to Offer. This will help you position yourself to each targeted area. Use one for each of your targets. Make a zillion copies of the Interview Record. Fill one out every time you go on an interview. Note to whom you spoke, to whom they referred you, their important issues, and so on. Two weeks later, you may not remember what you discussed.

If you are having a terrific search, you may meet with 5 to 15 people each week. Keep track of them with your Interview Record. Some people keep the records in a three-ring binder, alphabetically or by industry or target. Every time they write a follow-up letter, they attach a copy of that letter to the Interview Record. They cross-reference the information and become very methodical.

That way, when you conduct your networking follow-ups every two months, you will have the notes from your last discussion, and copies of the letters you had sent earlier.

Other things that can go wrong in the Interviewing Step include:

- Not thinking like a consultant.
- Not looking or acting like the level for which you are searching.

- Not seeing the interview as only the beginning of the process.
- Not getting information/giving information to move it along. "Where are you in the hiring process?" "How many other people are you talking to?" "How do I compare with them?" Be impersonal in the way you ask these questions so you can find out about your competition.
- Not preparing for the interview by having a 3x5 card or finding out with whom you will be meeting.
- Not being in sync with their timing (trying to close too soon or not moving quickly enough).
- Not listening to what's really going on.

During the Follow-Up Step: What Can Go Wrong?

In addition to targeting, follow-up is the most important reason Five O'Clock Clubbers land jobs quickly. This is the brainiest part of the process. Notice that the earlier diagram showed the three parts as equal: Preparation, Interviewing, and Follow-Ups. Spend an equal amount of time on each.

Study thoroughly those parts of this book. Some of the obvious things that go wrong include:

- **Taking the first offer.** Try to get three offers at the same time. Then select the one that positions you best for the long run.
- **Not recontacting your contacts.** If you have been in search awhile, the most important action you can take to develop new momentum is to recontact those with whom you have already met—perhaps every two to three months. That way they have a better chance of thinking of you when they come across news that may help you in your search.

Tell them, "It's been a while since we've met, and I am having a very interesting time. My search has taken a different direction, and I now find there is a lot of activity in the roof-repair market, which I am currently exploring. You were such a help to me before that I would like to call you again to find out what is going on at your end, and to tell you a little about what I've been doing." However you do it, recontact your contacts.

- **Not studying the books or listening to the audios.** Follow-up is covered in great detail in this book. Study it and spend the time it takes to think through what you can do next to move along the job contacts you have made. While those you have networked with should be contacted every few months, job follow-up is more complicated.
- **Stating your salary requirements too soon.** The discussion of salary negotiation in this book is another thing you should read thoroughly *at the beginning of your search*. Salary negotiation starts with the way you position yourself at your very first meeting.
- **Not reassessing where you stand in your search.** Let's say you have been in search awhile and would like to know where you stand. Take all of the contacts you have in the works (people you are in touch with on a regular basis), and divide them up into Stage-1, Stage-2, or Stage-3 contacts. You will probably have a ratio of 60 Stage 1 to 20 Stage 2 to 6 Stage 3. Therefore, to increase the number of contacts you have in Stage 3, your only recourse is to increase the number of contacts you have in Stage 1. Some will bubble up to Stage 2, and others to Stage 3.

Now that we've taken a break from your search to assess how you are doing, it's time to get back to work. Read on!

PART TWO

Preparing for the Interview

DON'T SKIP THIS STEP

Repositioning Yourself for a Job Change

*Greatness is not measured by what a man or woman
accomplishes, but by the opposition
he or she has overcome....*

DR. DOROTHY HEIGHT, PRESIDENT,
NATIONAL COUNCIL OF NEGRO WOMEN

Feel stuck in your present position? Peel off your old label, slap on a new one, and position yourself for something different.

Whether you're an accountant who wants to go into sales, or an operations person who dreams of being a trainer, the challenge you face is the same: You have to convince people that even though you don't have experience you can handle the new position.

It's a little like show biz: You play the same role for years and then you get typecast. It can be difficult for people to believe that you can play a different role. To move on to new challenges, you have to negotiate into the new job by offering seemingly unrelated skills as an added benefit to the employer. The key to these negotiations is positioning yourself.

Positioning

Simply put, positioning yourself means stating your skills and qualities in a way that makes it easy for the prospective employer to see you in the open position or in other positions down the road.

You may want to stay in your present organization, in which case you are positioning yourself to the person in charge of hiring for the particular department you want to enter. Or, you may want to go to a new organization or even a new industry. In this case, you are positioning yourself to a new employer. Either way, the steps are the same:

1. Determine what skills and qualities your prospective employer wants.
2. Search your background to see where you have demonstrated skills and qualities that would apply.
3. Write a summary at the top of your résumé to position yourself.
4. Use the same summary on your LinkedIn page and to sell yourself in an interview.

Your summary says it all. It should sell your ability, experience, and personality. It brings together all your accomplishments.

The rest of your résumé should support your summary. For example, if the summary says that you're a top-notch marketer, the résumé should support that. It's completely within your control to tell whatever story you want to tell. You can emphasize certain parts of your background and de-emphasize others.

> You can get typecast. To move on, you have to negotiate into the new job... by *positioning* yourself.

Thinking through your summary is not easy, but it focuses your entire job hunt. It forces you to clarify the sales pitch you will use in meetings.

However, many people *don't* put a summary that positions them on their résumés or on their

LinkedIn page. They say they want "a challenging job in a progressive and growth-oriented organization that uses all my strengths and abilities." That doesn't say anything at all, and it doesn't do you any good.

Résumé: Your Written Pitch

Make sure the first words on your résumé position you for the kind of job you want next, such as *Accounting Manager*. Line two of your résumé, also centered, should separate you from all those other accounting managers. For example, it could say, "specializing in the publishing industry." These headlines in your summary could then be followed by bulleted accomplishments that would be of interest to your target market.

Most people write boring résumés. To avoid this, keep in mind to *whom you are pitching*. Tell readers the most important things you want them to know about you. List your most important accomplishments right there in your summary.

It all starts with the Seven Stories Exercise. After you have done this exercise, you will talk about your accomplishments very differently than if you just sit down and try to write a résumé. The Seven Stories Exercise is the foundation for your résumé. Write out your work-related stories in a way that is *expressive* of you as an individual. Brag about yourself the way you would brag to the people in your family or your friends. Put *those* words at the top of your résumé to make it much more compelling.

Let's consider a few examples of summaries that will work for you:

Pursuing the Dream Job

Jane, a client-relationship manager at a major bank, has handled high-net-worth clients for more than 20 years. She is taking early retirement and thinking about a second career. Two directions are of interest to her: a job similar to what she has done but in a smaller bank; or, the job of her dreams—working as one of the top adminis-

trative people for a high-net-worth family (such as the Rockefellers), handling their business office and perhaps doing things that involve her interests: staffing and decorating.

If Jane were to continue on her current career path and go for a position as a relationship manager at a smaller bank, she would highlight the years she has worked at the bank. Her summary, if used in her résumé, would look like this:

More than 20 years handling all aspects of fiduciary relationships for PremierBank's private banking clients. Successfully increased revenue through new business efforts, client cultivation, and account assessment. Consistently achieved fee increases. Received regular bonus awards.

However, to pursue her dream job, Jane's regular résumé won't do. She has to reposition herself to show that her experience fits what her prospective employer needs. Her summary would read like this:

**Administrative manager
with broad experience in running operations**

- In-depth work with accountants, lawyers, agents, and others.
- More than 20 years' experience handling all aspects of fiduciary relationships for bank's private banking clients (overall net worth of $800 million).
- Expert in all financial arrangements (trust and estate accounts, asset management, nonprofits, and tenant shareholder negotiations).

Her résumé would also focus on her work *outside* PremierBank because these activities would interest her prospective employer: first, her work on the board of the luxury apartment building of which she was president for 14 years, and then the post she held for 10 years as treasurer of a nonprofit organization. Finally, Jane would highlight accomplishments at PremierBank that would be of interest to a prospective employer, such as saving a client $300,000 in taxes.

Ready to Take Charge

Robert had worked in every area of benefits administration. Now he would like to head up the entire benefits administration area—a move to management. His summary:

14 years in the design and administration of all areas of employee benefit plans

- 5 years with Borgash Benefits Consultants
- Advised some of the largest, most prestigious companies in the country
- Excellent training and communications skills
- MBA in finance

From Supporting to Selling

Jack wants to move into sales after being in marketing support. His prior résumé lacked a summary. Therefore people saw him as a marketing support person rather than as a salesperson—because his most recent job was in marketing support. He has been an executive in the sales promotion area, so his summary stresses his internal sales and marketing, as well as his management, experience:

Sales and marketing professional with strong managerial experience

- Devise superior marketing strategies through qualitative analysis and product repositioning
- Skillful at completing the difficult internal sale, coupled with the ability to attract business and retain clients
- Built strong relationships with the top consulting firms
- A team player with an enthusiastic approach to top-level challenges

Notice how he packages his experience running a marketing department as sales. His pitch will be, "It's even more difficult to sell inside because, in order to keep my job, I have to get other people in my company to use my marketing services. I have to do a good job, or they won't use me again."

If you do not have a summary, then, by default, you are positioned by the last job you held. In Jack's case, the employer would receive the new résumé with the new summary and say, "Ah-ha! Just what we need—a salesperson!"

Sophisticated Positioning

Here are how some people repositioned their backgrounds in a sophisticated way. Jeff had been in loan-processing operations in a bank. Outside of financial services, not many organizations do loan processing. To position himself to work in a hospital, Jeff changed his positioning to say transaction processing because hospitals process a large numbers of *transactions*, but not loans. Otherwise, they would look at his résumé and say, "We don't need to have loans processed."

In fact, many people who work in banking see themselves as working for information services companies. Money is sent via computer networks and wire transfers. They are passing information, not currency.

Nydia had worked at both banks and pharmaceutical companies. Because of her target, she positioned herself as having worked in *regulated industries*.

David saw himself as an international human resources generalist, but was having difficulty with his search. Since there were no international jobs in his field, he should not have positioned himself as *international*.

Now, think about *your* target market and how you should position your background for your target.

Making a Career Change

Elliott had been in sports marketing years ago, and had enjoyed it tremendously. However, he had spent the past four years in the mortgage industry, and was having a hard time getting back into sports marketing.

The sports people saw him as a career changer and a mortgage man. Even when he explained how marketing mortgages is the same as marketing sports, people did not believe him. He was being positioned by his most recent experience, which was derailing his search.

When job hunters want to change industries—or go back to an old industry—they cannot let their most recent positions act as a handicap. For example, if a person has always been in pharmaceuticals marketing, and now wants to do marketing in another industry, his or her résumé should be rewritten to highlight generic marketing, with most references to pharmaceuticals removed.

In Elliott's case, the summary in his new résumé helps a great deal to bring his old work experience right to the top of the résumé. In addition, Elliott removed the word "mortgage" from the description of his most recent job; his title at the mortgage company now stands out more than the company name. And he removed company and industry jargon, such as the job title *segment director*, which is not easily understood outside his company. He also updated his Linkedin profile to represent his new positioning of himself as a sports marketing person.

Notice that Elliott's description of what he did for the mortgage business is now written generically—it can apply to the marketing of any product. With his new résumé, Elliott had no trouble speaking to people in the sports industry. They no longer saw his most recent experience as a handicap, and he soon had a terrific job as head of marketing for a prestigious sporting-goods company.

If you want to move into a new industry or profession, state what you did generically so people will not see you as tied to the old.

Bring Something to the Party

When it comes down to negotiating yourself into a new position, seemingly unrelated skills from former positions may actually help you get the job.

For example, some of my background had been in accounting and computers when I decided to go into coaching and my CFO (chief financial officer) experience helped me ease into this new career. I agreed to be CFO at a 90-person career-coaching company provided I was also assigned clients to coach. My ability to create a cost-accounting system for them was what I "brought to the party." I was willing to give the company something they wanted (my business expertise) in exchange for doing something I really wanted to do (coaching executives).

Combining the new with the old, rather than jumping feet first into something completely new is often the best way to move your career in a different direction. You gain the experience you need in the new field without having to come in at the entry level. Equally important, it is less stressful because you are using some of your old strengths while you build new ones.

Coming from a background different from the field you are targeting can also give you a bargaining chip. If you are looking at an area where you have no experience, you will almost certainly be competing with people who do have experience. You can separate yourself from the competition by saying, "I'm different. I have the skills to do this job, and I can also do other things these people can't do." It works!

Our résumé book contains dozens of additional positioning (summary) statements. In addition, you will see how the positioning statements are used to set the tone for the rest of the résumé.

Elliott's positioning (summary) statement is on the next page.

ELLIOTT JONES

421 Morton Street Chase   Fortune, KY 23097

SEARS MORTGAGE COMPANY   2012-present
Vice President, Segment Director, Shelter Business
- Director of $4.6 billion residential mortgage business for largest mortgage lender
- Organized and established regional marketing division for largest mortgage lender, including first and second mortgages and mortgage life insurance

SportsLife Magazine   2009-2012
Publisher and Editor
- Published and edited largest health/fitness magazine. Increased circulation by 175%. and so on...

ELLIOTT JONES

421 Morton Street, Chase Fortune, KY 23097   ejones@yahoo.com

Fifteen years: domestic and international marketing management in the leisure/sporting goods industry

- Multibrand expertise specializing in marketing, new business development, strategic planning, and market research.
- Identified customer segments, developed differentiable product platforms, implemented communication strategies, managed sales, oversaw share growth, and generated profit.

SEARS MORTGAGE COMPANY   2012-present
VICE PRESIDENT, BUSINESS DIRECTOR
Residential Real Estate Business

- Business Director of a $4.6 billion business. **Managed strategic planning, marketing, product development, and compliance**.
- Consolidated four regional business entities into one; doubled product offerings. Grew market share 150 basis points and solidified #1 market position.
- **Developed and executed nationally recognized consumer and trade advertising, public relations, and direct-response programs**.
- Structured a product-development process, integrating product introductions into the operations and sales segments of the business.
- Organized and established regional marketing division.

SPORTSLIFE MAGAZINE   2009-2012
Publisher and Editor
- Published and edited largest health/fitness magazine. Increased circulation by 175%.

and so on...

The Five O'Clock Club®

Your Two-Minute Pitch: The Keystone of Your Search

If I venture to displace, by even the billionth part of an inch, the microscopical speck of dust which lies now upon the point of my finger, what is the character of that act upon which I have adventured? I have done a deed which shakes the Moon in her path, which causes the Sun to be no longer the Sun, and which alters forever the destiny of the multitudinous myriads of stars that roll and glow in the majestic presence of their Creator.

EDGAR ALLEN POE, *AN ESSAY ON THE MATERIAL AND SPIRITUAL UNIVERSE*

If your pitch—the way you position yourself—is wrong, everything else about your search is wrong.

Navigating the Minefield

The *Two-Minute Pitch* is the answer to the question, "So, tell me about yourself." With a great pitch, people are more likely to see you as *appropriate* for the kind of job you're going after. However, as we say at The Five O'Clock Club, "If your pitch is wrong, everything is wrong." You may have an interview every day and be absolutely brilliant in those meetings, but employers will not see you as appropriate for their jobs if your pitch is wrong.

The top of your résumé is the *written* positioning of yourself, as is your LinkedIn posting. The Two-Minute Pitch is the *verbal* positioning

of yourself. And they all must correspond. So, in spite of having spent the past four years in the mortgage industry, the top of Elliott's résumé could read:

Domestic and International Marketing Manager with 15 years' experience in the leisure and sporting goods industry

This will help him get back into the field he loved. In an interview, when an employer asks, "So tell me about yourself," Elliott could start with the verbal version of that same pitch: "I'm a domestic and international marketing manager with more than 15 years' experience in leisure and sporting goods. I've always emphasized quality and productivity. For example,..." And then he could talk about examples of his accomplishments, which would correspond to some of the bulleted accomplishments at the top of his résumé. When your pitch is correct, you will use it throughout your entire search.

If your résumé is done well, I should be able to pick it up and recite a pretty good Two-Minute Pitch right from your summary, as I could do with Elliott's. Test your own résumé and see if your pitch is that clear.

People tend to pitch themselves incorrectly unless they're thinking clearly about their positioning. Here's a typical example. I was chatting with Kathy before the start of a Five O'Clock Club meeting. Here's the way the conversation went:

Kate: So, what field are you in, Kathy?

Kathy: Banking.

Kate (sensing her positioning was incorrect): Well, I doubt that. What do you *do* in banking?

Kathy: Customer service.

Kathy worked in customer service, *not* banking. She was positioning herself incorrectly. This doesn't matter so much when she's talking to *me*, but it does matter when she's trying to get a customer service job.

Many job hunters have to reposition themselves, if only to emphasize certain parts of their backgrounds and downplay others. Figure out the kind of job you want to have next, and make sure that your résumé—and your verbal pitch—make you look appropriate to that target market.

Sugar, Sugar, Sugar: Use the Jargon of the Industry You Are Targeting

Cheryl had been in a sales position in the sugar business. In her small group, Cheryl talked about bulk sugar, liquid sugar, brown sugar, white sugar, sugar cubes, truckloads of sugar, and train-carloads of sugar. Everything was sugar, sugar, sugar! Yet Cheryl wanted a job in the bulk food business.

It's easy for an outsider to see that Cheryl simply needs to say *bulk food* instead of *sugar*. But when it's happening to you, it can be much more difficult to see that *you are positioning yourself incorrectly*.

Use the jargon and the words of your new industry. If you don't *know* the new jargon, then you must learn it. You cannot pass the translation responsibility on to the people who will be interviewing you.

Cheryl may think, "If I can sell sugar, they should be able to see that I can sell food." But they think Cheryl's committed to the sugar industry. It is *her* responsibility to show them that she understands and can fit into the new target industry by using their jargon.

Eventually Cheryl learned to say *food* instead of *sugar*. She soon got a terrific job in the food industry. A few years later, she repositioned

herself again and got a terrific job in the computer software industry!

Great minds have purposes, others have wishes.

WASHINGTON IRVING

Where Your Pitch Is Used

Your Two-Minute Pitch is the backbone of your search. You'll use it in job and networking interviews, and in your cover letters. You'll be ready when someone calls and says, "So tell me about yourself."

Your résumé summary statement could serve as the starting point for your pitch. Keep in mind:

- to whom you are pitching
- what they are interested in
- who your likely competitors are
- and what you bring to the party that your competitors do not.

Think about your target audience and what you want to say to them. Examine your background to find things that fit.

All managers establish relationships over their careers... the unsavvy [managers] form fewer of those relationships. They are also more likely to let relationships fade when they move on to new positions.... The savvy managers...consistently seek to build relationships and then keep them up once they move on. It doesn't take much time, just a phone call now and then to ask, How are you doing?

JOEL M. DELUCA, PH.D., *POLITICAL SAVVY*

Your Pitch in a Networking Meeting

The format for a networking meeting is covered in much more detail elsewhere. Use this same format whether you get in to see someone through a targeted mailing or by using someone else's name. They are both networking meetings.

Here is the format, briefly, so you can see where your Pitch fits in:

1. Exchange pleasantries—so the manager will focus on you.
2. Tell the manager why you're there, such as, "Jane suggested I contact you because she thought that you could give me the information I need. I'm interested in moving into the sports marketing field."
3. Then the manager will say, "Fine. What questions would you like to ask me?" Rather than ask questions at this point, say, "I do have questions, but first I'd like to tell you a little about myself." And then you give your Two-Minute Pitch: "I'm an accounting manager with strong Sarbanes-Oxley background," and so on.

That's how the Two-Minute Pitch fits into the networking meeting.

Your Pitch in a Job Interview

When you have a job interview, you are likely to be asked, "So Jane, tell me a little bit about yourself." If you have not done your homework and you know nothing about the company, you will be in trouble. Find out something about them *before* you give your pitch. Otherwise, you will not know how to position yourself.

So, for example, you could say, "There are a lot of things I have to say about myself, but I'd like to keep it relevant to your situation. What do you see as your needs right now?" Or say, "I can tell you a lot about myself, but first I'd like to know what it was about my cover letter or résumé that made you call me in."

Once they tell you something about what is going on in the organization, then you will be able to position yourself appropriately. Know something about them before you give your Two-Minute Pitch.

Your Pitch in the Cover Letter

Your cover letters will be much more effective if you use The Five O'Clock Club format.

1. Paragraph one is your introduction. You might say, "I have been following Apex Chemicals for some time and admire your emphasis on tight controls. I, too, focus on the close monitoring of business units and would like to work in a place like yours. I think we should meet because you never know when you may need someone like me." Your opening paragraph is generally *specific to the company.*
2. Paragraph two contains your summary. *That is your pitch.* "I am a senior accountant with over five years' experience in Lotus Notes."
3. Paragraph three contains the bulleted accomplishments you think would be of most interest to this target market. "You may be interested in some of the specific things I've done:
   • Reduced expenses in 4 units, saving the company over $200,000. And so on.
4. Paragraph four is the close, where you ask for a meeting, such as: "I will call you in a few days to set up a mutually convenient time to meet." Then you'll follow up with a few phone calls.

The heights by great men reached and kept
Were not attained by sudden flight,
But they, while their companions slept,
Were toiling upward in the night.

Henry Wadsworth Longfellow

What's Wrong with This Pitch?

Take a look at the beginning of my client Joshua's pitch, and see if you can tell what's wrong: "I have 18 years' experience in education and training: in developing training programs, in running training centers, etc."

What's wrong with this pitch? We can't know for sure until we know *to whom he is talking.* It turned out that the pitch was wrong because the interviewer was not interested in training but in personal computers. How much did Joshua know about PCs? A lot. "Why, I can make PCs dance," he said. "The only problem is that the hiring manager would probably want someone who could network them together, and I've never done that."

"*Can* you do that?" I asked.

"Of course, I can do it," Joshua replied.

"Then go *do* it," I said, "so you can tell her you have already done it. Network together the computers you have at home. And join a group that specializes in that. Ask one of the people if you can go along and help him or her network computers together."

Here's the pitch one week later: "I have 18 years' experience in computers, specializing in PCs. I have built PCs from scratch, and I've done software and applications programming on PCs. I also understand how important networking is. I've even networked together the PCs I have at home, and I belong to a group of PC experts, so I always know whom to talk to when tricky things come up."

But Joshua was feeling some frustration because he was an older guy aiming at a field full of mostly young people. He said to me, almost pleadingly, "I can do *anything* that has to do with PCs. Kate, I can make PCs dance!"

Joshua is speaking out of his *passion* and his love of PCs. I said, "Joshua, you have to say that in your Two-Minute Pitch." So, then Joshua's pitch ended on this note: "I can do anything, *anything* that needs to be done with PCs. I can make PCs dance. And I am very excited about talking to you today because I know that your shop relies on PCs. Maybe you can tell me more about that." Of course, Joshua got the job.

You, too, have to convey your passion, if indeed you're feeling any. Your passion will *dramatically* separate you from your competitors.

The Outline of Your Pitch

When developing your own pitch, first ask yourself, "What is the most important thing that I want them to know about me?" No, it's not that you're a hard worker and dedicated. That doesn't separate you from your competition, and it's a useless thing to say. Your opening statement should be a *positioning* statement having to do with the field you're in or the one you're going after. For example, "I'm an international marketing manager."

Now what's the *second* most important thing you want them to know about you? This thought should separate you from all the other international marketing managers, such as "with a strong operations background." What is the third most important thing? This statement usually supports the first two and may be an overarching statement that introduces the *accomplishments* that will follow, such as "My experience includes strategic planning, business generation, and people development. On the strategy side, I wrote the business plan for the division, which encompassed . . ." Here you would give concrete examples of your accomplishments—but not *too* detailed because you can give the details later. You don't have to cover your entire career in two minutes. Give them an overview, and you can interject, "I can tell you more about that later."

The final statement in your pitch could be something like, "I'm excited about talking to you today because of the strong international component of your business."

That is how you can think through the formulation of your pitch. It has an overarching statement with organized details to enable the listener to grasp the key points you are trying to make.

Know how to ask. There is nothing more difficult for some people. Nor for others, easier.

BALTASAR GRACIAN, *THE ART OF WORLDLY WISDOM*

Courage is doing what you are afraid to do. There can be no courage unless you're scared.

EDDIE RICKENBACKER

Repositioning Yourself in Your Pitch

Remember, *most* people have to reposition themselves based on the kind of job that they want to go after next. For example, when we asked Janie to "tell us a little bit about yourself," Janie said, "I've worked for big consulting firms my entire life."

If Janie still wanted to work for a big consulting firm, *then* her pitch would have been okay. However, Janie now wanted to work in international communications. In fact, when we dug into her background, we could see that she had been *doing* international communications with the big consulting firms.

So Janie had to reposition the top of her résumé to read, "Communications Executive— with 10 years of international experience."

Here's the start of Janie's revised verbal pitch, which now matches her résumé: "I'm a communications executive with 10 years of international experience." Now, notice how you *feel* about the next sentence of her pitch: "I have 10 years of international experience [now pay attention] in Europe, Latin America, South Africa, the Far East, Eastern Europe, and Russia." See how much more *interesting* it is with the geographic details rather than if she had said only, "I have 10 years of international experience." That would have been boring!

> **The richness of a pitch is in the details. You need to include details about yourself, too.**

Otherwise, yours will be a generic pitch, and it will not capture the imagination of your listeners.

And so Janie went on. "In fact, I was based in Amsterdam for three years." That adds even more interest.

And then: "I am known for getting new business. I've trained people all over the world in proposal writing and 50 percent of their pitches have resulted in new business." Now pay attention to this next part:

". . . These pitches were aimed at companies such as IBM, Philips, Natwest and GE." Again, see

how the details add interest to Janie's pitch. You have to do that too.

So decide on a *key statement* about yourself. Janie's pitch was "I am a communications executive." What's yours? Then, what's your sub-pitch? Janie's sub-pitch is "with 10 years of international experience including the following countries." And then, what are the most important additional points that you want to make about yourself that would be of interest to your target market? Janie added a few accomplishments that had to do with international communications, and this is the pattern you should follow.

Interviewers Need to Know Your Level

One final word about the beginning of your pitch. Prospective employers need to be able to tell what your level is. So if, for example, you say, "I install computer systems," they can't tell if you're making $25,000, $50,000, or $200,000 a year installing computer systems. So that's not a good pitch.

The listener needs to be able to identify your level quickly, within the first two or three lines on your résumé, and in the first few words of your pitch.

More Customization

In your pitch, do not tell your whole life story. Instead, say things that are relevant. Position yourself, and tell accomplishments that would be of interest to the organization. You memorize your pitch, and then *modify* it depending on whom you are talking to.

Philip, for example, was in marketing and specialized in developing new products. He interviewed at one company that already had dozens of new products. They wanted their products taken to market. Philip had to change his pitch. Instead of saying, "I develop new products," he said, "I'm an expert at taking products to market."

Be sensitive about your target market. Find out their needs, what they're missing, and their problem areas. Then position yourself accordingly.

Practice Your Pitch

Most people write out their Two-Minute Pitch, or the key points, and rehearse it in front of a mirror or with their small group.

Alice, a senior human resources executive, landed a prestigious job with a large company. When she reported on her successful job search at the Club, she said that she had met with the president of the company as well as with people on the board of directors and other very senior people. Alice said that she had practiced so much that she felt as though she were having an out-of-body experience when she gave her Two-Minute Pitch: The words just flowed out of her mouth! You want to get to where the words just flow. And that takes practice.

There are a lot of surprises during the interview process, but some things are *certain*. "Tell me about yourself" is not a surprise question. The answer to that question is your Two-Minute Pitch.

If you're following The Five O'Clock Club technique, you have highlighted certain accomplishments on your résumé, and the hiring team is going to ask you about them! You know these questions are coming. Make sure your answers are smooth; make sure they flow.

You have complete control over this aspect of the interview. If you do it The Five O'Clock Club way, your résumé will help to guide the interview process and make it more likely that the hiring team will ask you about certain accomplishments.

What Point Are You Trying to Make?

When you rehearse your Two-Minute Pitch, ask yourself: What *point* am I trying to make? What impression do I hope people will get about me?

I was listening to a client's pitch, and could not understand the point this executive woman was trying to make. After she had finished:

Kate: I don't get it. What point are you trying to make?

Client: Look, I want them to know that I have 20 years' experience in capital markets, whether

it's in aerospace or petroleum, metals and mining, or real estate. *My experience is in capital markets.*

Kate: That's a great pitch. Why don't you just tell them exactly that up front?

They Won't "Get It" on Their Own, So Just Tell Them.

Most job hunters think: I'll just tell them my background, and they'll see how it fits in with their needs. But they probably won't see.

> **Don't expect the hiring team to figure out something about you. If you have a conclusion you'd like them to reach about you, tell them what it is.**

If you want them to see how all of your jobs have somehow been involved in international, say, "All of my jobs have somehow been involved in international." Isn't that easy?

If you want them to notice that you have always been willing to move wherever the company wanted you to move, then say just that. If you want them to know that you have done things treasury executives rarely do, then tell them that.

If you want them to see that you have developed intensive product knowledge while handling various operations areas, tell them that. Do you want them to know that Java is your favorite programming language? Then don't say, "I have five years of Java experience." That's not your point. Do you want them to know that you can make computers dance? Tell them. Don't make them figure it out for themselves. They won't.

Don't think to yourself, "I thought that if I told them that I had done 12 years of Java programming, they would just understand that I also know how to manage project teams." No! *Tell* them what you want them to know and how your background fits in with their needs.

Make your message so clear that if someone says, "Tell me about John," they will know what to tell the other person about you.

What Will They Say about You When You're Gone?

If you're an accounting manager and your résumé says *Accounting Manager* in the summary, and you're applying for an accounting manager job, chances are good that everyone else they're interviewing is also an accounting manager. When you leave, the hiring manager is not going to say, "Oh, my gosh! I just met an accounting manager." Instead, you want them to say, "Oh, my gosh. I just met somebody who is an expert in developing new accounting systems. And he worked on a project in our industry doing exactly what we're trying to do."

What do you want them to say about you when you're gone? *That's* your pitch. Repeat it enough during the interview so that you know how they'll position you to *other* people after you leave.

Communicating Your Pitch

Many job hunters try to cram everything they can into their Two-Minute Pitch, but when your pitch is too densely packed, people won't hear what you want them to hear. Think about those who are considered the great communicators today. We judge communicators very differently from the way we did in the past, when the Winston Churchill type was ideal.

Today, our standards are based on the medium of TV. The best communicators speak on a personal level—the way people talk on TV. Whether you are addressing a big audience or are on a job interview, cultivate a TV style—a friendly, one-on-one conversational style, not a *listing of what I've done* style. Speak the way you would normally speak.

The interviewer is assessing what it would be like to work with you. Make your pitch understandable. Before people go on TV, they decide the three major points they want to make—what they want the audience to *remember*. For example,

don't say, "I started out in this job as a trainer, where I traveled to x and y and worked on special projects, etc.," if what you *really* want them to know is "That was a great assignment. My programs accounted for more than two thirds of the company's revenue."

Many job hunters have pitches that are too heavy in content. Let's return to the woman executive we were discussing: "I have 20 years' experience in capital markets in airlines, real estate and petroleum, metals and mining—assessing customers' and prospects' financial requirements based on the industry's point within the business cycle as well as the specific company's. I assess client credit, etc."

People can't listen to that. It's too dense. It needs some filler around the important words to resemble the way people really talk: "I have 20 years' experience in capital markets—capital markets has always been my chief interest. I had this experience in three different areas, but the area where I spent the most time was in the airlines. I was also most recently involved in petroleum, metals and mining, and earlier on in my career, I was involved in real estate."

The new pitch is more conversational than a list and will be more effective than simply getting all the facts out.

Vary Your Pitch by Organization

Change your pitch for every organization with which you meet. If you're pitching yourself to a large organization, you will probably have a different pitch than if you are pitching to a small organization. When you know something about the organization that you're interviewing with, you should be able to modify your pitch. Now, this does not contradict what I said earlier about having your pitch down pat. You *can* have it down pat, then you can ad lib a bit and modify it to suit this target market. Know your main point and your subordinate points, and modify those for each organization.

Emphasis and Tempo

When you say something important, emphasize it by slowing down. For example, in the sentence "I worked on that project for over nine months," you could slow down on "nine months" to give it emphasis. Like this: "I worked on that project for over [slowly] *nine months*." That's what TV announcers do. They speed up background words and slow down on the important words. Then your listener will not miss what you consider important.

I speak quickly, but when I am on an interview with somebody who is laid back and casual, even *I* can change tempo and slow myself down a little bit so that I match their pace.

But if I were meeting with somebody who is more fast-paced and chop-chop, then I can operate at the fast-paced end of my spectrum. If you speak very slowly to someone who is fast-paced, they'll think you're slow and won't fit in.

More about Filler Words and Pointer Words

As indicated earlier, filler words can be useful. They help *engage* your listener. Words can highlight important points that are coming up. You might say, for example, "One of the most interesting things that I've ever done was..." Those are highlight words. They point to whatever you're going to tell them next. You're saying, "What I'm about to say will be important." And then you may name an accomplishment. You may want to follow that (or a different accomplishment) with "That was one of the most satisfying things I have ever done because [slowly] I was in charge and I was able to operate on my own." That phrase points *back* to what you just said, so they don't miss it.

Smile

When I rehearse people for interviews, I find that I commonly tell people to *smile*. When you smile, it has an impact on the viewer. Even if you're on the phone, when you are smiling, it impacts the listener.

When you smile, people see you as more competent and more self-confident. If you do not smile, then you look worried and you look less qualified than you really are.

When you smile, the other person has a *visceral reaction* to you. Their tendency, unless the person is a brick wall, is to smile back. A good healthy smile helps you during the interview, and the hiring manager is more likely to think that there is good chemistry between you.

Use your hands as you would in a normal conversation. Don't sit there like a rock. Pay attention to the hiring manager's style. Take a look at the things around their room. Is the person more formal or more laid back? You can adjust your presentation accordingly.

Two Minutes Is a Long Time, So Show Enthusiasm

In this TV society, people are used to 15-second sound bites on the news. As the communicator, you have to engage the listener. Reinforce your main points. Don't say too many things.

Show *enthusiasm* during those two minutes. If you're an introvert and a low-key person, force yourself to sit *forward* in your chair. Sit almost on the edge of your seat. It will thrust your body forward and make you look more energetic. And using your hands a little will also give much more energy to your presentation. The interview process is an extroverted process, and low-key people are at a disadvantage. So, *act* a little extroverted on the interview; whether you're extroverted or not, you have to act that way more than you normally would. Otherwise, people may doubt that you have the energy to get work done. The good news is that you do not have to act that way on the job!

I once did a magazine article on who got jobs and who got to keep them. I talked to the deans of business and engineering schools.

I learned that the person most likely to get the job was the one who sounded enthusiastic. And the one who got to keep the job was the enthusiastic one—even more than people who were more qualified. Employers decided to keep someone who was willing to pitch in and do anything to help the company.

Even more interesting to me is that this same thing is true for senior executives. In my line of work, I sometimes have the opportunity to follow up with organizations when someone doesn't get a job. I am amazed by the number of times I am told (about people making from $150,000 to $600,000) that the applicant lacked enthusiasm: "He was managing 1,300 people, and I don't know how he did it. He just doesn't sound enthusiastic. How could he motivate his troops if he can't motivate me? Anyway, I don't know that he really wants the job. He didn't sound interested."

If you're in the interview thinking, "I don't know whether or not I want to do this job," that's the wrong attitude. The safest route is to be enthusiastic and act as *if* you want the job anyway. Later on, you can decide that you don't want it. But if you act unenthusiastically during the interview process and decide later that you're indeed interested, it's usually too late. So, when you go in for that interview, try to make it work. Try to get that next meeting. Whether you want the job or not, *act* like you do. Enthusiasm from start to finish, by the way, gives you the advantage when salary negotiation gets under way.

Depend on Your Small Group

Your group is terrific at giving feedback on the Two-Minute Pitch. Tell the other people in the group who they should pretend to be. That is, should they pretend that they are the marketing manager, accounting manager, or operations manager? Then they say to you, "So tell us about yourself." Then you say your pitch—you can refer to your notes—and ask them for their comments. Your group can comment on both the delivery and the content. They can tell if your pitch is clear, if you're being too modest about your accomplishments, or if your pitch is too general. Then refine your pitch and practice it again in your group the following week. Keep practicing it until you get it right. (Sometimes people use tape recorders to record the pitch.) It may take you three or four weeks to get it perfect, but that's what your small group is for.

Remember: The Two-Minute Pitch is one of the most important parts of the entire Five O'Clock Club job-search process. Most successful Five O'Clock clubbers said that once they got their pitch down, things seemed to work out better in their search. So practice your Two-Minute Pitch in your small group and take it to the world!

A very large amount of human suffering and frustration is caused by the fact that many men and women are not content to be the sort of beings that God had made them, but try to persuade themselves that they are really beings of some different kind.

Eric Mascall, *The Importance of Being Human*

Summary of What I Have/Want to Offer—Target 1

To Help Me Develop My Written Pitch to That Target

You must know:
- to whom you are pitching; you have to know something about them.
- what they ideally want in a candidate.
- what they are interested in.
- who your likely competitors are.
- what you bring to the party that your competitors do not.

For Target 1: Geographic area: _____

Industry or organization size: _____

Positionfunction: _____

1. What is the most important thing I want this target to know about me? (This is where you position yourself. If they know nothing else about you, this is what you want them to know.) _____

_____

2. What is the second most important thing I want this target to know about me? (This could support and/or broaden your introductory statement.) _____

_____

3. Key selling points: statements/accomplishments that support/**prove** the first two statements:

a. _____

b. _____

c. _____

d. _____

e. _____

4. Statement of why they should be interested in me/what separates me from my competition: _____

_____

_____

_____

5. Other key selling points that may apply even indirectly to this industry or position: _____

_____

_____

_____

6. Any objection I'm afraid the interviewer may bring up, and how I will handle it: _____

_____

Summary of What I Have/Want to Offer—Target 2

To Help Me Develop My Written Pitch to That Target

You must know:
- to whom you are pitching; you have to know something about them.
- what they ideally want in a candidate.
- what they are interested in.
- who your likely competitors are.
- what you bring to the party that your competitors do not.

For Target 1:   Geographic area: _____
Industry or organization size:_____
Positionfunction: _____

1. What is the most important thing I want this target to know about me? (This is where you position yourself. If they know nothing else about you, this is what you want them to know.) _____
_____

2. What is the second most important thing I want this target to know about me? (This could support and/or broaden your introductory statement.) _____
_____

3. Key selling points: statements/accomplishments that support/**prove** the first two statements:

a. _____
b. _____
c. _____
d. _____
e. _____

4. Statement of why they should be interested in me/what separates me from my competition: _____
_____
_____
_____

5. Other key selling points that may apply even indirectly to this industry or position: _____
_____
_____
_____

6. Any objection I'm afraid the interviewer may bring up, and how I will handle it: _____
_____

Summary of What I Have/Want to Offer—Target 3

To Help Me Develop My Written Pitch to That Target

You must know:
- to whom you are pitching; you have to know something about them.
- what they ideally want in a candidate.
- what they are interested in.
- who your likely competitors are.
- what you bring to the party that your competitors do not.

For Target 1: Geographic area: _____

Industry or organization size: _____

Positionfunction: _____

1. What is the most important thing I want this target to know about me? (This is where you position yourself. If they know nothing else about you, this is what you want them to know.) _____

_____

2. What is the second most important thing I want this target to know about me? (This could support and/or broaden your introductory statement.) _____

_____

3. Key selling points: statements/accomplishments that support/**prove** the first two statements:

a. _____

b. _____

c. _____

d. _____

e. _____

4. Statement of why they should be interested in me/what separates me from my competition: _____

_____

_____

_____

5. Other key selling points that may apply even indirectly to this industry or position: _____

_____

_____

_____

6. Any objection I'm afraid the interviewer may bring up, and how I will handle it: _____

_____

Additional Thoughts

Hints for Seemingly Low-Key People

In this country, we often think that people who are openly assertive, forceful, and dynamic are more able to get work done through others than those who are thoughtful, persistent—and perhaps relentless. These seemingly low-key, quiet types may have their abilities undervalued and their working style misunderstood. The hiring team may incorrectly see them as unable to make a strong impression on a customer, sell their ideas internally, or push projects through. They may even seem less intelligent than they actually are. Sometimes these people do not get the jobs they deserve because the interviewer is not able to see the full force of their personality at the interview itself.

If you are a low-key person, you may come across as meeker in the interview than you have been in your jobs. So be sure to sit forward in your seat, use more hand gestures than may be usual for you, and constantly put active, dynamic words into your conversation. Help the hiring team to understand your true style on the job. For example:

"I aggressively promoted products."

"I inspire and motivate people to go beyond whatever goals are set."

"Despite my low-key demeanor, I'm seen as a person who is relentless in meeting goals through others."

"I'm able to sell to anyone by using a low-key approach that disarms people."

"Once I am on the job, people see me as someone to be reckoned with, and I am able to convince them to do what needs to be done."

Make sure the hiring team sees you the way you really are on the job and also sees the benefit of having someone with your style.

It's Not Necessarily Easier to Get a Lower-Level Job

When job hunters have problems finding a job at their current level, they often want to lower their sights. They think, I'll take a job two levels lower than the one I just had. But there is competition at that level, too.

A man was forced into early retirement after having been president of a major chain of retail stores. He didn't need much money, and he simply wanted to work at an easy job. He admired The Five O'Clock Club and asked if he could do junior-level office work for a modest salary. He said he was willing to run errands, stuff envelopes, and do other mundane assignments. He assumed that we would be eager to hire him for that job, because he was such a bargain.

But many people wanted that office-administration position, and most were more qualified for the job than he was. The other candidates knew how to use computers, would be better at taking phone messages and following up than he would have been, and had actually had experience doing those tasks.

If you honestly want a lower-level job, present a logical rationale to the hiring team, and think about your competition exactly the same way you would if you were going after a job at your most recent level.

Darest thou, now O soul,
Walk out with me toward
the unknown region
Where neither ground is
for the feet nor any path to follow?

WALT WHITMAN

How to Handle Your References

In an exploratory meeting, the ball ends up in the savvy manager's court, which is exactly the intent. An observant manager also gains valuable information about the political lay of the land from such a meeting.

The manager should come out with a good sense of how hard a sell the idea is going to be. A great number of objections indicate a tough road but still can be used to develop strategy. Every objection or reservation shows a concern that needs to be taken into account or an agenda item of the manager who is objecting.

JOEL M. DeLUCA, PH.D., *POLITICAL SAVVY*

Navigating the Minefield

When you reach the reference-checking stage, two opposing forces are at work: prospective employers (sometimes) want to find out as much as possible about you, while previous employers (usually) want to say as *little* as possible about you—and all *you* want, when the dust has settled, is that *a few nice things* have been said about you. You must play a role in achieving this, and it requires strategy and savvy. Leave as little as possible to chance.

Companies need to protect themselves against lawsuits and tend to clam up when they are asked for references. Their policy, officially, is to give out your dates of employment and title—that is, name, rank and serial number—only. In some cases, this could work to your advantage, but actually it would not be good if your prospective employer makes inquiries and *everybody* pleads the fifth. Your future boss would worry that something was wrong. Of course, everyone expects that the HR people at your former

employer will be sticklers for policy and disclose almost nothing. But, as we all know, that's not really how business works. That's not the way the game is played: people will find a way to find out about you—if they want to. And you can't afford to be passive.

Thus, it's best if prospective employers are able to get *good* information about you, and you have some control over that. *You* need to be prepared to provide the names of good references and be *thorough* in preparing for this part of the search process.

What commonly happens, however? You go through the entire interview process, and then they ask for references. The dot.com you worked for has gone out of business. They loved you there. Too bad you don't know where to find your old boss. The previous manager you worked for didn't like you all that much, and you didn't like him either. And you forgot to ask any of your coworkers to serve as a reference for you, and now it's job-offer time.

Don't wait until you get a job offer to think about your references. Take care of them now. Take care of them always.

Here's some advice to help get you through this important process.

1. **Make a list of people you want to use as references.** Depending on the relationships you've forged over the years, former bosses, your boss's boss, and even former coworkers or clients can be used as references. If you are in a consulting or part-time job, be sure to add your current boss to the list. If there is no way you can risk giving your *former* boss's name as a reference, be prepared

with names of peers, subordinates, your former boss's boss, or boss's peers as backup references.

Come up with a list of names appropriate for the position you're going after. For example, the prospective employer may be interested in hearing from a few former clients of yours, as well as one boss and one peer. Of course, you would rarely use your *present* place of employment as a reference. If you confide in your boss that you are looking, chances are strong that you will be shut out and forced out—or maybe even fired on the spot.

2. **Next, get permission.** Ask the people on your list if they would serve as a reference for you. Get the agreement of three or four people, at least one of whom should be a boss or former boss. Tell everyone about the kinds of jobs you are looking at, and remind them of the good things you did for them— things you would like them to tell others about you. In other words, help people with the reference process. For more about this, see Point 4.

You can say to the prospective reference: "I was hoping to use your name as a reference in my job search. Do you think you would feel comfortable providing a strong reference for me?" If you sense that a person is lukewarm (that is, not inclined to give you a *great* reference), you don't want to use that person. If the person promises to be "very fair" and "provide a balanced picture," get someone else. Hiring managers *expect* you to give them the names of people who will have glowing reports about you. Remember: This is a game— it's a game when an interviewer asks you why you left your last two jobs (she doesn't want to hear all the gory details!)—she wants to hear positive things. If a reference talks frankly to a prospective employer about your good and bad points, you may not stack up well against the other applicants.

3. **Do your best to make sure that the hiring company talks to your best references first**. For example, tell any interviewer who asks for your references that you would like to call them first, as a courtesy, and you'll let them know which ones you have contacted. Your best reference may be from five years ago—and you'll be positioned better if this is the first reference checked. Say, "I was able to reach George Duke and Agnes Forrest, so you can contact them now." This is just another aspect of staying in control of the process. Ask George and Agnes to get back to you when they have spoken to your prospective employer (see Point 7). Then you'll know it's okay to release a few more names, saving the weakest till last.

Give a little warning about the weak references. Be sure to say, "You can call Jacob now, but don't expect to hear great things. He was very upset at my leaving, (or he tends not to give good references)." Get your two cents' worth in before they contact that person. That way, if they do hear something negative about you, they'll think to themselves, "Oh, that's what Kevin said they would say." You don't want people to be surprised by what they hear.

4. **Help your references to help you**. Some time ago, I received a call from a prospective employer checking on Bessie, a woman who had worked for me and used to head the accounting department. The caller asked, "Is Bessie the type who was happiest heading the accounting department?" I raved about Bessie's managerial and organizational skills. The caller said, "That's just what I was afraid of. We were considering her for an analytical position." So I had to backtrack and praise Bessie's analytical skills and ability to work alone. Call your references and tell them the kind of job you are applying for and what you would like them to say about you. Help them help you. You can even put some points in writing so the

references can refer to your sheet when they get a call about you. This leaves little to chance.It may sound pushy to prompt your references this way, but they'll usually appreciate having a script to follow.

Sometimes, after you receive an offer, you will be asked to sign a statement releasing your former employers from liability about anything they may say about you. This means that your former employers can feel free to tell the truth about you as they see it. So then it's especially important to guide who they call about you, if possible.

5. **Keep in touch with your references on an ongoing basis.** People change jobs a lot, and that includes your former bosses; you don't want to discover that you can't find your favorite old boss. If a company looks as though it is folding, get the home address and phone numbers of those you would like to use as references. Send these people a holiday card each year—just so you can keep tabs. If the card is returned by the post office, you need to make calls right away before the trail goes really cold.

When I had run The Five O'Clock Club for 20 years, I didn't need references anymore, but I still had on my mailing list a boss I had 20 years earlier. I didn't want to lose touch with him.

Work hard to eliminate the problem of not being able to locate someone who could provide the perfect reference when you need it. Of course, if you don't want anyone to contact a boss from five years ago who didn't like you, then let the guy disappear. Then you can honestly say you can't locate them.

6. **Protect your references from too many phone calls.** If lots of prospective employers call the same person, your references will get annoyed and you will look like a loser: "I wonder why Joe is having such a hard time finding a job." So don't give out your references too soon or too freely. If an employer

asks for references before you've even had a meeting, that is too soon— except in academia, where it is more standard to give references up front.

Don't let people call your references unless they are on the verge of making you an offer that's acceptable to you. Just say, "My references are very important to me, and I don't want to bother them with phone calls until we're really sure we want to work together."

7. **Ask your references to follow up with you**. You need to know when a reference has actually been called, so ask your references to let you know when they are contacted. Then debrief them. Remember, the ball is always in your court. Your references may be able to shed some light on how a prospective employer feels about you, and you may get information to help you with more follow-up.

Also, if you have given out three names and none of them has been called within a week or two, you are probably not as close to an offer as you think. Call the hiring company and try to uncover any possible hidden objections.

8. **Thank your references.** After you get a job, let them know what happened and thank them for their help. Keep Point 5 in mind: These are people who have helped you; keep in touch on an ongoing basis.

If You Left under Bad Circumstances

Think of it this way: Many of the people we meet at The Five O'Clock Club have had a recent problem despite an otherwise fine career. Yet they get new jobs.

In the case of an unhappy departure, it's best if you and your former manager can settle on a mutually agreeable story. If this is impossible, think of a substitute reference, such as someone who used to be your boss, even if it was a while back. Then say, "I worked for Jane for five years, so she knows me better than my most recent boss."

If they *still* insist on speaking with your former boss, it's time for a preemptive strike to warn them that they might not hear good things. You might want to say something like this: "I'll be happy to give you Jonathan's phone number. I'm sure he'll be able to tell you details about the work I did. But I wanted to become part of a productive and organized team, which was not the case in my last position. Jonathan's style is more flamboyant and seat-of-the-pants, so please keep that in mind when you speak with him. And definitely do give him a call. But I really want you to hear about a special project I worked on when Jane was my boss, so be sure to call her as well...."

If you've been at one place for a long time but had problems only with your most recent boss, then you have a long track record of success with that employer. If you'd been there a short time, then you probably had a long track record of success elsewhere. Focus on your past successes, not on your most recent failure.

For example, if you worked for your last employer only 6 months but worked for the prior one for 10 years, you would obviously prefer that they contact the employer for whom you worked for 10 years. Then you need to say to your prospective employer, "I worked at that place for only 6 months, and it didn't work out. You'd get better information about me if you contacted the employer where I worked for 10 years."

You need a rationale for why interviewers should *not* contact your most recent employer. Don't fabricate a story. Chances are, you have a good reason. Just BRIEFLY state your reason. Don't go on and on about it. If it's true, you could say, for example, "I had four bosses in two years." Or perhaps your style is more like the style of the company where you are now interviewing. Or point out where you have learned from your past about the kind of firm where you would work best, and that's why you're so excited about this new opportunity.

Or my favorite, which I used in my own search: "Everyone makes one mistake in his or her career, and going to that firm was mine. If you would like a more balanced feedback of my per-

formance, it would be better if your contacted Bob Johnson at Acme instead, and here's why." Remember this is a game. People who have decided to hire you want to hear positive things about you, so get good at positioning your strengths during the reference-checking stage.

If You Work in a Field Where Everyone Knows Everyone Else

In a very small, tight field where everyone knows the people where you used to work, you may not have a chance to give out references. Prospective employers simply pick up the phone and call people where you used to work—even if HR has a strict policy against such informal reference checking. You will have to develop a strategy about how to handle this in your particular case. Often, there are key players in the industry—people whom everyone calls. Try to make sure those people think well of you. If that's not possible, do a preemptive strike and suggest names of people the prospective employer can call. One good rule that flows out of this reality of "reference by reputation" is: Work to establish a sterling reputation. Become known as a great boss and peer. There are consequences when you don't; if you are difficult to get along with, your reputation will precede you.

Gaining Leverage in the Reference Game

What if things did not work out well in your last job, and you're afraid prospective employers will want to call them as a reference? Get on with your search, line up some other references—perhaps someone you worked with earlier or someone at your last organization who liked you—and *have three or four job possibilities in the works.* When you're in demand, your prospective employers won't care so much about a few bumps in your past. They'll care more about beating out the other companies that are interested in you.

By the way, if you're talking to a small- to mid-sized company, and you have 6 to 10 things in the works, they are less likely to do a reference check. And if they do, it's likely to be perfunctory, because they're influenced by your marketability.

If a Former Boss Is Sabotaging You

If you're getting interviews everywhere, second interviews, and then no job offers, then your references may be suspect.

If you think a former boss is doing you in, you could have a friend call your former employer and pretend to be interested in hiring you. Your friend can probe to see what your former boss says about you. If it really is a problem, you could approach your former boss and say that you are having a problem getting a job and think that it's because of his references. Ask him directly what he is saying about you. Tell him what you'd like him to say, and negotiate with him. Focus on whatever you did well in that organization, not on your most recent failure. As we said earlier, job hunters can write out a script for a former employer, listing the good things you think the former employer might be willing to say. Then, when your former employer gets a call, he or she can just refer to the script.

If he *insists* on saying bad things:

- Figure out a way not to use him as a reference.
- Bring your concerns to human resources. Believe me, they *will* care (see below).
- Or tell prospective employers that you've been working for 20 years and have lots of great references, but your latest employer is unlikely to give you a good reference because he (for example) tends to say negative things about everyone. That way, when they call him, they will not expect to hear good things and will somewhat discount what he says.

A former employer should not have the power to derail your career. In fact, employers are not allowed to say whatever they want, and human resources above all will be sensitive to this. Terminated employees can sue for defamation if they think they have been *wrongly* maligned by a former employer. A former employee can sue for what a former employer tells prospective employers who seek a reference, and they can sue for what a former employer tells former coworkers about the termination. (Amy DelPo, *Dealing With Problem Employees: A Legal Guide*, Nolo Press, 6th edition, 2011).

We're not suggesting you sue your former employer. On the contrary, lawsuits are usually a bad idea. These cases are difficult to win, even though your employer can say only things he can prove are true. However, knowing that your employer is not allowed to say just any old thing about you gives you some clout. Most employers know they should be careful when giving out references; they know there's a reason why many companies have a strict policy about giving out only your title and dates of employment. But if your former boss doesn't use judgment when giving references, go to human resources and tell them that someone ought to talk to your former boss because he is ruining your chances of getting another job. Then give them your evidence of this (such as "I had a friend call and my former boss said...").

One final note on lawsuits. Not only are they difficult to win but also they are a huge distraction. *You should be focusing on your job search.* Furthermore, if word gets out that you're suing your former boss, prospective employers are likely to lose interest in you—*fast.*

Asking for a Written Reference

It's more common for young people, but even seasoned professionals may ask an employer for a written reference (especially via LinkedIn). While a letter of reference or a LinkedIn reference may not be considered as good as a reference done via the phone—which allows for probing during the give-and-take of conversation—enthusiastic praise captured forever can be valuable. And if you do lose contact with the reference, you've always got what they said in writing.

But make it easy for your reference to provide the letter. Don't be like Jeff, who was young, naive—and just a little bit lazy. Jeff was about two years out of college, working for a company whose president had great influence in the industry. Jeff thought a letter of reference would help him tremendously as he applied for positions in the future.

Jeff sent an email to the company president asking for a written letter of recommendation. The president said he would help Jeff in any way he could, but Jeff was aghast when "he wanted *me* to write the letter, and then pass it along to him for editing."

Jeff should count his blessings. You can only imagine how many requests for references the president of a company gets. He cannot spend his time writing references—he has to manage the company. Yet, what a nice guy he is for offering to "help in any way he could."

But Jeff has to make the president's job easier. He has to put in a little effort if he wants a reference. I often ask employees to give me a draft when they want a reference from me. Then I know what aspects of their personalities and their jobs they want to have emphasized. They are also reminding me of what they have done. If I'm trying to help them, the last thing I need is someone complaining that I left out an important project he or she worked on!

So, if you want a written reference, ask your boss and volunteer to write a draft. You'll see how difficult it is to do.

Writing is easy. All you have to do is stare at a blank sheet of paper till drops of blood form on your forehead.

GENE FOWLER (WRITER)

How to Write a Reference Letter (Also Called a "Letter of Commendation")

The following guidelines can be used as a template:

- Put "To Whom It May Concern" at the

top, then use the first sentence to place you in context: "Jeff worked with us for two years in the capacity of...."
- Next, give a general appraisal ("Through-out his time with the company he was a top-notch employee and...").
- Follow with some details of what you've accomplished. Don't be afraid to brag a little.
- Finally, you could conclude with something like "I would highly recommend Jeff for whatever position he believes is appropriate."

Then your manager will modify your letter to suit her style and perhaps include things she knows about you.

Then, Keep Up the Good Work

Don't forget you've got to live up to the letter of recommendation!

I once wrote a terrific letter of reference for Stan, an employee who was also a student, about to graduate and move on (of course, at my request, he first wrote a draft). Once Stan had that letter in his hot little hands, he slacked off; he missed days and showed up late. He figured he had what he needed.

Au contraire! A few weeks later, I received a phone call from a vice president of a venture capital firm who asked about Stan. This would be a plum opportunity for a recent graduate. Stan would be the assistant to the president of an organization. He would travel with the president and help him get ready for meetings. All of the other students who worked there did copying and stuffing envelopes but were glad just to be in that firm.

I urged them to hire Stan but mentioned that he sometimes had to take off from work for personal reasons, although I thought those reasons were behind him (this was true). I was trying to give them a hint that he may have problems, although I didn't want to ruin his chances of getting this great job.

A few months later, the venture capital firm

called me again to say that they *had* hired Stan—but they had just *fired* him, too! He routinely missed work and gave very lame excuses. The vice president said to me, "He must have thought we were stupid!"

Developing Your Character

Young people can get away with character flaws: arrogance, pettiness, impatience, recklessness, impulsiveness, distractedness (to name a few suggested by the students in our office!). Managers excuse them because of their youth, and they expect that young people will grow out of it. But as employees get older, managers are less tolerant—they figure you ought to know better. When you are older, you are likely to *lose* your job because of your arrogance—and other character flaws.

I once coached Jane, whose reputation preceded her. She was brilliant but irritating and unpopular with her bosses and peers. By her mid40s, she had chewed up so many relationships that she couldn't find a job. I explained to her that she had achieved her previous high level not because of her personality but in spite of it. Like so many obnoxious people, she mistook being difficult for being strong and committed. When she was younger, she could get away with being arrogant, but managers expect mature behavior from adult employees. After all, there are *lots* of bright people around, and employers can choose the *nice ones*. Many studies have shown that managers prefer ability to get along over high IQ.

Jane decided to reform. She went to those she had offended and apologized. Did she turn into a charmer? No. But she learned a little humility and how to bite her tongue. She realized that if she couldn't keep a job, maybe she wasn't so bright after all! She's now been with her present employer seven years.

If You've Made a Big Mistake

Here's a sticky one, and I'm sure some readers (especially older ones) will not agree with me on this case. I received an email from the mother of Julian. Her 16-year-old son and three other teenage boys were fired from their jobs at a local grocery store because they stole soda, candy, and/or money. Julian made restitution, wrote a letter of apology, and asked the owner for forgiveness. The owner said he'd forgive him but could not give him a job reference.

People of all ages make mistakes. Julian seemed to have learned his lesson. Here's the sticky part—and remember that the topic right now is protecting your references. If Julian were my son, I would advise him *not* to put the grocery job on his record. Just pretend this part of his life never happened, resolve to do better in the future, and get a fresh start at age 16 ½.

Now, what if you're older and have had a problem? According to the National WorkRights Institute, a nonprofit human rights organization (and reported in the *New York Times*), "Forty-six million people in the United States have been convicted of something sometime in their lives and our economy would collapse if none of them could get jobs.... That figure includes everybody in the FBI's criminal records database, which includes people convicted of a relatively minor misdemeanor." Where would we be without forgiveness and fresh starts?

Remember that George W. Bush was convicted of driving while intoxicated quite a long time ago, but he was still considered for a very important job. Generally speaking, everyone should have a chance at redemption. I asked a few human resources people for their thoughts, and I heard that companies are only supposed to ask about felonies. But I've seen applications that ask if you have ever been arrested. That's outrageous. And even when someone has been convicted of a crime, hiring systems should be flexible. People should not be branded for life. One woman who emailed me said she was convicted of battery years ago after hitting a woman she found in bed with her husband. It's unfair that she should be punished for life. None of us is perfect, after all. We're supposed to believe in second chances. In fact, as of this writing, many states are passing reforms that say a person may not be excluded from consideration for a job because of a criminal record unless the crime relates specifically to the job. Check out the situation in the state where you live.

In the meantime, if your record includes an arrest, misdemeanor, or felony, stay away from large corporations, which are more likely to have more rigid policies and more thorough background checks. Go after the smaller firms (fewer than 1,000 employees) and not-for-profit organizations. Certain convictions will limit a person from entering fields such as banking, health careers, and computer information systems. Work hard at getting letters of reference or introductions from previous employers. As a matter of routine, attach these to your resume. This may help move the hiring team past the reference issue.

Some people have been able to have their convictions expunged (erased). This varies from state to state, and the laws are changing all the time, so see an attorney.

If you have made mistakes in your past, don't let your fears run away with you. References may seem like an impossible mountain to climb. But are they? If you perfect your interviewing skills, you may win people over. They may not care all that much about references. Don't believe me? A survey for the *New York Times* advertising department found that two-thirds of hiring managers thought interviews were the most effective way to judge job candidates, while "fewer than one in six hiring managers said that references are an effective manner of determining whether to hire a candidate."

In closing, I want to point out that the job-search process is a research process: finding out where you fit in and who will accept you. Your life might have to change—but life goes on, often for the better. I have been inspired by former New York State Court of Appeals Judge Sol Wachtler, who was on his way to becoming governor. He spent 15 months in prison for stalking an ex-lover (while self-medicating at the rate of 5,000 pills in an 18-month period while serving on the bench). After his astonishing fall, Wachtler, now rehabilitated, teaches at a small college and lectures to keep others off unprescribed drugs. Of his long, dark period when his life fell apart, Wachtler says, "It's true that when one door closes, another opens, but the hallways are hell."

At no point in the job search should you go it alone, and references are no exception, because references can be a complicated matter. Every individual has a unique situation, all the more reason to get help in brainstorming what to do. That's why we have small groups, so you can discuss your reference strategies with your small group and your coach.

Being entirely honest with oneself is a good exercise.

Dr. Sigmund Freud

The Five O'Clock Club

How to Handle Rejection Personally and Professionally

In nature, there are neither rewards nor punishments—there are consequences.

ROBERT GREEN INGERSOLL

First, the pragmatics:

Rejection in Response to a Networking Contact You Tried to Make

The person did not understand you were seeking information. If many people respond to you this way, reassess your approach to networking.

Rejection Following a Job Interview

This is a true rejection letter. It used to be it took seven job interviews to get one offer, but the figure may now be higher. If you are still interested in the organization, don't give up. (Read what Michael did in the chapter "Following Up When There Is No Immediate Job.")

Lessons to Learn

When you get rejected after a job interview, think about it. How interested are you in that firm? Did you hit it off with the interviewer? If you think there was some mutual interest, see if there might be other jobs with the organization later—perhaps in another department. Or perhaps the person hired instead of you might not work out. Keep in touch. Job hunters rarely do, but employers like to hire people who truly want to work for them and show it by keeping in touch.

CASE STUDY Stan
Turning a Rejection into an Offer

Stan was told an offer was being made to another candidate. He was crushed, but he immediately dashed off a letter to the hiring manager and hand-delivered it. The brief letter said in part:

I was disappointed to hear you have offered the position to someone else. I truly believe I am right for the position and wish you would keep me in mind anyway. You never know—something could happen to the new person, and you may need a replacement. Please consider me no matter when this may occur, because I believe I belong at your institution.

The next day, Stan received a call with an offer. Some people may think the offer to the other candidate fell through. However, I believe Stan's letter influenced the hiring manager. When he saw the letter, he thought to himself, We're offering the position to the wrong person! and he allowed the negotiation with the other candidate to lapse.

And now, handling your emotions.

Cut down on stress and you'll increase your chances of finding a new job. If you've been out of work a while, you're really feeing it. Money woes. A sense of rejection. Questions and pressure from family and friends. If you've lost your job, you know this dismal laundry list all too well.

It's all too easy to convince yourself that you will never find another job, a mindset that can turn into a self-fulfilling prophecy. Here are a few suggestions that will help you push through your job-hunt stress:

- **It is OK to be "between jobs."** When you don't have a job, "So what do you do?" becomes a dreaded question. We resort to a euphemism, "I'm between jobs."

   You must learn to ignore the inner voice that in your darkest moments says, "I'll never get a good job again." Even if you have just been turned down for three jobs, remind yourself that you got three interviews and you can get three more.

- **Stay in touch with colleagues and friends from your former workplace.** When you are unemployed, the daily camaraderie of the office is gone. One of the most painful aspects of not going to work every day is missing people who were fun to be around. In addition, they will be able to remind you of your past achievements.

- **Treat your job search like a job**. The lack of a job-day routine can be disorienting. You can feel that you have been cut loose.

   The best way to overcome the loss of your daily routine is to create a new one. Treat your job search as your new job. Providing yourself with the day-to-day structure you are familiar with will help you keep your sanity and get you going in your job search more quickly.

- **Exercise regularly and keep a healthy lifestyle**. Regular physical exercise and a healthy diet help to reduce tension and stress. If your former routine involved going to the gym and you can still afford it, keep going. If you can't, a half-hour walk every day will do the trick.

Keep an eye on what you're eating as well. Healthy foods give you energy.

- **Take time to enjoy the change of pace**. Being freed from the 9-to-5 grind means you finally have time to take stock of what you really want to achieve in your life. Think about your life and plot course corrections. Some questions to consider as you plan your job search:

   1. What matters to me the most?
   2. What do I want to do differently?
   3. What hasn't worked for me in the past?
   4. What was my own role in my job loss? What can I do better the next time?
   5. How am I taking care of myself?

- **Stay away from negative news and naysayers**. Even in good economic times, you don't have to go far to find negative news about the world situation. During a recession, it's in your face 24/7, and it's something you should stay away from if you can. Similarly, stay away from naysayers. Their negativity will only get you down.

- **If you need to vent, vent!** Getting it all out does have healing power, and there is nothing especially heroic or brave about trying to go it alone. Find support groups at churches and synagogues, libraries and community centers. You will find people who will listen and whose stories will help you to feel less isolated.

- **Your unemployment is a business problem**. When you had bad days at work, you analyzed whatever problem was plaguing you, marshaled resources and people, and came up with solutions. In the same way, set your objective: To find a satisfying job that pays the bills. And develop your business strategy for achieving it.

- **Celebrate short-term successes**. When you get up in the morning, set up some achievable goals for the day so that you can end it with a sense of accomplishment. Write five more targeted letters. Identify 10 more companies to contact. Make 10 follow-up phone calls. Set up one or two meetings to network. Just being able to cross these goals off your list at the end of the day is a good feeling. And, of course, they often lead to something even better.

- **Keep on top of your game**. Not going into the office is no excuse to let your skills and knowledge slip. There's no better time than a job search to make sure you stay current and sharp. Catch up on reading journals and attending meetings of your professional associations. You might consider taking a course, one that you could never find the time for when you were employed.
- **Have fun**. In the same way that you get burned out on your job after working nonstop for a month or two, you can get burned out on your job search. You need to stay fresh.

If you stay positive and make, "I will persevere!" your motto, you will land a great job, sooner or later.

One of the best ways to properly evaluate and adapt to the many environmental stresses of life is to view them as normal. The adversity and failures in our lives, if adapted to and viewed as normal corrective feedback to use to get back on target, serve to develop in us an immunity against anxiety, depression, and the adverse responses to stress. Instead of tackling the most important priorities that would make us successful and effective in life, we prefer the path of least resistance and do things simply that will relieve our tension, such as shuffling papers and majoring in minors.

DENIS WAITLEY
© 2010 THE WAITLEY INSTITUTE, INC.

PART THREE

The Five O'Clock Club Approach to Interviewing

THINK LIKE A CONSULTANT

Basic Interviewing Techniques

Just know your lines and don't bump into the furniture.

SPENCER TRACY'S ADVICE ON ACTING

Most people think of the interview as the *end* of the job-search process. They think: "Thank goodness. I finally got an interview!" But at The Five O'Clock Club, we think of the interview as the *beginning* of the process. So far, you've searched to line up *meetings*, but your *job* search is just beginning.

What an Interview Really Is—and What It Isn't

An interview is a business meeting—a time to exchange information between an organization's representative and a person, namely you. As many Five O'Clock Club coaches suggest, it is helpful to your self-esteem to think of interviews as *meetings* and even refer to them that way.

The purpose of the interview is *not* to get a job. Perhaps you find this shocking, but the purpose of the interview is to get information and give information—so you'll get another meeting.

Most job hunters try to close too soon. They're under a lot of pressure. When they're going in for their first meeting, everyone says: "I hope you get the job!" At The Five O'Clock Club, we hope you *don't*. We hope you get the next *meeting*. It is unlikely that you will get an offer for a good job after just one meeting. I would wonder what's wrong with the company: Is it the type that hires easily and fires easily?

Instead of trying to land a job immediately, conduct yourself at the first interview so that they

will want you back for a second one. Get enough information so that you can follow up intelligently. It is not uncommon in today's market to have 12 to 15 meetings at one company for one job. You may have fewer, but don't count on it. Instead, plan to be in this for the long haul with each company, perhaps with 6 to 10 meetings.

The *primary* purpose of the first meeting is to start to uncover information about:

- the organization
- the job
- the environment
- the opportunity
- the boss
- your prospective peers

Another purpose of your interview is to uncover their objections—to find out if there's any reason they might be *reluctant* to bring someone like you on board. Any salesperson will tell you that the sale begins *after* the customer reveals the reason for his or her reluctance to buy. Once this is done, you have a chance of *overcoming* objections. Later, we'll tell you how to uncover this information and increase your chances of turning a job interview into a job offer.

The First Two Minutes

Many people have heard that the hiring decision is made during the first two minutes. *That's* a lot of pressure, and it's wrong! So forget about everything hinging on the first few minutes, or even the conventional wisdom that an interview is a *selling* opportunity. Yes, that's true, but it's far more complex than that. And it's not over when an interview is finished. Many people say, "It's in God's hands now," but that's the attitude of someone who has *given up*. Chances are, there's a lot more you can do—and God wouldn't want you to be so passive! At The Five O'Clock Club we say, "After the interview, you're just getting *started*."

While it is true that a hiring manager will quickly decide against you if you look like a slob or have tattoos and piercings all over your face, the average job hunter has *many* more chances than the first two minutes. By following The Five O'Clock Club approach, you can turn around a situation that normally would have ended in failure. In fact, many a Five O'Clock Clubber that got an actual *rejection* letter after a job interview have still been able to turn the situation around and wind up getting hired.

Obviously the way you move will be affected by the character you are playing; but natural movement comes from your "center," from the same place as a natural voice. When you walk from your center, you will project a solid perspective of yourself. Walk with that certainty and ease, and your path becomes a center of gravity. Your force pulls all eyes to you.

Slouch or poke your head forward, or pull your shoulders back uncomfortably, and that power seeps away. Only a relaxed, centered walk creates a sense of strength. A centered walk can be very menacing, too. Even if you don't get film work on the basis of this advice, follow it and you'll never get mugged, either.

MICHAEL CAINE, *ACTING IN FILM*

CASE STUDY Dorothy
Overcoming Their Objections

Dorothy, a reserved but highly intelligent and refined woman, was interviewing for a position as a consultant. She prepared thoroughly, dressed in a manner that she thought was appropriate, and conducted the meeting the best way she could.

She asked the interviewer if there was any reason that she might be hesitant to bring her on

board, compared with some of the other people they had seen. The interviewer responded that she was afraid that Dorothy would not come across as strong enough in her meetings with prospective clients: "In this business, you need to wow them."

When Dorothy did her follow-up letter, she stressed how successful she had been in the past with clients. She asked for another meeting.

This time she dressed in a power suit—a red one that would have been inappropriate for a first interview—and conducted herself very differently. The interviewer said she wondered why she had ever thought those negative things because they obviously were not true. Dorothy got the job and was very successful.

Each handicap is like a hurdle in a steeplechase, and when you ride up to it, if you throw your heart over, the horse will go along, too.

LAWRENCE BIXBY, "COMEBACK FROM A BRAIN OPERATION," HARPER'S

Dress and Act the Part

If you've worked in the same place for 10 years, your appearance may get a little sloppy and your coworkers will overlook it. But appearance counts on a job interview.

Here's an example. A coach had asked me to meet with his client, Gregory. Gregory was a banking vice president with excellent credentials who was having trouble getting a job. At the appointed time, I saw someone with a pronounced swagger coming down the hall with his suit jacket thrown over one shoulder. I said to myself, "This *can't* be him." But it was. As Gregory got closer, I could see that his shirt was dirty and terribly frayed around the collar and cuffs. During our meeting, however, Gregory presented himself well verbally, had intelligent things to say, and was not cocky or arrogant, but he just didn't *look* the part. I had expected to meet someone who looked like a bank vice president. Obviously, Gregory's dress and the way he walked were working against him. He was smart enough to believe me when I told him what had to be changed. He shaped up and got a job quickly.

Now, if you want to move up a level in your next job, dress for *that* level. I worked with Angie, who was going after a high-powered job, but her clothes just didn't look like she *deserved* that kind of money. It's important to look like you're worth what the job pays. Sara, on the other hand, dressed like a glamorous model when interviewing for a back-office job at a party planning company. She looked as if she wanted to be the hostess at the parties, and the employer was afraid Sara would be unhappy doing operations work. Sara realized she'd rather be a hostess and she applied for those kinds of jobs instead.

Dress consistently with the culture and for the job you're going after. If you're going for a job in a very conservative culture, dress conservatively. Play the game. Look the part. Don't have body odor. Have a crisp-looking hair style or whatever is appropriate for the industry.

It's true that employees in certain fields may wear jeans and sneakers to work, but that's rarely a standard for interviews.

> **A rule of thumb is to wear an outfit that's one or two levels above the job you're interviewing for.**

Dressing this way shows respect. It shows seriousness on your part. In the dot.com boom days, when there was a labor shortage in certain fields, some job applicants showed up in all sorts of attire and still got hired. But when the market tightened up, employers had *other* people to choose from, and they didn't have to settle for employees who showed such disdain for their work appearance. Employers usually want employees who don't look radical and who are in tune with a business environment. Employers want people who will go along, get along, and take their jobs seriously.

Remember, this is like show biz. Even if you don't feel self-confident, act as if you do, and that is reflected in how well you're put together. If you come in looking defeated, like a loser, why would anyone want to hire you? Act as if you are successful and feel good about yourself, and you will increase your chances of actually *feeling* that way. Enthusiasm counts. Every manager is receptive to someone who is sincerely interested in the company and the position—and dresses that way.

Here's a little number I do before a long take: take a slow deep breath in, then bend over and let your arms dangle, really relaxed. Straighten up slowly, breathing out gently and evenly. This exercise relaxes you, helps concentration and gives you control... it gets the oxygen to the brain. You feel and look like a twit, panting away, but you find you get a rush to your head, your eyes begin to sparkle a bit, and you're ready to play an energetic scene, mental or physical. Just be careful not to overdo the panting or you will hyperventilate and pass out.

MICHAEL CAINE, *ACTING IN FILM*

With Whom Will You Meet?

If you were invited to a business meeting—especially one where you were going to be the topic of discussion—you would naturally want to know who else would be there, and you might want to know something about them, such as:

- their names and job titles
- the issues important to each of them
- their personalities
- their ages
- the length of time they have been with the company

Yet most job hunters go into interviews—which, of course, are business meetings—unprepared, knowing little about the people.

At The Five O'Clock Club, we work to change your thinking on this issue. Matt, for example, was going to be screened by telephone by *five* recruiters from an out-of-town search firm. All five would be on the phone at the same time.

He told his Five O'Clock Club group about his upcoming meeting and said, "Wish me luck." And we thought, wish me luck? *Nobody* trained The Five O'Clock Club way says, "I'm going in blindly to a meeting with five other people. I don't even know who they are and just wish me luck." So we told him, "Call the search firm and get some information."

Even though Matt was talking to search firm people and not members of the hiring team, he needed to prepare as he would prepare for any other business meeting by simply asking about *each* of the people who'd be on the phone. What were their names? Their titles? What issues tended to be important to each of them?

Frankly, it's also nice to know a person's age beforehand. *You* know that it's very different if you're in a meeting with 28-year-old versus, say, a 58-year-old. You can't ask directly for a person's age, but you can get a feel for it. How long has the person been in the industry? How long in this organization? Those answers will give you a hint.

By the way, we also told Matt that he should ask the people to identify themselves as they spoke so he would know who said what during the call, and he should take notes so he can analyze the meeting later.

The meeting of two personalities is like the contact of two chemical substances; if there is any reaction, both are transformed.

CARL JUNG, MODERN MAN IN SEARCH OF A SOUL

The people you want to reach, whether they're your coworkers, your boss, or an organizational president, should be viewed as distinct target audiences that require different approaches and strategies.

JEFFREY P. DAVIDSON, MANAGEMENT WORLD,

Other Advice about Telephone Meetings

For most people, it's best if you can have an in-person meeting rather than be screened over the telephone. You can gather more information when you're there, watch the person's expressions, and have eye contact. So tell the interviewer, "I'd much prefer to meet with you in person—even for a brief meeting."

If you are forced into a telephone meeting, here are some extra words of advice from Dale Dauten, with whom I write a nationally syndicated newspaper column, "Kate and Dale Talk Jobs," published by King Features:

I've had many telephone interviews for various consulting jobs or speaking assignments, often by committees. I've done a bit of experimenting and can offer a couple of suggestions. First, sit at a desk or table, clear the area of any distractions and then spread in front before you the following: your résumé, a list of accomplishments, a list of questions you can ask them, research on the company, along with a blank pad of paper. I like to draw a rectangle on the blank pad, and think of that rectangle as a *conference table*. I find out in advance who'll be in on the conversation and put them around the *table*. Then as the members of the committee introduce themselves, I put key words next to each name. If they don't tell you their positions, ask. They'll be flattered. If, along the way, you can refer back to something one of them said, or ask each of them a question, you'll win them over, one by one.

Feel free to ask each of them, "What would you like most from the new hire?" and/or "What problems have you had in the past and what would you like to see done differently?" Find out their fears, their hopes, and what you can do to make their lives easier. Having that information, you can impress them during the call, and more important, address those issues in your follow-up letters, which you can be sure will be shared around. The committee will want to meet you in person, and that is the sole measure of victory in a phone interview. Do your preparation, and your panic will dissipate as you say to yourself, No one could be better prepared than I'm going to be.

Ask the Person Who Arranged the Meetings

To be better prepared, ask whoever set up the meeting—whether it was human resources, the hiring manager, a search firm, or an administrative assistant—to give you the information you need. You can say, "I'm excited about the meeting next week and want to prepare. I'd like to know something about the people I'll be meeting and the issues that are of concern to them." You may not find out everything you would like to, but even a little bit of information will help.

Let's say that the person who set up the meeting says to you, "Jane, you'll be meeting with Mr. Jack and Ms. Jill." Then you say, "Thanks very much. I'd like to prepare for the meeting. Could you tell me a little bit about each person?"

Or the scheduler says, "John, when you come in, we'll have you meet with five people." John should say, "Thanks very much. Could you tell me who they are and a little bit about each one of them?" And, as John is told each person's name and title, John should ask, "Do you know what Mr. Jones is like, or what issues tend to be important to him? I'd like to be prepared."

Try it. If it doesn't work out perfectly, you're still likely to have more information than you would have had. And you'll get better at asking for this kind of information before a meeting.

Develop Your Script

This is a basic, but important, Five O'Clock Club technique. Prepare a 3x5 card for each organization with which you'll meet. Write the following on it:

- Your pitch—your summary about yourself for this particular organization. "I'm an international marketing manager."

- Then write the headlines of three or four accomplishments you want to tell this specific company. "Increased sales 17% average per year over three years."
- Also write the question *you're most afraid they're going to ask you* at this specific company and how you're going to handle it.
- An answer to what you think might be the employer's main objection to you, if any.
- A statement of why you would want to work for this company.

> **Keep your 3x5 card in your pocket or purse and review it just before going in for the interview so that you will know your lines.**

Here's a scenario you can imagine. In the morning, you have to meet with one organization and in the afternoon you're meeting with another. It's hard to get your thoughts together for each of these meetings. *All* you have to do is pull the appropriate card out of your pocket or purse, look at it on the way into the meeting or in the elevator. Those are your *lines*. This is the information you'll cover during the interview— whether they ask for it or not. Then when you *leave* the meeting, just pull your card out again— to see whether you've covered those things. It's like testing yourself. Did you *cover* those points or didn't you? If you did *not* cover them during the interview, you can cover them in your follow-up letter. Those 3x5 cards are critically important.

It can become even more complex and sophisticated than that. It may be that you need a different 3x5 card for each person with whom you meet within one organization. You may want to make *different* points to the heads of research, finance, manufacturing, sales, and operations. Each of these people has different issues. Therefore, form a *hypothesis* ahead of time about what each person would be interested in—considering the kind of job that you're going after.

You're meeting with each of them for a reason. They're each *worried* about the person who's going to land the job. They're worried that *their* part of the organization might be ignored or that the new hire might make their lives difficult. The finance person may be interested in your budgeting skills. The salesperson may be interested in your interface with the sales people and the support you're going to give them. The manufacturing people may be wondering if you're going to give them sufficient information ahead of time so they can do their jobs well.

So it is important to form a hypothesis about the *concerns* of each person with whom you're going to meet. Prepare your 3x5 card for each. Then cover that information with each person and let them know *how* you'll make their lives easier if *you're* the one who gets the job. *Say* to them, "What would you like from this new hire? How can I make your life easier if I'm the one in this new job?" Tell the finance person some bulleted accomplishments about how you worked with finance in the past. Tell the marketing person how you worked with marketing in the past and how you would like to work with them in the future. You can see how *sophisticated* this simple 3x5 card approach can become.

Finally, for each of these people, list on that person's 3x5 card *the question you're most afraid they might ask* and how you'd handle it. For example, if you've never been in charge of a budget before, what's your answer to that? If you've never formally managed people, what's your answer to that? Your answer has to be something like "Well, I've managed dozens of people informally on projects when I was the project head."

Today, managing direct reports versus indirect reports is not as important as it used to be. Nor is it important whether you supervised people who are on payroll versus consultants.

Write down all of the difficult questions you hate the most. Then write your answers. Your 3x5 cards are your best friend in being prepared.

> **During the meeting, write down what they each say—so you can follow up more intelligently.**

If you don't take notes during the interview, it's all going to be a big blur. Chances are, you want to be able to recall what the finance person said versus the manufacturing person and the operations person. You'll be following up with each of these people so you *need* to know what *each* of them said—their key issues and concerns. For example, if the person's main issue is "I hope you have a good sense of humor"—and this happened to me once—then you'd better stress your sense of humor in your follow-up. If the person's main issue is the long hours the job requires and they're afraid you may have a problem with that, then make sure you address it. Whatever is important to them is important to you.

I am a great believer, if you have a meeting, in knowing where you want to come out before you start the meeting. Excuse me if that doesn't sound very democratic.

NELSON ROCKEFELLER

Think about Their Issues

In formulating your follow-up, try to think beyond what's been verbalized. That is, anticipate additional issues that are likely to be important to each person. Decide how you will address these issues. A financial person, for example, will most likely be concerned about the bottom line. An operations person, a marketing person, or someone in human resources will probably have different concerns.

You can also think about a person's concerns based on his or her position in the hierarchy. People higher up are generally more concerned about the direction of the department, division, or company, while those lower down are usually more concerned about the day-to-day workings of the job. Each person will care about whether you can do the job from their own perspective and perhaps whether you will fit in.

If they ask if you own a horse, say yes.
If they ask if you are a horse, say yes.
And you'll learn how to do it that night.

ROBERT PARRISH, AWARD-WINNING FILM EDITOR-DIRECTOR.
ADVICE HE RECEIVED FROM HIS MOTHER.
QUOTED IN *THE NEW YORK TIMES*

CASE STUDY Bob
Prepared for the Meetings

Bob, a marketing executive, had been looking for a job for a while when I met him, and he was very tired. He was now applying for a plum marketing job at a major information services company and was going in for his initial meeting.

Before the meeting, he researched to find out what was going on in the company. He formed a hypothesis about why they wanted to see him. He prepared his 3x5 card to address the issues he thought would be important to them, and wrote out a Two-Minute Pitch specifically for this company.

At this first meeting, he probed to find out the problems the company faced. He also tried to get a feel for the company culture.

When Bob had interviewed at other companies, they loved his ability to think up new product ideas. But he learned that this company already had plenty of new products; they wanted someone who could make their products successful.

He decided that his next step should be to meet more people. Bob did a thorough follow-up after the first round of interviews. He addressed the issues that were important to each person with whom he met, reminded each of the positives they found in him, and handled the negatives (the reasons why each person might not want to have him on board).

A man's accomplishments in life are the cumulative effect of his attention to detail.

JOHN FOSTER DULLES, QUOTED BY
LEONARD MOSLEY, *DULLES*

The Second Round of Interviews

Bob was called back to meet with five more people. Before the meetings, he asked their names and titles, found out a little about each person, including the issues that might be important to him or her, and the number of years he or she had been with the company.

Bob typed up a sheet with every name and job title and a hypothesis about what each person's concerns might be, how he could address those concerns, and the questions he wanted to ask each person. His sheets included, in brief:

- the head of sales, who Bob thought might be threatened by a new marketing person
- the head of finance, who would probably be concerned about the profitability of the new products
- the head of operations, who might be worried about being ignored by sales and marketing
- the head of human resources, who may be concerned about how well Bob would fit in
- his future boss, the head of all marketing (Bob prepared three pages of notes on this person!)

Courtesy of Jerry King, Cartoons, Inc.

"You're cute, very cute. But in this business cute just doesn't cut it. We need computer savvy individuals."

With this kind of preparation, Bob had hypotheses and solutions in mind, rather than going into each meeting cold. Thus he would be in a position to have the best meetings possible.

In addition to the questions he designed specifically for each individual, he asked them all:

- What would you like from whomever you hire for the new job?
- What are the things you would be afraid he or she might do in the new marketing position?
- How could the new person make your life easier?
- What are your most important concerns about this job and the new hire?
- He also asked questions that had to do specifically with this company and the job, such as:
- Who are your key competitors for these new products?
- Have you targeted new growth industries?
- I've heard that your company wants to move toward greater predictive offerings. Is this true? Have you been successful?

He also asked questions having to do with organizational issues, such as:

- The job seems to be in a state of flux. What is your impression of it?
- How would the new person work with each of the department heads?
- What would you like to see this person accomplish after the first year? After three to four years?
- What support could the new person look forward to from you?
- Would the new person work only within this one division or explore appropriate opportunities with other divisions?

In addition, Bob asked other selected people:

- Where are they in the hiring process?
- How many others are they considering?
- How do I stack up against them?

Questions You Might Ask in an Interview

You are there not only to answer the interviewer's questions, but also to make sure you get the information you need. Ask questions that are appropriate. What do you really want to know? Here are a few possibilities to get you thinking in the right direction:

Questions to Ask Human Resources

- Can you tell me more about the responsibilities of the job?
- What skills do you think would be most critical for this job?
- Is there a current organization chart available for this area?
- What happened to the person who held this job before?
- What kinds of people are most successful in this area?
- What do you see as the department's strengths and weaknesses?

Questions to Ask Managers (and Perhaps Peers)

- What are the key responsibilities of the job?
- What is the most important part of the job?
- What is the first problem that would need the attention of the person you hire?
- What other problems need attention now? Over the next six months?
- How has this job been performed in the past?
- Are there other things you would like someone to do that are not a formal part of the job?
- What would you like to be able to say about the new hire one year from now?
- What significant changes do you see in the future?
- May I ask what your background is?
- What do you find most satisfying about working here? Most frustrating?
- How would you describe your management style?
- How is the department organized?
- May I meet the other people who work in the area?
- How is one's performance evaluated? By whom? How often?
- What skills are in short supply here?

You can never enslave somebody who knows who he is.

ALEX HALEY

Bob treated everyone he met as an individual to be reckoned with and courted, and he handled them all *differently*.

> **His goal was to have each person see him as the ideal candidate.**

Being seen as *ideal* means emerging from the pack. To do this, he probed to understand thoroughly the situation for each department head.

During all this, Bob had to resist his natural tendency to think up new product ideas, since this was not something they wanted.

> **Don't ask: "Is there anything I can do to convince you that I'm the right person?" The answer is always no. Decide for *yourself* what you must do to convince them.**

If you have an important point to make, don't try to be subtle or clever. Use a pile driver. Hit the point once. Then come back and hit it again. Then hit it a third time—a tremendous whack.

WINSTON CHURCHILL, ON PUBLIC SPEAKING, QUOTED BY EDWARD, DUKE OF WINDSOR, *A KING'S STORY*

Problem Areas

There were a few problem areas:

- Bob's future boss seemed weak and might feel threatened by him. He had to reassure the boss in his follow-up that he would be a support and not a threat.
- Bob was not happy with the way he had come across to the operations head. When he wrote his follow-up, he said he was not pleased with the way he had addressed some

issues and went into great detail explaining his position.

Bob was able to write a very tailored follow-up to each person only because he had thoroughly prepared—he also took notes during the meetings so he would accurately remember what each person said.

Bob asked to meet with his future boss again to discuss some details and followed up in writing again after that meeting. Since this was a protracted process, Bob decided the human resources person, who was smart and also open, was the best one to keep in touch with for the status of the situation. In addition to all of his follow-up in writing, he wanted to have a feel for how things were going so that he could decide whether additional effort would be needed—for instance, if another candidate were to enter the race.

There are no hopeless situations. There are only men who have grown hopeless about them.

CLARE BOOTH LUCE, *EUROPE IN THE SPRING*

Round Three

Bob was called back for another round of meetings, this time with the head of management information services, the division head, and the human resources manager. When he went back for this round of interviews, Bob made a point of stopping in to see his future boss and also the operations head—to keep the contacts alive.

> **Your goal is to have each person be an advocate of having you on board. If there is anyone who objects to you, make sure you handle it now.**

I have always tried to be true to myself, to pick those battles I felt were important.

ARTHUR ASHE

A Hold in the Countdown

Human resources had already asked for six to eight references and had checked them out. Everything was fine. The head of human resources said, "They want you. In five years, I've never seen such enthusiasm. I'm sure they're about to make you an offer. Are you interested? When do you think you could start?"

Then suddenly everything was put on hold for seven weeks while the company decided to reengineer (reorganize). They assured Bob that everything was okay, and that he would be happy with the results—especially the money.

But Bob panicked. He couldn't stand the stress any more. He had been in search mode a long time, and his nerves were giving way. He was anxious to force their hand. If they wanted him, they could make him an offer now. What on earth could make them wait seven more weeks?

Midway in our life's journey,
I went astray from the straight road
and woke to find myself alone in a dark wood.

Dante, *The Inferno*

Don't Force It; Instead, Make Sure You Have 6 to 10 Things in the Works

As his career coach, it was all I could do to get Bob to focus on a broader search while he stayed in touch with them. Because he had such a good relationship with the human resources manager, Bob spoke mostly with that person. For the next seven weeks, the manager continued to assure Bob that things were going well, and he should just hang in there.

Bob said I couldn't possibly imagine the strain he was under. He told me of his daughter's health problems at home.

I warned him that the strain he was under now would be nothing compared to what he would feel if this job fell through and he had *nothing* else in the works. Starting a job search from scratch truly would be a nightmare. It's much better not to let one's momentum slip. So Bob bravely mustered the energy to focus on other possibilities, and he got a lot of other things in the works. However, he never relaxed.

Finally, the seven weeks was up. The company asked him to wait one more week. Then they made him an offer.

Do not drop your search activities when an offer seems almost certain. If it doesn't materialize, the lost momentum is difficult to recover.

—Advice from a successful job hunter at The Five O'Clock Club

---

Whensoever a man desires anything inordinately,
he is presently disquieted within himself.

Thomas à Kempis

Finally . . . the Offer

Bob was stunned by the offer: It was for the boss's job! Bob was not the only one who had seen the boss as weak; the rest of management did too. They offered Bob the job because he did not try to undermine his prospective manager or make him look bad. They saw that he played by the rules. The pay was phenomenal, and Bob deserved it.

Look at all the planning that Bob put into wooing this one company. Make sure you plan for each person with whom you will meet and keep notes on each (use the Interview Record in this book). Make sure everyone you meet wants to have you on board. Be in sync with their time frame, not your own. And be sure to have 6 to 10 things in the works—just in case. That is what's required in a successful job hunt.

Until you value yourself, you will not value your time.
Until you value your time, you will not do anything
with it.

Dr. M. Scott Peck

Courtesy of Jerry King, Cartoons, Inc.

"You're in luck. Word from upstairs
is that a position just opened up."

Research: Preparing for the Interview

There is no knowledge that is not power.

RALPH WALDO EMERSON, *OLD AGE*

Do Your Homework

Before the meeting, research the company and the industry. There's no excuse for going into an interview without knowing something about the organization. Interviewers expect you to know, at the very least, basic information available on the company website. They also expect you to know what has been written in the press about them. If you're asked why you are interested in the organization, you will have your answer if you've done this kind of homework. So do your research—through the library or the Internet and also through friends or contacts you may have in associations you belong to.

You don't want to look foolish. The hiring manager will probably ask, "So why would you like to work here at Smithfield Labs?" Often, the job hunter looks at the person as if to say, "Oh, is that where I am? I forgot what company I was interviewing with."

In most cases, of course, you will have plenty of time for research—but here's what one job hunter did when an interview came up with almost no warning. She knew she couldn't go in without research. Denise had a job interview scheduled at a major company—for a position in which she had no direct experience. The job had to do with organizational development.

But before she went on the interview, she went on the Internet. She had only about 45 minutes before the meeting, and she spent it doing research. She found what had been written about this company in the press in the last 6 months to a year, as well as other information having to do with the organizational development field. She found out when organizational development started and what company had developed it first. She looked up the various key players on LinkedIn and also Googled them. With this quick and dirty research under her belt, she ran over to the company for her interview. She had to meet with 18 people that one day! Interviewers followed her into the ladies' room asking her questions.

But when she met with person after person, all of this Internet information was fresh in her mind. She was able to speak knowledgably about the trends in the company and also the trends in the profession. She got the job—and she credits it 100 percent to the research she did ahead of time.

The ability to learn faster than your competitors may be the only sustainable competitive advantage.

ARIE P. DE GEUS, *HARVARD BUSINESS REVIEW*

In our book, *Shortcut Your Job Search*, read the chapter on research and study the bibliography at the back of the book.

Make yourself necessary to someone.

RALPH WALDO EMERSON

The will to persevere is often the difference between failure and success.

David Sarnoff,
Wisdom of Sarnoff and the World of RCA

Two Kinds of Research

There are two kinds of research. *Primary* research means talking to people who are doing the kind of work you're interested in or people who *know* something about those industries or organizations. You can get in touch with those people through networking or by contacting them directly.

Secondary research is materials in print, generally at the library, or information online. Secondary research is removed from the source—removed from the people themselves.

Conduct both primary and secondary research, and keep a balance between the two. Some job hunters would rather spend their time talking with people during their job search. They need to do more library and Internet research. Others prefer to spend their time in the library or working on their computers. They need to get out more and talk to people. Whichever *you* prefer, do more of the other. You need a balanced source of information in your search.

Primary research—talking to people—doesn't just happen in an office. You're researching when you're talking to a person on a plane or at a bus stop. Someone asks, "What do *you* do for a living?" You say, "This is what I do, and this is what I am interested in doing next." They may be able to tell you something about the industry you're interested in. That's research!

You're researching when you go to an *association* meeting, talk to people there, and find out more about what's happening in your target industry. You can research while you're at a party. Those are all examples of primary research—talking to people.

You're also researching when you go to a website that has to do with the organization that you're targeting. That, of course, is secondary research. But be honest. Job hunters often waste time on the Internet. They start exploring and go off on side journeys that may not be relevant to their search. Be careful about how you spend your time online.

Before your interview, you need information on the organization—and the people in it—so you can go in prepared. In addition to the sources listed in the *Shortcut Your Job Search* book, here are a few other research resources that are helpful specifically before an interview.

- Study the **organization's website**. Even for very low-level jobs, a hiring manager is likely to ask, "So how much do you know about us?"

- Often, they'll expect you to know the information in their **annual report**, which may appear on their website. Or you can call and ask investor relations or public relations to send you a copy of their annual report.

- Many organizations have a **press release** section on their websites. Or you can go to prnewswire.com or to the "News" section of Google. Organizations will expect you to know *whatever* they have made public. You may go on an interview, and they may say, "Oh, don't worry about having to work in the Acme building." Maybe they've put out a lot of press releases announcing that they are moving a lot of employees to the Acme building in a remote part of town. If you're interested in this organization, they expect you to know about the things that are of most interest to them.

- **Former and current employees**. One Five O'Clock Clubber met with a former employee before he went on an interview. The employee told him all about the projects the department was working on and gave him great information about the personalities of all the managers he would be dealing with. Dig in before you go on interviews. The more senior you are, the more research you must do before the interview.

- **Journalists** are another source, especially trade journalists and bloggers. If they cover the industry you're targeting, they can probably tell you a lot about this organization.

  If you're reading a trade journal having to do with health care, banking, opera, association management, or whatever you're targeting, find an article that interests you, and write to that journalist. Nobody writes to them— except you, of course.

  Just follow the standard Five O'Clock Club format for cover letters. Paragraph one is your introduction. You can say, "I was reading your article in *Association Management* magazine and I thought it was interesting. I'd like to talk to you because I'm conducting a job search aimed at that industry." Paragraph two is your summary about yourself. Paragraph three in a standard Five O'Clock Club letter contains three or four bulleted accomplishments. Paragraph four is the close, where you ask for a meeting.

- **Network with Five O'Clock Club Alumni**

  Thousands of successful Five O'Clock Club graduates have volunteered to help current job hunters who are attending the Club. The profile of our alumni is impressive: 40 percent of our attendees earn more than $100,000 per year and a growing number earn in excess of $200,000 (60 percent earn under $100,000 a year).

  If you have attended four small group sessions at the Club (so we're sure you know how to network properly, The Five O'Clock Club way), you can join our LinkedIn group yourself. Here is the way it works right now (although the Internet changes all the time):

✓ Go to www.linkedin.com. Sign in or join.

✓ The menu on the left of the page has "home" followed by "groups." Click on "groups."

✓ At the top of the Groups page, there are tabs. The second one says "Groups Directory."

✓ On the right-hand side, it says, "Search Groups." Enter "Five O'Clock Club".

✓ You will be taken to the Five O'Clock Club main page. Click on "Join this group." If you are eligible, you request to join will be accepted.

After you join, you will not have to go through all of this. Instead, **The Five O'Clock Club will be listed as one of the groups you belong to and you will be able to simply click on our group.**

- **www.linkedin.com** is a network of professional-level job seekers. The idea behind this site is that since members refer each other, it is a network of *trusted professionals*. Service is free, and people join by being referred online (via email) by a classmate, coworker, colleague, or other professional. Members fill out a profile, which allows others to contact them, as well as search the network for contacts by such things as job title, job function, or location. Members can access those who are not in their own network but are in the overall database via these searches. There are over 300,000 job listings from over 1,000 employers worldwide. Jobs are posted directly on the employers' own sites. This network allows users to get needed introductions to a hiring manager or recruiter. For example, a member can call a hiring manager and say, "Joan Smith of Exco recommended that I call you"—even if the member knows Joan only via a network search.

- **Association members**. Another important part of your research into specific organizations is deciding whether you actually want to *work* there. Ask about this organization at association meetings. Say to everyone you meet: "I'm going on an interview at XYZ organization. What do you know about them? Do you think this is a good organization or a bad organization? What are they like in our field? Are they ahead in the field or are they behind in the field? What's going on there?"
- **Discussion boards** helped George, a Five O'Clock Clubber. George was going on an interview at a rather small organization, and when he searched online, he found information and gossip about the *president* of the organization. People were saying that she was difficult to work with and that she was not willing to move to the next stage in the growth in the organization.

  Often, the online gossip is untrue. Disgruntled current or former employees may be trying to hurt the organization. But when George met with the president, the way she acted reflected what he had read online. He landed a very significant-sized contract with that organization because he knew a lot about their weaknesses, and he also felt that he knew how to talk to the president. (Many more sources are covered in our book *Shortcut Your Job Search*.)

Every exit is an entry somewhere else.

Tom Stoppard

- Research for the **follow-up step** is covered in great detail in the chapter on follow-up in this book. However, I'll mention some of the more important points here. In the follow-up step, consider the *issues* that came up in the meeting and think of how you can address

those issues. For example, if the hiring team is concerned that you have no experience in mergers, you may have to talk to a few people who work in mergers and ask them how *they* would handle the meeting. Then you would get back to the organization and say, "I've been giving some thought to how I would handle mergers in this job and would like to meet with you again to discuss it."

So, depending on what happened in the meeting and what reservations they may have about you, you're likely to have to do some kind of research *after* the interview. It may be that you talk to others in the field, research online or at the library, or simply think hard to *develop a plan* of what you could do for them. Whatever you're considering, mull it over with your small group. This step of the process is too difficult to go alone. You want to turn that job interview into an offer!

After the interview, you may need to conduct primary as well as secondary research so you can write a proposal. You may have to talk to people in the field, read trade journals, or search the Internet. Then you'd get back to the organization and say, "I've been giving this some thought and here is what I think I would do if I got this job with your organization."

- Finally, you'll need to research **salary information** to find out what you're worth in the market. You can go to websites such as salary.com or look at the salary surveys on yahoo.com—or find sites having to do with your field. Or you can look at job postings for your field and see what's being offered. But the best source of information for what *you're* worth in *this* market is to talk to people.

  When you're talking to hiring managers who have no openings right now, say to them, "If you had an opening right now for someone like me, what kind of salary range would you bring that person in at?" You're worth different amounts in different fields, different industries, and different geographic markets, so you have to test yourself in various markets.

The crisis consists precisely in the fact that the old is dying and the new cannot be born. In this interregnum, a great variety of morbid symptoms appear.

ANTONIO GRAMSCI

Research While You're There, Too

Research can be done in person as well. That is, go to the company beforehand or at least get there very early. Look around, get a feel, check out the culture. Is it compatible with your style? Do you need to adapt your style for the interview? Is the company formal or informal?

I like to go to the building an hour ahead of time. I don't know how long it's going to take in traffic. I want to get there and get relaxed. I tell the receptionist, "I'm very early for the meeting, so please don't tell Miss Jones that I'm here. I'd like to sit here quietly. I even brought work with me."

Then I sit and observe while I work on other things. I gather a lot of information. I observe how people interact with each other. If there's company literature, I study it. I also ask questions. For example, I say to the receptionist—and this is a key question you're going to ask of *every* person you meet—"What's it like to work here?" Their answers will tell you about the company culture.

People—*especially* lower-level people—will volunteer important information. Don't rely only on your prospective boss for information, because he or she wants to paint a positive picture and will give you a one-sided view. Instead, ask the receptionist, "What's it like to work here?" If the receptionist says, "Honey, do yourself a favor and leave now," *that's* important information.

The other question to ask each person is "How long have *you* been working here?" because you want to know the turnover rate. I say to the receptionist, "It's such a pretty reception area. I'm very excited about coming for an interview—and by the way what's it like to work here? Oh, that's interesting—and how long have you been working here?" And she says four months. "Oh, great. You must be really excited about working here."

Then somebody invariably comes by and offers me a cup of coffee and I usually say, "Thanks so much. If you don't mind, I'd like to get up and follow you—just to stretch my legs a little." I actually want to get into some other areas, maybe the kitchen area. I get a chance to observe and overhear things I might not see on the interview. Then I'll say to the person who is offering coffee, "I'm very excited about interviewing here. I hear great things about the company. It's such a pretty office layout. What's it like to work here?" and the person will tell me about the long hours or anything else that's important to *them*. And then I ask, "Oh and by the way how long have you been working here?" And that person says "Five months." Mmm. That's interesting.

Some job hunters may worry that one of those people might be the hiring manager. But the questions are innocuous. Of course, I'm actually probing to find out the turnover rate and the critical problems.

If everybody tells you "we're working 70-hour weeks" and if everybody's been there only 4 or 5 months, you know that you're going to be working 70-hour weeks, and you know how long you'll last there. Don't rely only on the hiring manager. Get information informally from lots of people.

Don't necessarily ask about something specific. Instead, ask an open-ended question. If you've been burnt in a prior job, you'll be on the lookout for that one thing that bothered you before. One job hunter was now afraid because, in the past, she was assigned to an office in a different building from everyone else's. She said to herself, "*That's* never going to happen to me again." So when she went on interviews, the most important thing for her was to see the office she would be in. Chances are, she was too focused on that and apt to overlook something else critically wrong in the organization. Of course, the purpose of all this is to get a handle on the company culture. Find out if it feels compatible with your style or if you need to adapt your style for the interview process. Find out if the company is more formal or more informal. By the time you actually get in for the interview with the hiring manager, you'll already know something about what's going on there, and you'll be more relaxed.

We can become anything. That is why injustice is impossible here. There may be the accident of birth, there is no accident of death. Nothing forces us to remain what we were.

JOHN BERGER, *PIG EARTH*

Surround the Hiring Manager

At The Five O'Clock Club, we're always talking about campaigns aimed at various target industries. You may conduct a campaign aimed at specific *companies* as well. Most job hunters think about the hiring manager, and only the hiring manager. We talk about *surrounding the hiring manager* and influencing the people around her. Then, by the time you get in to *see* the hiring manager, you'll know the issues, you'll know the organization, and you'll have advocates who want you to work there.

Often a job hunter finds out that there's an opening somewhere, and then they just want to find out exactly who the hiring manager is and get in to see that person. After all, that person is the one with the job, so why would you contact anyone else? But consider contacting someone other than the hiring manager. He is being inun-

dated with requests for meetings by people who have heard about the job. To the hiring manager, those who network in may seem just like those who responded to the ad: another job hunter who knows there is an opening.

But you're different. You're not a grubby job hunter. You're sincerely interested in this organization, aren't you? You want to meet with someone regardless of whether he or she has an opening, don't you? In fact, you are so interested in this organization that you would be glad to speak with other people there, not just the hiring manager.

If you first meet with others, you will learn a lot about the hiring manager, the organization, its needs, and the kinds of people who work there. They can refer you to the hiring manager—with their recommendation. You will be much better prepared than those who got in through the ad. After the formal interview, you will have advocates in the organization who can coach you and speak to the hiring manager on your behalf.

Some job hunters worry that the job may be filled before they get to the hiring manager. That's possible, but most jobs take a long time to fill.

What we want you to do is counterintuitive. We have other ideas for you, and you can read more in the next section.

"I've never said this before, but I hope it's you who gets this job."

Advanced Interviewing Techniques

If you don't go, you'll never know. You have to not look at it like a rejection. There are so many reasons you're not picked that you can't even worry about it.

ROBERT DeNIRO, ACTOR

Think and Act Like a Consultant

Pretend for a minute that you own a small consulting company. When you first meet a prospective client, you'll probe to better understand the problems this person is facing.

> **If the manager has no problems,
> or if you cannot solve them,
> there is no place for you.**

You are also there to sell your company. Therefore, as the manager talks about company problems, you reveal your own company's experience and credentials by asking questions or by telling how you have handled similar situations. You want to see how *your* company fits in with *this* company.

If the conversation goes astray, as a consultant you would lead it back to the topics on your 3x5 card—the work you would do for them and your abilities. That way, you can make your points in context.

It is your responsibility, as a consultant, to reassure the hiring manager that everything will work out. The manager does not want to be embarrassed later by discovering he's made a hiring mistake. It is almost as if you are patting the manager on the arm and saying, "Everything will be just fine. You can count on me."

You must display self-confidence in your ability to handle the position. If you are not confident, why should the hiring manager take a chance on you? If you want the job, take a stand and say that you believe it will work.

If you are asked how you would handle a situation, there are several approaches you can use to reassure the manager.

- It won't be a problem. I'm good at these things. I can figure it out.
- I'm very resourceful. Here's what I did as company controller...
- I've been in that situation before. I can handle your situation even though I don't know the specifics (since I'm not on the job yet).

Let the manager air doubts about you. If you are told what these reservations are, you can reassure the manager on the spot or you can mull it over later and reassure the manager in writing.

Do not appear to be *shopping around*. Be sincerely interested in this particular company, at least during the interview.

Follow up on your meetings. Address the important issues, stress your interest and enthusiasm for the job, and state your major selling points—especially since you now know what is of interest to the interviewer.

> **Thoughtful follow-up will dramatically
> increase the number of job offers you
> get. It is one of the most powerful tools
> you have to influence the situation.**

We've been preaching the consultative approach for decades. It will make you much more powerful and calmer during the interview process—instead of sitting there like a grubby job hunter pleading, hoping that they'll hire you, and passively trying to answer the questions correctly so that you'll win the big prize.

With the consultant mentality, you'll be much more proactive. A consultant is trying to land an assignment—an assignment that pays $40,000, $60,000, $100,000—whatever your salary is. You know that a consultant doesn't expect to breeze through one meeting and then get handed a $100,000 or a $40,000 consulting assignment.

What do consultants do at a first meeting? Imagine me right now, holding an 8½ x 11 pad of paper. I've got my pen in hand and I'm thinking— thinking really hard. I'm thinking the way a consultant thinks. They're not just sitting there answering questions as if they were on a quiz show. They're trying to understand the situation and what the organization's needs might be, maybe even squinting because they're thinking so hard. They're thinking and asking questions that reveal:

- What's going on with this organization?
- What's the flow of work? Who does what exactly?
- And what's handled by this department versus what's handled by that department?
- Have you thought about perhaps needing a person who can handle *this* thing and *that* thing?

Let's be more specific. Pretend that you really are a consultant on the job truly trying to advise this manager. *Pretend you have no stake in the outcome of this meeting. That is, you're not trying to land an assignment.* You're just trying to think about what is right for this organization, not what's right for you. What do they need to have done— *whether it includes you or not*? What's the political situation in the organization? What are the things that are holding them up? You may ask the hiring manager, "What's your vision for this department

going forward? What's keeping you from having this department work the way that you want it to work?" Ask questions that help you to help this organization.

The secret of science is to ask the right question, and it is the choice of problem more than anything that marks the man of genius in the scientific world.

HENRY TIZARD

Let's pretend, for example, that they have an opening for a marketing management position in a subsidiary of a company. You may want to ask:

- Exactly what is your *relationship* with the parent company?
- Do any of their marketing people get involved in the marketing efforts here?
- Are you forced to use any of the marketing solutions that they might have at the parent company?
- Are you allowed to do pretty much whatever you want to do here?
- What's this division's sales volume right now?
- What sales volume would you like it to be?
- What do you think is stopping the division from getting there?
- What is your time frame for getting the sales volume to that new level?
- Is there a problem with your marketing literature, or are you satisfied with it?
- Is there a problem with your sales force? Are you satisfied with that?
- Who exactly on staff is doing whatever affects marketing right now?
- Do you feel like you're understaffed or overstaffed? (What do you think is going on?)
- Do you think your employees are stars or not stars?
- Who are your major competitors? How do you see them in comparison to you?
- Have you been gaining ground or losing ground?

These are not the standard interview questions you might find in some other interview books. These are real questions—as if I was working with a job-hunter client who was preparing for a meeting. I'm thinking, "Well, what are some of the things that I'd like to know if I were meeting with these people, if I wanted to get a good feel for what's going on?"

> **Ask yourself what you would *really* like to know if you were actually about to get a job there—rather than repeating generalized questions job hunters always ask in interviews.**

Now, don't just shoot all those questions out one after another. Write them on your notepad, and as interviewers are answering, make comments and tell them something about your experience. "Gee, that's interesting, because when I worked with ABC International, we had the same kind of problem with the parent, and here's what we did about it." Or you say, "The staffing problems seem to be an important issue here. Let me give some thought to how jobs could be combined." Ask questions that are appropriate to the job you're going after. Give them ideas and suggestions that are appropriate to the job. All this gives you a chance to talk about yourself. Have a **consultative mind-set**—probe to really understand what's going on so you can figure out the kind of solutions they need.

What convinces is conviction. Believe in the argument you're advancing. If you don't, you're as good as dead. The other person will sense that something isn't there, and no chain of reasoning, no matter how logical or brilliant, will win your case for you.

LYNDON BAINES JOHNSON

Now what does a consultant do to *follow up*?

> **Consultants ask questions, they take notes, and then they go away and they work on the problems.**

They don't just ask questions and shoot the breeze as if it doesn't take any brainpower. It takes brainpower. After the meeting, you'll do your homework. We'll cover this in depth later in *Turning Job Interviews into Offers*, but at the very least, your homework includes doing Internet research on other organizations that are in the same situation and finding out what they're doing. In the case of one Five O'Clock Clubber, it meant going far beyond that. He visited all of the company's car dealerships and talked to the manager of each about the insurance coverage they had, then went back to the hiring manager and said, "Since I last met with you, I've stopped by a lot of your dealerships and I talked to each manager to uncover their attitudes about the insurance they use. Here's what I learned."

Of course, he got the job. He was able to do intelligent follow-up because he found out during the interview what was of concern to the hiring manager and others with whom he was meeting. He had a consultative mentality.

Help hiring managers define the job: Remember that most jobs are created for people. Some job hunters come away from a meeting and say, "They don't even know what kind of job they want filled here." *Most* companies don't know. You're the consultant. Help them! Of course, don't be an arrogant know-it-all. Show some humility in your suggestions. After all, you couldn't possibly know as an outsider what they know as insiders, and you can admit that to them.

Uncover any political problems. It may affect whether or not you want to work with them. Get the offer, and then decide later if you want to take the job.

*That is the essence of science:
ask an impertinent question, and you are
on the way to a pertinent answer.*

JACOB BRONOWSKI, MATHEMATICIAN, BIOLOGIST,
HISTORIAN OF SCIENCE

*"Jerkins and I worked it out. He can
have the office with the window."*

Consultants also find out about their competitors. Consultants know that others are being considered. So, a consultant asks,

- How many other consulting firms are you talking to?
- How far along are you with them?
- How do you see our firm comparing with the other firms you're talking to?

Consultants try to measure how they stack up against their competitors. You, too, need to find out how you stack up against your competitors. Otherwise, you go away dumb and happy, thinking, "They liked me, they really liked me." Well, they liked you, but are they going to hire you? And how do they see you versus your competition? So you have to ask,

Where are you in the hiring process?
- How many others are you talking to?
- Now that you've met with some of these other people, how do you see me compared with them?
- What kind of person might you be tending toward hiring and why?
- Can you think of any reason why you *wouldn't* want to have someone like me on board?

You could also ask, "What kind of person would be your ideal candidate, and how do you see me in comparison with your ideal?"

Interview Practice

Even experienced job hunters need practice. Each interview smooths out your presentation and responses. As you get better, your self-confidence grows.

By now, you've had networking or information-gathering interviews. You will have practiced talking about yourself and will have information about your area of interest and the possibilities for someone like you.

When I was unemployed, I had lots of interviews, but I was not doing well. I was under so much stress that I kept talking about what I wanted to do rather than what I could do *for the company.* I knew better, but I could not think straight. An old friend, who belongs to The Five O'Clock Club, helped me *develop my lines* for my 3x5 card. Then we practiced. After that, my interviews went well.

Be sure to record every networking and job interview on the Interview Record.

People who are in weekly Five O'Clock Club small group strategy sessions do better on interviews for a number of reasons. One is that they get to hear the experiences and the blunders of those who are ahead of them in the job search so they don't make those same mistakes later. But another reason is that they're practicing every week how to speak, keep things concise, and get to the point. When it's your turn in the small group, you tell other people what is happening in your search and what you need help with.

The way you seem in the small group bears some resemblance to the way you are in interviews. It's better to get feedback from friendly peers and your career coach rather than lose one job offer after another and not know why. Every Five O'Clock Club session gets you more ready for your meetings with prospective employers.

It may sound like a contradiction, but you achieve spontaneity on the set through preparation of the dialogue at home. As you prepare, find ways of making your responses seem newly minted, not preprogrammed.

MICHAEL CAINE, *ACTING IN FILM*

Consider Your Emotions

You can get all the techniques right, but *controlling your attitude and emotions* is another matter. Try your best to be positive, confident, and upbeat. Tell yourself—as actors and athletes do—"this is a performance," and it doesn't *matter* if you're throwing up five minutes before. You just have to remember, "It's showtime, folks!"

Be prepared with your 3x5 card, with your research, with your hypothesis about each person you'll be meeting, and with all your questions.

But they need to see your personality, too. You can't act a piece of cardboard. I know this is difficult—but smile during the interview *performance*.

As you read in the discussion of your *Two-Minute Pitch*, when I do interview training with job hunters, I usually have to tell them to smile. When you smile, it makes you feel better. And it makes an unconscious impact on the hiring manager: They see you as more competent and more self-confident. So smile and let your person-

ality come through. In the final analysis, there's chemistry involved, and interviewers will be asking themselves: "Do we *want* to work with this person?"

I recently met with the president of a technology company who said they hire a lot of writers and they had interviewed Ed, whom he described as a star. Ed was very young, brilliant— and full of himself. During the interview, Ed kept saying, "When I come in here, I'm going to do this, and then I'm going to do that." Everyone who interviewed Ed was reluctant to have someone like him on board, but since he was such a star, they didn't want to turn him down. The president, however, felt that Ed's arrogance would hurt others in the firm.

Organizations want team players who help the productivity of the group. I'm sure Ed was shocked when he didn't get the offer. But he hadn't shown any deference to the company and its goals or any concern for his prospective peers. He didn't try to establish chemistry. He wasn't a fit.

Employers want to know if you *can* do the job, if you're *willing* to do the job, and if you'll *fit in*. So keep all three in mind.

The trouble with most people is that they think with their hopes or fears or wishes rather than with their minds.

WILL DURANT, RECALLED BY FRIENDS
AT THE TIME OF HIS DEATH, 1981

Get a Job Offer

Be sure to treat each interview as an *opportunity*, even if you're skeptical. ("Do I really want to work there?") That is, sincerely intend to turn each interview into a solid job offer. Do your best to make the position and the pay into something acceptable. Believe it or not, people have turned bad situations around that way. Making the most of each interview is just good practice, if nothing else. Negotiate changes in the job itself. Suggest additional things you can do for the company—jobs often can be upgraded a level or two. Or perhaps the manager could refer you to another area of the company. You should make every effort to turn an interview into a reasonable job offer.

- This is an opportunity to practice your negotiation skills and increase the number of interviews you turn into offers. You can always turn the job down later. Job hunters are under tremendous pressure from family, friends, and former colleagues who want to know "how your job hunt is going" or "do you have a job yet?" If you say you are still looking and have not gotten any offers, you may feel bad. That's another reason why you may want to get a few offers—even though you are not interested in those particular jobs. Only if your job hunt seems to be going very quickly should you let up on trying to get practice offers.
- Getting job offers helps your self-esteem and morale.
- Getting offers puts you in a stronger negotiating position as well. You can say you received a number of offers, but they didn't seem right for you.
- Even if you turn down an offer, stay friendly with the hiring manager. This may lead to another offer later that is more appropriate.
- When you get an offer you are not sure about, say that you have a few other things you must attend to but will get back to them in a week. Then contact other companies that were of real interest to you. Tell them you have received an offer but were hoping to work something out with them. They may tell you to take the other offer—or they may consider you more seriously because the other offer makes you more valuable. Sometimes knowing you have another offer is the only thing that will make a company act.
- You may be surprised: Perhaps what you originally found objectionable can be

changed to your liking. If you end the process too early, you lose the possibility of changing the situation to suit you. Having a job created especially for you is the best outcome.

To take what there is and use it, without waiting forever in vain for the preconceived—to dig deep into the actual and get something out of that—this doubtless is the right way to live.

HENRY JAMES

Keep an Open Mind before the Meeting

Don't accept or reject any opportunities until you *get an offer.* You have objections to them, and they have objections to you. Try to overcome their objections to you, as well as your objections to them. For example, if the travel hours are just too long, see if that can be negotiated. It may be worth a shot. Try to turn these interviews into offers even if you don't want to work there. Otherwise, you'll never wind up with 6 to 10 job possibilities in the works. To get this quantity of offers and be more attractive to the organizations where you would like to work, you need to get some offers from crummy organizations.

One Five O'Clock Club client had a major objection to one company: It was in the wrong city! Maria's group urged her to go on the interview anyway, because the organization was the ideal one for her career path. After four meetings, Maria told the prospective employer that she really did not want to relocate. But a compromise was reached. She ended up working in that city three days a week and working at home two days a week in her ideal job!

We have a maxim at the Club, "Don't chase jobs, chase companies." Try to work it out within the organization rather than focusing exclusively on one job. It happens: They may interview you for one job and hire you for a completely different job. You never know. If you don't get an offer and they liked you even a little, turn it into a networking meeting and meet with people in other parts of the organization or even in other companies.

Be enthusiastic. Get offers. You don't have to say *yes* to every offer. To get 6 to 10 things in the works, not all the *jobs* you're going after will be terrific ones—nor will all the *offers* be terrific. That's not what matters. Getting offers at least helps you in your negotiation with other employers.

Any job that has defeated two or three men in succession, even though each performed well in his previous assignments, should be deemed unfit for human beings and must be redesigned.

PETER DRUCKER

Follow-Up

After interviews, job hunters typically send bland cookie-cutter thank-you notes: "It was a pleasure meeting with you and finding out so much about your organization. I know that we're right for each other." Remember, the purpose of your follow-up is to *get the next meeting* and you'll read more about that later in *Turning Job Interviews into Offers*.

In your follow-up letters, cover the specific, relevant, individualized information you gathered from each person you met. *Address their issues, whatever they were.* Counter their negatives and address their concerns about you.

Coming in as a Freelancer or Consultant—and Using Leverage

Some job hunters are willing to work for a company as a freelancer or consultant and hope the company will later put them on the payroll. But guess what? This may never happen. If you are doing a great job for little money, the company has no incentive to change that arrangement. If you want to be on *salary*, consult only if you are sure you have the self-discipline to *continue job hunting after you start consulting*.

You can parlay a consulting assignment into a full-time job at a decent salary *if* you do outstanding work on the assignment and *if* you get a decent offer somewhere else. Then tell your manager that you enjoy what you are doing and would like to be a salaried employee—but have received another job offer. You would prefer working for this company, but this temporary arrangement is not what you want.

Aiming for the Second Job Out

Sometimes the job you really want is too big a step for you right now. Instead of trying to get it in one move, go for it in two moves. Make your next job one that will qualify you for the job you really want.

What Do You Really Want?

To get ahead, many people compromise on what they want. A lot of compromising can result in material success but also feelings of self-betrayal and not knowing who you really are.

It can be difficult to hold on to your values and live the kind of life that is right for you. You may feel there is no hope for change. If you are really honest, you may discover that you have tried very little to make changes. Ask yourself what you have done to improve your situation.

Deciding where you want to work is a complex problem. Many unhappy professionals, managers, and executives admit they made a mistake in deciding to work for their present companies. They think they should have done more research and more thinking before they took the job.

The stress of job hunting can impair your judgment. You may make a decision without enough information simply because you want to *get a job*.

Ego can also be involved: you want to get an offer quickly so you can tell others and yourself that you are worth something. Or you may deceive yourself into thinking you have enough information. Even if you are normally a good decision maker, you can short-circuit the decision-making process when it comes to your own career.

You will make better decisions when you are not deciding under pressure. Start now to see what your options are. Then you already will have thought them through in case you have to make a move quickly later.

Objectively evaluate the information you come up with, and develop contingency plans. Decide whether to leave your present position, and evaluate new opportunities for each possibility. List the pros and cons for you and those close to you.

You may realize, for example, that a certain position is at a higher level, pays more, and offers more prestige, *but* you will have less time for your family, and the job will make demands on your income because you will have to take on a more expensive lifestyle. You may even decide that you don't like the kind of work, the conditions, or the people, or that your lack of leisure time will push you farther away from the way you want to live.

Depending on your values, the job may or may not be worth it. If you list the pros and cons and evaluate them objectively, you are more likely to be at peace with your decision and have fewer regrets. You are more likely to weigh the tradeoffs and perhaps think of other alternatives. You will decide what is important to you. You will have fewer negative surprises later and will be warned of areas where you may need more information. You will make better decisions and have more realistic expectations about the future.

I am proud of the fact that I never invented weapons to kill.

THOMAS A. EDISON

If I had known, I should have become a watchmaker.

ALBERT EINSTEIN, ON HIS ROLE IN MAKING THE ATOMIC BOMB POSSIBLE

What If Your Interviews Are Not Turning into Job Offers?

Here are a few suggestions for diagnosing stalled interviewing.

- **Listen to gather better information.** You may find that your target market is declining, you don't have the required background, your positioning is off, or whatever. Going on interview after interview with no callback and no offers means something is wrong. One of my clients kept saying that managers insulted her. If you have the same experiences again and again, find out what you are doing wrong.

- **Perhaps you are unconsciously turning people down.** A job hunter may make unreasonable demands because, deep inside, he or she knows there are things dramatically wrong with a situation. The requests for more money or a better title may be intended to make up for the unacceptable working conditions. One job hunter thought he was turned down for the job. In reality, he turned down the job. He did not let an offer happen because he knew the job was not right, and he made it fall through. There is nothing wrong with this—so long as he knows he could have had a job offer if he had wanted one.

- **Make sure you are addressing the company's problems—not your own.** A major mistake that I have made myself is focusing on what I wanted rather than on what the company or the manager needed.

- **Perhaps you are not talking to the right people.** Are you interviewing with people two levels higher than you are— those in a position to hire you? If you are spending a lot of time talking to people at your own level, you can learn about the field, but this is unlikely to result in job offers.

- **If you don't know why you didn't get the job, don't be afraid to call**. If appropriate, you may want to call a few of the people with whom you interviewed to find out why you did not get the job. If you are really stuck and feel you are not interviewing well, this can be very valuable feedback for you. You may even be able to turn a negative situation around.

Do Your Best, Then Let It Go

You are trying to find a match between yourself and a company. You are not going to click with everyone, any more than everyone is going to click with you. Don't expect every interview to turn into a job offer. The more interviews you have, the better you will do at each one.

And don't punish yourself later. Do your best, and then do your best again.

Hang in there. Get a lot of interviews. Know your lines. And don't bump into the furniture. You will find the right job. As M. H. Anderson said: "If at first you don't succeed, you are running about average."

So to avoid all that horror, prepare. Apart from anything else, preparation uses up a lot of the nervous energy that otherwise might rise up to betray you. Channel that energy; focus it into areas that you control. The first step in preparation is to learn your lines until saying them becomes a predictable reflex. And don't mouth them silently; say them aloud until they become totally your property. Hear yourself say them, because the last thing you want is the sound of your own voice taking you by surprise or not striking you as completely convincing.

Michael Caine, *Acting in Film*

Remember that the interview is the start of the job-search process, not the end. This is now the *beginning* of your search, and from here on your emphasis will be on trying to turn that interview into an offer. With this new mind-set, I hope:

- You'll never interview again the way you've interviewed in the past.
- You'll never sit there like a passive job hunter just pleading with someone to hire you.
- You'll be more proactive, and you'll think like a consultant.
- You'll write out your 3x5 card and go in prepared.
- You'll find out ahead of time who you'll be meeting with, what their issues are, and something about them so you can tailor your approach and your mind-set to each person.
- You'll take notes during every meeting.
- You'll never say to a job hunter who is going on a first interview, "Good luck, I hope you get the job." I hope instead you'll start saying, "Gee, I hope you do great, and I hope you get more meetings with that same organization."

That's what I wish for you and for everyone else in your Five O'Clock Club strategy group.

...You ought to say, "If it is the Lord's will."

James 4:15

How to Use the Interview Record

Shy persons often act like they were captured and are being interrogated.

GARRISON KEILLOR

On the next page is a very important worksheet: the Interview Record. Make a lot of copies of this page for your own personal search. Every time you have a meeting—**whether a networking meeting or a job interview**—fill it out. Make note of with whom you met, to whom they referred you, and what happened in the meeting. Attach to the Interview Record a copy of your notes from the meeting, the follow-up letter you sent, and perhaps the letter that led to the meeting.

Two weeks after the meeting, you may not remember what you discussed. If you are having a productive search and you are meeting with 10 to 15 people each week, you will not be able to remember what each person said, let alone how you met that person. To keep track of your meetings, maintain a record of each one.

Some job hunters use a three-ring binder, and arrange all of the Interview Records alphabetically or by industry or in some other logical order, with their letters attached.

Some job hunters methodically cross-reference the names by noting who referred whom.

At the beginning of your search, you may think you will be searching for a short time. But part of a good search is to follow up with your contacts at least every two months. You can have a more intelligent follow-up if you have an Interview Record to refer to.

Interview Record

Name: _____

Position: _____

Company: _____

Address: _____

Phone: Business_____

      Home: _____

Email: _____

Referred by: _____

Link to referral: _____

People spoken to (may require separate sheets.):

_____

_____

Issues (advice, problems, plans, etc.): _____

_____

_____

Key points to remember: _____

_____

_____

Referrals (write additional names on back):

Name: _____

Position: _____

Company: _____

Address: _____

_____

Phone: Business: _____

      Home/cell: _____

Date of initial contact: _____

Method used: _____

        (if letter or email, copy and attach to this sheet)

Planned date of follow-up call to set up

   appointment: _____

        (also record date on job-hunting calendar)

Actual dates of calls to set up appointment:

_____

_____

_____

_____

Appointment: _____

Follow-up note mailed: _____

        (copy attached)

Follow-up 2: _____

Follow-up 3: _____

Follow-up 4: _____

Follow-up 5: _____

Follow-up 6: _____

        (copy attached)

Other comments:
- tone of the meeting
- positives about you
- objections to you
- key issues to address
- logical next steps
- influencers
- your feelings about the job

The Five O'Clock Club

How to Handle Those Difficult Interview Questions

A sudden, bold, and unexpected question doth many times surprise a man and lay him open.

Francis Bacon, *"Of Cunning"*

It doesn't help you to read those books that say, "Here are a thousand interview questions and here are a thousand answers." The Five O'Clock Club takes a strategic approach to this issue. Remember the strategies—not the memorized answers you find in those books.

#1. Have the Right Attitude: Business Is a Game

When an interviewer asks you a question, don't ask yourself, "I wonder what the answer to that question is?" Instead, ask yourself, "I wonder how I should *play* it?" Because *job hunting* is a game. *Interviewing* is a game. So be a little light-hearted, have a lot of meetings, and get good at playing the game.

But when an answer isn't working for you, change your answer! Don't use a bad answer on dozens on interviews, hoping you will find someone who values you. Find another way to answer the question.

Have positive answers to everything. If people ask about your former boss or your former place of employment, the game is to see how positive can you keep it. Don't tell the gory, irrelevant truth. If someone says, "Tell me about your former boss," what will they think if you say, "My boss didn't have a lot of time for us"? They'll wonder

what's wrong with you that you needed a lot of your boss's time. You'll leave a negative impression if you say negative things.

Keep your answers brief. Pay attention—to keep from rambling when you're trying to explain something. Others don't care. *You* care. This is probably your sensitive spot. You're probably trying to explain exactly where you were in the hierarchy or exactly why you left your last job. *They don't care.* Keep your answers brief. Practice in your small group. Decide how you want to *play* this.

Most often, when interviewers ask you a question, they're hopeful about your answer. They want to find the right person, and they're hopeful that you're the one! Sometimes I have the opportunity to talk to prospective employers, and they say to me, "Why did he have to tell me that? I didn't want to know so many details about why he left that job."

Don't be like a little kid who mindlessly says, "I'm just going to tell them the truth." I don't want someone working for *me* who's obsessed with the truth. Because somebody is going to call my office and ask, "Where's Kate?" "Kate's out bowling." Even if something like that were the truth, it's not the right answer. I need people who are business savvy rather than obsessively truthful.

I worked with David, a senior person, and I asked him what he told people on interviews when they asked, "Why did you lose your last job?" David said, "I tell them I lost my job because

I did my boss in. I really killed him. I even ruined his marriage. Later on, when he had the chance, he did me in. That's why." You've got to have a better answer than that.

Don't take questions so literally. This is not like a discussion with a friend. For example, if the interviewer asks you why you didn't finish college, should you tell the truth? Should you say, for example:

- I couldn't decide on a major.
- My mother died and I had to help out.
- I ran out of money.

These answers are not wise because they're negative, and they also take you both away from what should be the main discussion: the company's needs and how you can help.

The interviewer is not interested in you and your mother. There is a job to fill. Talking about certain subjects weakens your position—regardless of who brought them up. Keep the interview positive, and try not to discuss subjects that detract from your case. Many times hiring managers say to me, "Why did Joe (the applicant) have to tell me that? I was ready to hire him, but now I'm not so sure. When my boss confronts me about Joe's lack of college, I don't have a good answer."

As I mentioned earlier, some job hunters insist on being *honest*. They think, "I'll just tell them the way it is, and if they don't hire me, then so be it." These job hunters are putting the responsibility on the interviewer. We've all had problems. The interviewer doesn't have to hear about them.

A businesslike answer, however, moves the

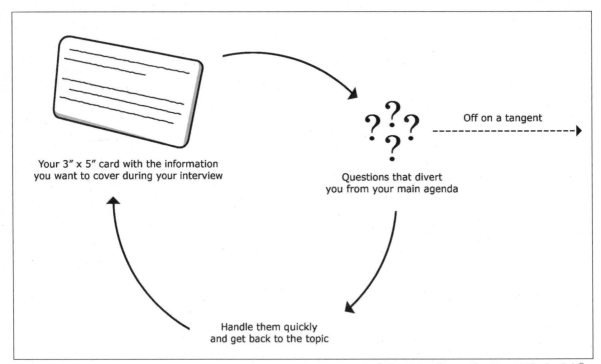

Your 3" x 5" card with the information you want to cover during your interview

Questions that divert you from your main agenda

Off on a tangent

Handle them quickly and get back to the topic

© Kate Wendleton, The Five O'Clock Club®

interview along. Let's try the question again, keeping the goal of the interview in mind.

Do not allow the interview to get off track. When the interviewer brings up something that takes you in a direction in which you don't want to go, briefly give a response that satisfies the interviewer, and then get back on track. Give your answer, and then say, for example, "But I really wanted to tell you about a special project I worked on." It is your responsibility to get the conversation back on track.

Why Didn't You Finish College?

"I like to be out there doing things. I finished several semesters, but I wanted to get more done. And that's what my bosses have always said about me: I'm someone who gets things done. They've all been happy with me."

Do not go into long discussions. *Briefly and politely* handle those questions that might take you off course, then smoothly move the conversation back to the company's needs or your abilities—the things on your 3x5 card that you had planned to cover. Give your answer, and then say, for example, "but I really wanted to tell you about a special project I worked on." It is your responsibility to get the conversation back on track.

Lettice: Let me play the interviewer for once: you be the victim.

PETER SCHAFFER, *LETTICE & LOVAGE*

There are no hopeless situations. There are only men who have grown hopeless about them.

CLARE BOOTH LUCE, *EUROPE IN THE SPRING*

#2. Be Prepared

Your 3x5 card will become your little bible. At the top of your 3x5 card, write your summary about yourself. That's your Two-Minute Pitch. You'll have three to five accomplishments you want to talk about, and you'll have the answer to what you consider a tough question. Master these. Carry your 3x5 card in your pocket or purse, and before you go into your interview, look at the card. This is what you want to tell people—regardless of what they ask you. It's like a politician: It doesn't matter what reporters ask the president, for example. He knows what he wants to talk about.

Difficult interview questions are *any* questions that take you off course—that get you away from what you should be talking about during the interview. So, if the interviewer says, "How's your tennis game?" get the conversation back on course: "Well, I don't know about tennis, but it reminds me of my last job. One of the things I did there is...." And talk about an accomplishment you have listed on your 3x5 card.

When anyone asks you a question that takes you off course, don't simply handle it and let those words hang out there. If *you* also talk about tennis, that's where the conversation will go. Later, you'll say to yourself, "How did we get on this?" Tennis is an innocuous example. But normally, it's something you really *don't* want to talk about, such as what happened in your last job, or the one assignment you didn't do well in. Then you wind up thinking that one assignment is killing your interviews, but it's not that at all. It's *your* fault because you didn't handle it briefly enough. Give enough of an answer, and then *get back to information on your card.* "You know another job I had that's even more interesting is...." Get back to your card.

If you've been unemployed for a long while, be prepared. You may be asked, "What have you been doing these last two years?" Employers don't want to hear that you've been a stay-at-home dad, regardless of how proud you are of it. That has nothing to do with business. Instead, say you've been taking care of a family situation and you've also been studying cost accounting via the Internet. And now you've become an expert in cost accounting, you've been going to accounting meetings, and you've done some cost accounting as a volunteer for a friend's business. If you haven't been doing anything, *do* something.

Before you start answering questions, know something about the employer's needs. So, for example, Angie's been an accounting manager and is great at managing a staff. But *this* employer wants a troubleshooter who can solve some of their long-term accounting problems. Angie can't stick with her regular pitch, which is "I'm great at managing the accounting staff and keeping the work reconciled." They'll say, "Too bad. We need someone who can help us analyze the business—and also manage a staff." So, probe first. If you don't know where the interview is headed, you can say, "There are a lot of different ways I can answer this, but can you tell me a little about your situation? What are your goals? What are you trying to do? What are the problems that keep you up at night?" Find out *something* so you'll know how to position yourself.

Remember that you're talking to a specific company, so do your research ahead of time. Then you can say what interests you about this organization, as opposed to "Oh, I'm at Xerox, is that where I am today?" Organizations want to hire people who want to work for them.

Midway in our life's journey, I went astray from the straight road and woke to find myself alone in a dark wood.

DANTE, *THE INFERNO*

#3: Level the Playing Field

Job hunters feel vulnerable. Employers seem to hold all the power. The best thing you can do to level the playing field is to have 6 to 10 things in the works. Then you won't feel intimidated by one company.

Having 6 to 10 things in the works is why Five O'Clock Clubbers who have been unemployed a very long time before they come to us can still get jobs at market rates. The issue is no longer "What have you been doing for the last 18 months and how much were you making in your last job?" If you're talking to 5 other potential employers about jobs in the $80,000 to $100,000 range, or whatever, you're in a strong negotiating position.

You can also level the playing field by thinking of yourself as a consultant, as opposed to thinking of yourself as a grubby little job hunter who just hopes somebody will have pity on you and hire you. A consultant asks questions, has pen and paper ready, and probes about the employer's situation. And a consultant asks about the competition.

Here's an important question to ask yourself: If an employer were to offer you a job and asks you to start work a week from Monday, what's the gap between what you know now and what you *need to know* before you can start working there? You might think, for example, "If I were really going to start there soon, I'd need to talk to the head of manufacturing, or the head of operations, and some of my prospective peers." Or "I'd need to do some research and find out more about this industry, and then come back here again for another meeting." If you think about actually *getting* the job, you may realize how little you know. Your whole thought process will change, and your demeanor in the interview will change along with it.

Don't tolerate extremely rude interviewers. Some interviewers take advantage of what they think is their power position. Jay, a client of mine, was a relatively senior person who worked on Wall Street. When he lost his job, he told me of a service offered by a financial information provider—let's call them Acme Information Services. When Jay lost his job, he assumed he would no longer have access to Acme's system. He was surprised when Acme said they would let Jay use the service for free for four months—a tremendous advantage in his job search. Jay said, "Wow, what a nice company."

Within two days, Acme asked Jay if he would like to come in for a job interview! It turned out to be a cattle call. He was in a room with 80 unemployed people standing in lines 10 or 15 deep. Jay, like almost everyone else there, was feeling fragile because he had just lost his job. He was wondering if he would ever work again.

Jay came away from there feeling beaten up. Then Acme called him back for another meeting where he would be interviewed by four people at the same time. Jay asked me, "Should I go?" I said, "How much do you loathe yourself? You're at the beginning of your job search, Jay, you happen to be in a terrific market, and will probably get a lot of offers. Do you want to get beaten up even more right now?" Then I added, "Instead of turning them down, which would make you nervous, just postpone the meeting and say, 'Gee, I'd love to come in and get beaten up some more by you, but I can't do it for another week and a half.' Just buy yourself some time."

Acme Information Services wanted unemployed people to feel weak so they could get them at a cheap price. Jay had multiple offers and never went back to Acme. But when things looked slow in his search, I'd say, "Would you like to go back to Acme?" That kept him going.

CASE STUDY George
Feeling at a Disadvantage

If life doesn't break your heart at least once a day,
I'd say that was a lack of imagination.

GARRISON KEILLOR

Some interviewers don't know how to interview! They can be unfocused or fail to observe simple interviewing etiquette. If a hiring manager allows interruptions—keeps making calls or answering them—consider saying, "I don't mind waiting outside for a few minutes while you take care of these emergencies. Then we can have a more quiet meeting." Unless that behavior is typical of the industry you're in, consider not putting up with it.

Let me give you an example of the problem a very senior person faced so you won't think that all of the rudeness is aimed at lower-level people. George met with four or five senior company executives. They liked him and then asked him to meet with a psychiatrist. The psychiatrist reported back to management erroneous impressions about George, such as that he was too detailed a person. In fact, George was an amazing strategist. One of the senior managers said to George, "The psychiatric report was not so good," and they told him about it.

How would such a report make you feel? George had a lot to offer, but that conversation made him feel deflated. My attitude was "Didn't these senior managers themselves have any impressions of George? Did they have to rely so completely on an outsider? And if he did go to work for them, would they be able to make up their own minds or will they have to call in outside experts? Don't they have any guts?"

So when George regained his composure, he wrote them a note to regain the offensive and bolster his self-esteem. He said, "I'm interviewing with six or seven other companies right now. I'm impressed by your company as well, but I wanted to give you some feedback. I don't think the method you are using for hiring is very sound. The psychiatrist's analysis did not accurately reflect my working style, and I think you should be a little cautious about this in the future when you're hiring senior executives."

When you feel you are being mistreated, you *can* respond. You can take the offensive—but not to the point that it takes you off-strategy. Above all, move on. And when you have 6 to 10 things in the works, it's easier to move on. George did not end up working there, nor did he want to. He had plenty of other offers.

You must have long-range goals to keep you
from being frustrated by short-range failures.

MAJOR GENERAL CHARLES C. NOBLE

#4. Stop Standing in Your Own Way

When you have your 6 to 10 things in the works, they're not all going to be brilliant possibilities. A good number will be with organizations you don't ever want to work for.

But getting the offers serves a purpose: It boosts your ego, helps you to better compare one situation with another, and increases your chances of getting offers from the companies that are of most interest to you. You will be able to say, "I've got four offers right now but I don't want to work for the others. I want to work for you." Prospective employers will see you as more marketable. So get some offers—even ones that are not right for you.

A Five O'Clock Clubber was having a hard time in his search, and I asked him what he thought the problem was. He said, "Companies don't want to hire me because I'm single." Over the years, I've heard a lot of reasons for getting turned down for jobs, but I'd never heard that one. So I asked him, "What is it about being single that's keeping you from getting a job?" He said, "Look, I've been living with this woman for nine years and I will not marry her." Because it bothered him, he would inadvertently bring up the fact that he was single during the interview process.

If you tell the interviewer, even in subtle ways, that there is something wrong with you, they are unlikely to take a chance. They'll think, "Well, it doesn't seem as though there is anything wrong with that, but if you tell me there is, then I trust you." And they're going to stay away from you.

Here's another example that doesn't sound as silly. I was doing a workshop for lower-level workers at a major retailer. Richard, the head of the mailroom, had supervised about 30 people—a responsible job. For some reason he was sensitive to the fact that he had been head of the mailroom for *only* two years.

When we practiced the Two-Minute Pitch, he himself brought up what he considered a weakness. He shot himself in the foot at the outset, "Well, I'm head of the mailroom, at Bloomingdale's, where I have 30 to 50 people reporting to me and it's going very well *despite the fact that I've been on the job for only two years.*"

When Richard positions himself that way, the hiring manager is going to think there's something wrong with his having been in the job two years. If you feel that something is a handicap for you, think twice about mentioning it—don't bring it up! If you think your age is a problem, you may inadvertently say, "Despite the fact that I'm older" or "Despite the fact I'm only recently out of school." Remember, positioning is everything. Be careful what you say.

Your attitude should be, "Problem? What problem?" Be sensitive to your own sensitivities—and get over them.

I know in my heart that man is good. That what is right will always eventually triumph. And there's purpose and worth to each and every life.

Quote by Ronald Reagan,
inscribed on his memorial, 2004

Let our advance worrying become advance thinking and planning.

Winston Churchill

Sample Questions

Let's try some sample questions, but remember that you must find your own answers, depending on your situation.

Tell me about yourself.

See Your Two-Minute Pitch.

Why are you looking? Why are you leaving?

You can count on being asked this because it's their job to ask it. Have your answer ready and then move back to the topics on your 3x5 card.

They're just checking off items on a list to make sure there are no problems. Keep it brief. You are the only one who cares about the gory details.

Some job hunters have very solid reasons for being out of a job. One Five O'Clock Clubber, a PR executive in his mid-50s, lost the best job of his life when his boss died and the new president brought in her own person. He was out through no fault of his own, and there was no better answer than what really happened to him.

Other than a story like that one, the best strategy is to describe your job loss as something you were proactive about—as if you had some say in the matter—and are also glad about. At the very least, do not describe your job loss as having to do with your own performance. Here are a few examples of positive responses:

"My company is going through a reorganization. I had the option of taking another job internally, but I decided to look elsewhere."

"X company has been great for me, but the career possibilities in the areas that interest me are extremely limited."

"Perhaps you heard that the _____ industry has been going through a major restructuring. I was caught, along with 3,000 others."

- If you're still employed, or if you're in outplacement and are allowed to look for a job back in your old firm:

    "I don't know that I *am* leaving. I'm talking to people around the company. They sure would like me to take another job there, but I feel like I want to look outside as well."

- If you lost your job and received even a little severance, you can say:

    "I had the opportunity to grab a package and I took it. I'm so lucky. I was not growing as much as I would have liked, and now I can move my career along. That's why I'm glad to be talking to you today. I understand that your department is very involved in the new technologies."

They'll rarely ask how long you will be getting paid, and it's none of their business anyway.

Do what's appropriate for you and for your comfort level. Talk it over with your coach or with those in your small group. Maybe there's a variation of these answers that's right for you.

- If you had been working long hours: "I decided I couldn't work 75 hours a week and also look for a job. I couldn't do justice to my staff or to my former employer. I left the company so I could conduct a proper search."

- If you didn't get along with your boss: Generally speaking, it's not a good idea to say that you left because of personality conflict. People may suspect that *you* are a difficult person. Sometimes those at very senior levels can get away with the *personality clash* excuse, but even then it's better to say, "We have differences on strategic issues."

When you're tempted to talk about conflict with a boss, it's best to say instead:

"I want to move my career in a different direction. My expertise is not the most important thing at my present company, and I want to move to a company where my skills will be put to better use."

What are you looking for?

It takes a lot of thinking to be ready for this question. Nothing turns off interviewers more than candidates who don't know what they want. So don't speak in generalities: "I'm looking for a job that excites me" or, even worse, "I'm not sure." This amounts to asking the interviewer to come up with ideas for you! You shouldn't be going on job interviews if you're not hungry and focused.

Be prepared to name the kinds of positions you think would be appropriate for you. If your Two-Minute Pitch is polished, you will be able to talk persuasively about the kind of things you can do for the company.

How long have you been unemployed?

If you've been unemployed for a long time, and you answer, "26 months," how likely are you to be hired? I have run job-hunt groups of people who have been unemployed 2 years or more. The first thing we work on is an answer to this question.

From a moral point of view, I must help these people develop a good story so they can get back to work. It would be cruel for me to insist that they tell the truth. Who will hire an applicant who says, "When I was fired, I got depressed for 6 months and couldn't move, and then my mother got sick and I had to help. By then, I had been unemployed 11 months, and no one would hire me. I'm hoping you will give me a chance."

Very few people are willing to give this person a chance, and you can't fault them for that. After all, the "truthful" job hunter is saying, "I've had all these problems, but I'm better now. Will you risk your organization for me?" It's not fair to burden the interviewer. All the interviewer wants to do is fill a job—not save lives.

The solution is to develop a good answer you can live with. Think of what you have actually been doing. Have you been working on your computer? Helping at your church or synagogue? Helping friends with their businesses? Most people can think of something they've been doing— even something little—that they can build a story around.

If you really haven't been doing anything at all, then *go do something*. You are unlikely to interview well if you haven't been out there at all. Get your adrenaline going. Walk dogs, pick strawberries, usher at church. Get active.

Better yet, learn a new skill. Master new software. Take refresher courses. Volunteer your skills, or get paid something nominally. You might even consider saying you were paid for volunteer work, if you think they would back you up. Then think up a good story:

1. "I've actually been *looking* only a month or so. After I left X company, I spent some time working on a special project for a small company."

2. "I've been looking only a few weeks now. After working for more than 20 years, this was my first time off, and I took advantage of the time to (fix up my house, take care of a sick family member, learn tax accounting, etc.). I was glad to have the opportunity to (help out, learn something new, etc.). But now I'm ready to get back to work and put in another 20 years."

3. Take the work you've done:

   "I've been doing public relations work for a small firm. I thought it would be fun to try after so many years with a big corporation, but now I know I like corporate life and I want to get back."

If your answers aren't working—if you're not getting second interviews or job offers—change your answers. Be creative, brainstorm with family and friends, and try new approaches. Positioning is everything; things won't go well until you've positioned yourself correctly.

What would you like to be doing five years from now?

"Actually, I'd like to do the best job I can possibly do in the position we're talking about right now. I know that if I do a great job, good things will happen to me later. They always have."

How would you handle this?

The interviewer describes a problem situation and asks how you would handle it. You can't think that quickly.

"I'd have to give it some thought. I'm the type who likes to think things through. I've been up against problems like this before, such as when we were behind schedule at X company. I thought about the problem, and quickly decided we should do a, b, c. This reduced our processing time and everyone was happy.

"Everywhere I've worked, I've been able to assess situations and resolve them, and I'd do the same for you. I don't know how to answer your question at the moment, but I know I would handle the problem the way I have handled things in the past. I have a good track record."

What are your greatest weaknesses?

After taking time to mull it over:

"Actually, I can't think of any work-related weakness. My bosses have always thought I was great. I'm the kind not only to do my own job but also to notice what else needed to be done in other areas and pitch in to help."

Or name a weakness and show how you have dealt with it, such as:

"Sometimes I get impatient with people because I want the job to get done, but I make sure I find out what's going on and help them with whatever may be stopping them."

What are your strengths?

Don't simply say, "I'm organized, dependable, and honest." They won't remember your strengths unless you also give an example to illustrate each one. For example: "I'm very organized. I was asked to straighten out a library of 30,000 boxes of files. Within just 3 months, everyone in the department could find anything they wanted."

Tell me about the worst boss you've ever had.

If you say that the worst boss you've ever had simply did not have enough time for his subordinates, they'll wonder why you needed so much of your boss's time. If you say your worst boss yelled and screamed at people, they'll wonder what you did to make your boss so angry.

No matter what your bosses have been like: "I've been really lucky. I've been blessed with good bosses. They've all been different, but I've learned from each of them."

What is your current salary?

(See Part Five of this book.)

The most important strategy is to postpone the discussion of salary until you get an offer. And remember, the person who names a number first is in a weak position.

They ask you to fill out your salary on a form

If you find you are always filling out forms before you get into the interview, it may mean that you are getting most of your interviews through search firms, ads, or human resources. Instead, try to get in through networking or through contacting someone directly. Then you won't find yourself filling out so many forms. If you are forced to fill out a form on a computer, see if it will take "0" as an answer.

How many other companies are you talking to?

"I've been very pleased with the response to my résumé. I'm looking at several opportunities." Don't tell them the names of the other companies unless you think it's in your best interest.

If you are *not* talking with other companies, you can say that you are just getting started and expect to be talking to a good number shortly. It is not a good strategy to pretend that you are on the verge of another offer if you are not. The hiring manager may tell you to take the other offer. Instead, get out there to talk to other companies.

We have two different positions. Which would you prefer?

Hedge your bets. "I could see myself doing [this] and I could also see myself doing [that]."

What is your management style?

This is a common question, so don't be blindsided by it. Be prepared to give examples. Think of stories that demonstrate your management style. Some may be fresh in your mind after having done the Seven Stories. "Four years ago, my staff was cut while workload was increasing..."

How good are you at ...?

If they ask, "How good are you at computer programming?" it's not good enough to say, "Very good." Instead, elaborate on how good you are: "I'm excellent at what I do, I have always been selected for the toughest assignments, the ones that no one else could do. For example..."

Don't Play Politics

About 15 years ago, I was being interviewed by a large company for a part-time consulting assignment. My prospective boss told me an idea she had that had nothing to do with my job. Her plans didn't make sense to me, but I would not risk discussing them with her until after I was hired.

Then she had me meet with her boss. He told me that he thought the project she was working on was idiotic, and he asked me what I thought. What I thought was "I'm not going to undermine my prospective boss on a job interview!"

So I said, "She's a smart woman. I couldn't possibly know as an outsider what she knows as an insider. I'm sure she's making the right decisions for the right reasons."

Don't let silly politics stand in the way of your getting a job that you know you can do well.

A horror story

My friend Sharon came to her first job in New York City from small-town, Monroeton, Pennsylvania. She was *fired* after only nine months in the Big Apple. It was unfair, and she was outraged. She decided that she was not going to let New York do this to her and so—as a ploy because the paperwork had not yet been filled out—she told her boss that she was on the verge of finding another job and would leave soon. By saying she needed "just one more week," she stayed for two more months—with pay.

During those two months, she felt a great deal of stress and caused Mike, her boss, considerable embarrassment. People knew she had been fired, but she was still there. But what could he do: Fire her again? She had nothing to lose.

She got an offer for a job that would be an acceptable next step. She would be managing a staff of seven, so it would look good on her résumé. The company itself was not a great fit for her, but she was desperate!

On the Thursday before Sharon was to start, Edgar, her prospective boss, took her out to lunch at a very nice restaurant to celebrate her coming on board. They had just sat down when Edgar leaned way over across the table and said to her, "Sharon, why did your former employer fire you?" And she thought, "I cannot believe this is happening!"

Now remember, Sharon had created a stir in that company and it was quite believable that Edgar had heard about it. Sharon was thinking, "How should I play this?" Edgar said, "I called a few people over there and they all told me the same thing: Sharon was fired."

Sharon's heart was pounding. Her ears were pounding. She thought that if she told Edgar the full truth he would never bring her on board. And so she said, "I don't know why people gossip and spread outrageous stories! I've already given my notice, so you should call my boss and ask him exactly what he thinks of me. Mike loves me."

By then, Mike was so afraid of Sharon that he would have said anything. Sharon's hunch was that he would not say that she had been fired.

Edgar leaned back in his chair and said, "I was just *kidding*. I never called anybody at your old company. But I hadn't done your reference checks, and my bosses are bothered about that. My bluff usually works. When I ask people why they were fired, they confess and tell me the truth." Then Edgar paused and said, "Let's eat!"

"Eat!" Sharon thought. "I can't eat. I want to throw up." For the rest of the meal, Sharon could not hear a word he said.

Now remember, Edgar wanted to hire her. Often a hiring manager asks questions because he or she *has* to ask them. I am not advising you to lie on interviews, but do use your judgment.

By the way, Mike himself was fired about four months after Sharon left.

What questions do you have for us?

I go into the interview with an 8 ½ x 11 pad. At the top of the pad, I put the four or five questions that I want to ask, and I integrate those questions into the conversation. I also take notes during the interview because I want to remember the details for the follow-up letters. If I meet with five people in one day, I cannot possibly remember what each person said. The notes are crucial even if you talk with only one person.

At the end of the meeting, when the interviewer asks, "Do you have any questions for us?" I make a point of looking at my questions (even though I know that I've already asked them all) and say, "No thanks, we've covered them all." But because the questions were written on the pad, I look prepared.

That's what consultants do. They go into a meeting with pen and paper in hand and try to figure out how things work so they can create an assignment for themselves.

What do you need to know? **If they were going to offer you a job that started a week from Monday, what is the gap between what you know now and what you need to know to get started there on Monday?** Ask those questions.

For example:

- "I'd like to talk to the head of manufacturing and also to the head of the operations department so I can get an idea of what they do."
- "I'd like to talk to some of my prospective peers so I can figure out exactly how I would interface with them."
- "I need to give this some thought and then I'd like to meet with you again. I'll have some ideas to discuss with you then." (Then do some research and find out more about this industry.)
- "What are some of the problems that keep you up at night?"
- "What are the most important things that need attention right now?"

And then a consultant will ask:

- "Where are you in the decision-making process?"

- "What other consultants are you talking to?"
- "How do you see me stacking up against them?"

If you ask questions like these—as if you were going to start working there a week from Monday—you will be much more proactive in the interview process. You will be thinking like a consultant.

The Good Interviewer

It probably won't happen to you during your entire job search, but be prepared for the person who conducts a good interview. In a good interview, the hiring manager may start with the beginning of your career, asking, "What did you do in this job?" "Why did you leave that job and go on to the next one?" "What did you like best about that job?" "What about your boss?"

Then he or she asks you about the next job in a methodical, organized way. "What did you enjoy?" "What did you do best in that job?" "Why did you leave it?" "Tell me about the next one."

You're not going to get very many interviewers like that.

How to Handle Discrimination

If the interviewer asks you questions that are illegal (such as questions about pregnancy or your plans to have children), assume they are not being asked maliciously. Instead of answering the question itself, answer the *concern* that may have prompted the question. For example, if someone asks, "Do you have small children at home? Are you married?" You cannot say, "It's illegal to ask that." They'll apologize, but you won't get the job. Who needs a troublemaker?

Instead, try to figure out why they're asking you that question and answer their concern. You could say, for example, "Are you concerned that I might not show up at work? I've never missed a day in 15 years."

Remember the following:

- Be prepared.
- Have your 6 to 10 things in the works so that you're not at a disadvantage.
- The purpose of the first interview is not to get a job offer. The purpose of the first interview is to get the second interview.
- You're trying to give and get information so that you can get that next meeting.
- Half of the interview process is being prepared, but the other half is having that right attitude. They'll sense your self-confidence, and you are less likely to buckle when they ask you idiotic questions—often they don't care about the answers anyway.

Human beings are actually created for the transcendent, for the sublime, for the beautiful, for the truthful, and you don't teach people these things. It comes with the package of being human, and all of us are given the task of trying to make this world a little more hospitable to these beautiful things—to love, to compassion, to caring, to sharing, just to being human.

NOBEL PEACE PRIZE RECIPIENT ARCHBISHOP DESMOND TUTU

My formula for success? Rise early, work late, strike oil.

J. PAUL GETTY

No Apologies Needed When Asked the 'Overqualified' Question

by Chip Conlin, certified Five O'Clock Club Master Career Coach

"Your resume states that you've worked with 2 presidents, won the Nobel Prize and climbed Mt. Everest. That's all fine and dandy, but how are you at telemarketing?"

Courtesy of Jerry King, Cartoons, Inc.

In my years of facilitating small groups and working with clients privately, the "overqualified" label has a way of rearing its ugly head every now and then. The trouble I have with the word itself is that it rarely makes sense. Most people are capable of doing a certain type of work or they are not. All of which leads me to believe that some other motive is operating below the surface when hiring managers or HR professionals raise the question, "Based on your work experience, why would you ever consider this job since you are obviously overqualified?"

That motive on the part of interviewers may be a concern that a person is only trying to get a job that pays less or has less responsibility while they look for another one at their previous level; would not work well under a younger boss; or even the fear that the person has no intention of staying in the job beyond a few months or years. Of course, the subtle implication here (often subtle as a sledge hammer) is the person's age. While age discrimination is against the law, age unfortunately can play a part in a hiring manager's decision although frequently under the guise of one of the above reasons.

For example, at The Five O'Clock Club, I see more members make the transition from the for-profit to the not-for-profit arena. However, in some instances they have had to overcome the overqualified label to demonstrate they are the best person for the job. In these cases, salary often becomes a key issue. In fact, utilizing many of the 5OCC methods, such as working on The Seven Stories and Forty-Year Vision exercises, crafting the appropriate Two-Minute Pitch, and positioning themselves correctly on their resume has been key to overcoming these potential objections. In the face of being labeled overqualified, having a clear focus and convincing the hiring manager you are the best answer to their needs will win every time.

Recently, I worked with two clients, both of whom have extensive corporate sales experience in the publishing arena. Of course, once the publishing industry started going digital their jobs were eliminated, but both took the opportunity to re-evaluate their careers and decided to transition into the not-for-profit world. By coming up with a strong Summary on their resumes, and a Two-Minute Pitch, which positioned them correctly, they were able to build on their sales skills, accomplishments and experiences to get meetings with the heads of development in several not-for-profit organizations. One landed and the other is now getting interviews within the not-for-profit arena.

In short, whether switching careers or looking for new opportunities in your current field and faced with the overqualified question, whether you fear it is your age, work experience, or that when you graduated from college you were still using a typewriter, you need to convince the hiring manager you are the best person for the job by sharing relevant experiences in your background, not hiding them. Have your Two-Minute Pitch ready so when asked "Why would I hire someone like you?" you are prepared to take control of the interview, and let the interviewer know why this job is the right career move for you. And lastly, do not apologize for who you are! If you miss out on an opportunity because of being labeled "overqualified," it was probably not the right job anyway.

You're Overqualified ... and You're Out!

by Ruth Robbins, certified Five O'Clock Club Master Career Coach

It's time to get back to work. You could really want this job, and it will look great on your résumé. The interview seems to be going well, then you hear the words you've heard all too often before—and it doesn't matter how respectfully or kindly they are said: "You're overqualified." Senior Five O'Clock Club coach Chip Conlin has pointed out that 'overqualified' is a way to get rid of you with what looks like a compliment. 'Overqualified' is actually a code word for other concerns and worries:

- You'll jump ship as soon as you get a better offer.
- You're settling for the job because the market is bad.
- You'll be unhappy with the compensation.
- You'll be a bored or impatient with the way we do things.
- You might be a know-it-all, and you'll be too difficult to manage.
- You're too old for us, i.e., for the culture of our department and company.
- You might not be able to keep up with our quick-paced digital environment or technology.

If you don't want 'overqualified' to end the conversation—if you want to remain in the game—these concerns must be anticipated prior to the interview. Your responses must be very carefully thought out ahead of time. The Five O'Clock Club methodology encourages thorough preparation for the interview, including how to address these kinds of concerns or worries.

For example, be prepared to explain

1. why you want to work in a position that's a level or two below where you've been;
2. how it fits in with your longer term vision or immediate short term goals;
3. why you strongly believe the company is a great fit for you. Explaining yourself on these topics is of paramount importance in overcoming the reservations people may have about you.

But you also have to be honest with yourself. Are the reservations about you justified? Will the job, in fact, work to your advantage (and not just be good for the paycheck)? At this point in your career, have you made progress toward your career goals, and will this position be a good fit for you? Can you afford to take a cut in salary or job title, and still keep your career on track? Above all, will you be excited about this position?

It goes without saying that doing due diligence on the job prior to the interview includes studying the company, its financial health and anticipated trajectory; you also need to find out the names and backgrounds of the individuals on the hiring team. But the Five O'Clock Club recommends digging deeply on the cultural and interpersonal fronts as well. Find out, for example, what kinds of experience members of the hiring team possess. Where are they in their careers? How much industry experience does the hiring manager have—maybe you can make a guess about his or her age. If you will be interviewed by several people, research their professional backgrounds: how many years have they been in the industry and with the company. Their profiles may be on the company website, and there will probably be a lot more information on LinkedIn. Check out how diverse the staff may be, in terms of background, culture and age. And talk to people: network ahead of time with everyone who may be able to shed light on the company culture.

Many job hunters are timid about asking probing questions at the time that the interview is set up. We understand that, but if you don't get good background information at the time the interview is scheduled, work up your courage and call a few days later. The Five O'Clock Club suggests that you say: "I want to be well prepared for the interview. Can you tell me a little bit about the people I'll be meeting with and their backgrounds?"

You don't want to be unpleasantly surprised. One of my clients landed an interview through a networking contact, but she failed to find out that the hiring manager had far less experience than she did. Had she known this, she could have anticipated the 'overqualified' objection. If you suspect that you'll encounter this situation, practice your responses. Note them on your 3 x 5 card and review them before the meeting.

Here are responses that some of my clients have used to counter the 'overqualified' fear:

- I'd like to address your concerns. I want to help make you feel more secure about my interest and desire to come on board and stay with the organization. For example…
- Well, I'd like to reframe 'overqualified' if I may. I'm 'more' than qualified for the position, which I think is a positive, reas-suring thing to say about someone. I'm proud of my experience / skills / knowledge and I'm excited about the position you've outlined, and know I can both contribute and learn from you.
- At this time in my career, I'm really more comfortable being a team player than the team leader. I've experienced that. I'm not wedded to empire building or anything close to that. I'm excited about the job you've described to me.
- I am very willing, and pleased to roll up my sleeves and do the work that has to be done for the job you outlined.
- End the response with: I'd love to keep my hat in the ring.

Five O'Clock Club job hunters should master the drill: go armed into interviews with

1. strong knowledge of themselves (based on the Seven Stories Exercise and the Forty-Year Vision),
2. in depth knowledge of hiring managers and the corporate cultures,
3. and carefully crafted answers to objections—including 'you're overqualified.'

It's also important to honestly analyze any ambivalence there might be about the prospective opportunity. If you're not convinced or clear that this is the job you want, you can be sure that the hiring team won't be either.

The Five O'Clock Club®

PART FOUR

Turning Job Interviews into Offers

THE BRAINIEST PART OF THE JOB-SEARCH PROCESS

The Five O'Clock Club®

Follow-Up after a Job Interview: Consider Your Competition

Bullock shrugged. He'd been thinking about Bill that afternoon, trying to decide how to fit him into Deadwood Brickworks, Inc. It wasn't a question he could be useful. Anybody could be useful when you decided where they fit. That was what business was.

PETE DEXTER, *DEADWOOD*

So far in the interview process, we have considered you and the hiring manager. By acting like a consultant, you can negotiate a job that's right for both you and him or her. But there are other players and other complexities in this drama. First, there are all the other people you meet during the hiring process. They are influencers and, in fact, may influence the hiring decision more than the hiring manager does. These are people the hiring manager trusts and on whose opinions he relies. In addition, there are complexities such as outside influencers, the timing of the hiring decision, and salary considerations. Finally, you have competitors. They may be other people the interviewer is seeing, or your competition can be an ideal candidate in the interviewer's mind.

This chapter contains case studies of how some people considered and dealt with their competition. In the next chapter, we'll give you the guidelines they followed, which helped them decide what they could do to win the job. Remember, the job hunt really starts after the interview. What can you do to turn the interview into an offer? This is the part of the process that requires the most analysis and strategic thinking. Think *objectively* about the needs of the organiza-

tion and of everyone you met, and think about what you can do to influence each person.

If you're in a seller's market, however, you may not need to follow up: You'll be brought back for more meetings before you have a chance to breathe. *If you're in a buyer's market*, you will probably have to do thoughtful follow-up to get the job.

Because effective follow-up is a lot of work, your first decision should be: Do I want to get an offer for this job? Do I want to *go for it?* If you are ambivalent, and are in a competitive market, you will probably *not* get the job. Someone else will do what he or she needs to do to get it.

Follow-ups will not guarantee you a specific job, but extensive follow-ups on a number of possibilities increase the number and quality of your offers. If you focus too much on one specific situation and how you can *make* them hire you, that won't work. You need both breadth and depth in your job hunt: You have both when you are in contact on a regular basis with 6 to 10 people who are in a position to hire you or recommend that you be hired. You must have 6 to 10 of these contacts in the works, *each* of whom you are trying to move along.

Ideally, you will get to a point where you are moving them along together, slowing certain ones down and speeding others up, so you wind up with 3 concurrent job offers. Then you can select the one that is best for you. This will usually be the job that positions you best for the long run— the one that fits best into your Forty-Year Vision.

It will rarely be sensible to make a decision based on money alone.

Therefore, if one situation is taking all of your energy, stop right now for 10 minutes and think of how you can quickly contact other people in your target area (through networking, direct contact, search firms, or ads). It will take the pressure off and prevent you from trying to close too soon on this one possibility.

CASE STUDY The Artist
Status Checks Rarely Work

Most people think follow-up means calling for the status of the search. This is not the case:

At Citibank, a project I managed needed an artist. I interviewed 20 and came up with two piles: one of 17 rejects and another of the 3 I would present to my boss and my boss's boss. A few people called to *follow up*. Here's one:

Artist: "I'm calling to find out the procedure and the status. Do you mind?"

Me: "Not at all. I interviewed 20 people. I'll select 3 and present them to my boss and my boss's boss."

Artist: "Thanks a lot. Do you mind if I call back later?"

Me: "No, I don't mind."

The artist called every couple of weeks for three months, asked the same thing, and stayed in the reject pile. To move out, he could have said things like:

- Is there more information I can give you?
- I've been giving a lot of thought to your project and have some new ideas. I'd like to show them to you.
- Where do I stand? How does my work compare with the work others presented?

If all you're doing is finding out where you are in the process, that's rarely enough. *The ball is always in your court.* It is your responsibility to figure out what the next step should be. Job hunters view the whole process as if it were a tennis game where—*thwack*—the ball is in the hiring manager's court. Wrong.

Me to job hunter: "How's it going?"

Job hunter to Kate: (*Thwack!*) "The ball's in their court now. They're going to call me."

When they call, it will probably be to say, "You are not included." If you wait, not many of your interviews will turn into offers.

CASE STUDY Rachel
Trust Me

Rachel had been unemployed for nine months. This was her first Five O'Clock Club meeting. She was disgusted. "I had an interview," she said. "I know what will happen: I'll be a finalist and they'll hire the other person."

Rachel was nice, enthusiastic, and smart: She was always a finalist. Yet the more experienced person was always hired.

Here's the story. Rachel, a lobbyist, was interviewing at a law firm. The firm liked her background, but it needed some public relations help and perhaps an internal newsletter. Rachel did not have experience in either of those areas, though she knew she could do those things. She wrote a typical thank-you note playing up her strengths, playing down her weaknesses, but essentially ignoring the firm's objections. She highlighted the lobbying and said that PR and a newsletter would not be a problem. She could do it. She was asking the firm to *trust* her.

A man is not finished when he's defeated;
he's finished when he quits.

RICHARD MILHOUS NIXON

Lots of Job Hunters Take the Trust Me Approach

The following occurred during a group meeting at The Five O'Clock Club:

Me: "Do you want this job? Are you willing to go through a brick wall to get it?"

Rachel: "Yes. I am. I really want this job."

Me: "Let's think about overcoming their objections. If you can write a PR plan after you get hired, why not do it now? Why ask them to trust you?"

Two people in the group had old PR plans, which they lent her. Remember: The proposals or ideas you write will probably be wrong. That's okay. You're showing the company you can think the problem through and actually come up with solutions.

Rachel's lack of experience with newsletters was also an objection. We suggested Rachel call law firms in other cities and get their newsletters.

After doing research, Rachel sent a very different note. In this one she said she had been giving it more thought and was very excited about working for the firm. She had put together a PR plan, which she would like to review with them, and had gotten copies of newsletters from other law firms, which gave her ideas of what she could do in a newsletter for them. Of course, she got the job.

Mediocrity obtains more with application than superiority without it.

BALTASAR GRACIAN, ORACULO MANUAL

Uncovering Their Objections

Rachel got the job because she overcame the objections of the hiring committee. Start thinking about how you can overcome objections. This will change the way you interview, and you will become more attuned to picking up valid objections rather than quashing them. Then you can even solicit negatives. For example, you can ask:

- Who else is being considered?
- What do they have to offer?
- How do I stand in comparison with them?
- What kind of person would be considered an ideal candidate?
- What would you like to say about a new hire one year from now?

Get good at interviewing so you can solicit valid objections to hiring you.

Without competitors there would be no need for strategy.

KENICHI OHMAE, THE MIND OF THE STRATEGIST

Act Like a Consultant

Since most jobs are created for people, find out what the manager needs. Hiring managers often decide to structure the job differently depending on who they hire. Why not influence the hiring manager to structure the job for you?

Probe—and don't expect anything to happen in the first meeting. If you were a consultant trying to sell a $30,000 or $130,000 project (your salary), you wouldn't expect someone to immediately say, "Fine. Start working." Yet job hunters often expect to get an offer during the first meeting.

Forget about job hunting. This is regular business. You're selling an expensive package. Do what a consultant or a salesperson does: Ask about the company's problems and its situation; think how you could get back to the interviewer later. Get enough information so you can follow up and give the interviewer enough information so he'll want to see you again. Move the process along: Suggest you meet with more people there. Do research. Have someone influence the interviewer on your behalf. Then get back to him again. That's what a consultant does. Remember to move the process along; outshine and outlast your competition.

CASE STUDY Ken
Identifying the Issues/Timing

Ken was the first person interviewed for a senior vice president of marketing position. When Ken asked, the interviewer said he would see five or six more people. As you will see shortly, being first is the weakest position. Get rid of your competition quickly, or find ways to maintain the interviewer's interest and meet with him or her again.

Ken identified the company's most important

issue. It was not wondering what Ken would do as the head of marketing but something more basic: It was debating the *role* marketing should play in the new organization.

Determining the real issues is critical in deciding your follow-up plan. And since the timing was against him, Ken acted fast. He wrote a handsome four-page proposal about the role marketing should play, and he sent it overnight.

When Ken was called for a second round of interviews, he found there were no other candidates. Ken had gotten rid of his competition. Ken not only identified the issues, he was in sync in terms of timing. The company was planning to decide quickly, so he acted quickly, too.

CASE STUDY Leon
How Did He Get the Job?

Leon came to The Five O'Clock Club after 15 months of interviews. After 3 Club meetings, he got 2 job offers simply because he followed the group's advice and wrote proposals. When he told the group his good news, someone asked him how he got the 2 jobs. He said that one offer was from a search firm, and one was from networking. Leon had been pursuing jobs through networking and search firms for 15 months, but it wasn't until he decided to do real follow-up on these that he was offered a job.

CASE STUDY John
Consider Your Likely Competitors and Go for It

Most job hunters think *anxiously* about the competition out there. Instead, be objective about your likely competitors.

John thought he had been job hunting for a year. He answered ads, met with search firms, and even went on interviews, but he wasn't job hunting: *In a tight market, the job hunt starts after the interview.*

At our first meeting, John recounted his activity. One ad he'd answered was for a job at the

Kennedy Foundation, and he'd met three people there two weeks earlier. He was waiting for their call. Before John went on, I stopped him.

"John," I said, "do you want that job?"

He replied, "I'll see what happens next. If they call me, I'll consider it."

"The way things stand, John, you are not going to get that job. If they call, they'll say they found a better match. Are you willing to go through a brick wall to get that job? If you are, I can help you—and it's a *lot* of work. But if you essentially want to sit on the bench answering ads, there's not much a coach can do."

John said he was willing to go after the job. A job hunter's total commitment is absolutely necessary, or he will not be willing to do—or even notice—what needs to be done to win the job.

He said, however, that the real secret of his fortune was that none of his mules worked as hard and with so much determination as he did himself.

GABRIEL GARCIA MARQUEZ,
LOVE IN THE TIME OF CHOLERA

Who Are John's Likely Competitors?

The Kennedy Foundation wanted a controller. John had been a controller in a major corporation for 20 years. What kind of controller would the Kennedy Foundation most likely want?

Develop a prototype of your likely competitors. You have to guess about your competition. But once you form a hypothesis about who your competitors are, you can figure out a plan to outshine and outlast them. It's better to have some hypothetical competitor in mind than nobody. Remember, your competition might not be real people but an ideal in the mind of the hiring manager. Get rid of that competitor, too, or the hiring manager will continue looking for that ideal person.

John thought his likely competitors were people who had been controllers in not-for-profit organizations. I suggested that he spend a day at the Foundation Center (a library) and research the controllership function at other foundations. I told him to make sure he could handle the work and knew the jargon.

John came back with good news: "I know how to do that kind of accounting. It's actually what I've done all along."

How Does John Now Stand in Relation to His Likely Competitors?

John now has 20 years of corporate controllership experience and a day in the library. His likely competitors have real hands-on experience. At this stage, John is *not* even with them. He has to do more if he wants the job.

John and I searched his background for areas that might interest the Kennedy Foundation—experience his likely competitors would not have, such as securities accounting.

Look at all the work and thought John has put in so far—without a request from the hiring manager. The ball is *always* in your court.

John had met with three people at the Kennedy Foundation. Among the three was a financial person and someone from human resources. His first draft of the letter to the financial person was negative: "Despite the fact that I have no not-for-profit experience, I believe my credentials...."

Wrong. Come up with something that beats out your competition. You must be in a position to say, in so many words, "Unlike others who have spent a lot of time doing this work, I bring something extra to the party."

Also remember that you are interviewing with individuals, not organizations. You are *not* interviewing with the Kennedy Foundation or with IBM. Each person you meet has his or her own opinions about the issues that are important, the things that person likes about you, and the reasons he or she might not want you there. Address these points with *each* person.

Don't forget that it (your product or service) is not differentiated until the customer understands the difference.

Tom Peters, *Thriving on Chaos*

The Other Decision Makers/Influencers

Many job hunters assume the hiring manager is the only person who matters. Big mistake. Others are not only influencers; in some cases, they may actually be the decision makers.

I'm a good example. I make terrible hiring decisions: Everyone I interview seems fine to me. So I have others meet with the candidates. Their opinions weigh more than mine. Any applicant who ignores them is ignoring the decision makers—or at least the serious influencers.

Take seriously every person you meet. Don't be rude to the receptionist. She may say to the boss, "If you hire him, I'm quitting." That receptionist is definitely an influencer.

The people you want to reach... should be viewed as distinct target audiences that require different approaches and strategies.

Jeffrey P. Davidson, marketing consultant
Management World

Identifying the Issues

When John first met with the human resources person at the Kennedy Foundation, she asked him questions such as, "So, what do you do on weekends?" and "Where do your kids go to school?" Assuming these were not idle questions, what issue was she getting at?

We decided the issue was *fit*. When John wrote his first follow-up letter to her, he said he was excited about the position and had spent a day doing research—and he addressed the issue of fit. He did this by emphasizing his qualities of loyalty and commitment. Also, he correctly sensed that they would be impressed with where he went to college and his relationship with his family.

Three months, 11 grueling interviews, and 7 in-depth reference checks later, John's credentials were presented to the board of directors for approval. To make sure his important arguments were brought before the board, John prepared one more follow-up letter (see the next page). By the way, John had 3 more interviews after the board meeting. He got the job—and he's still there.

Many job hunters ask John how he got the job. They are asking the wrong question. They mean, "How did you get the interview?" John is forced to reply, "I got it through an ad." I hope you can see that John got the *job* through his analysis and follow-up. It was just the *interview* that he got through an ad.

---

*You must call each thing by its proper name
or that which must get done will not.*

A. HARVEY BLOCK

What Happens as Time Passes

Most jobs are *created* for people: Most interviewers don't know clearly what they will want the new person to do. Yet job hunters expect the hiring manager to tell them exactly what the job will be like and get annoyed when the manager can't tell them.

Generally, the job description depends on who will be in the job. Therefore, help the hiring manager figure out what the new person should do. If you don't help him, another job hunter will. This is called "negotiating the job." You are trying to remove all of the company's objections to hiring you, as well as all of *your* objections to working for them. Try to make it work for both of you. But time is your enemy. Imagine what happens in the hiring process as time passes:

You have an interview. When I, your coach, ask how it went, you tell me how great it was: The two of you hit it off, and you are sure you will be called back. You see this interview as something frozen in time, and you wait for the magical phone call.

But after you left, the manager met with someone else, who brought up new issues. Now his criteria for what he wants have changed somewhat, and consequently, his impression of you has also changed. He was honest when he said he liked you, but things look different to him now. Perhaps you have what he needs to meet his new criteria, or perhaps you could convince him that his new direction is wrong, but you don't know what is now on his mind.

You call to find out "how things are going." He says he is still interviewing and will call you later when he has decided. Actually, then it will probably be too late for you. His thinking is constantly evolving as he meets with people. You were already out of the running. *Your call did nothing to influence his thinking:* You did not address his new concerns. You asked for a status report of where he was in the hiring process, and that's what you got. You did nothing to get back into the loop of people he might consider or to find out the new issues that are now on his mind.

---

*Oh I could show my prowess, be a lion
not a mou-esse, if I only had the nerve.*

THE COWARDLY LION IN THE MOVIE THE WIZARD OF OZ
(FROM THE BOOK BY L. FRANK BAUM)
BY E. Y. HARBURG AND HAROLD ARLEN

The manager meets more people and further defines the position. Interviewing helps him decide what he wants. You are getting further and further away from his new requirements.

You are not aware of this. You remember the great meeting you two had. You remind me that he said he really liked you. You insist on freezing that moment in time. You don't want to do anything to rock the boat or appear desperate. You hope it works out. "The ball is in his court," you say. "I gave it my best. There's nothing I can do but wait." So you decide to give it more time... time to go wrong.

---

*Annie: ...you want to give it time—
Henry: Yes—
Annie: . . . time to go wrong, change, spoil.
Then you'll know it wasn't the real thing.*

TOM STOPPARD, THE REAL THING

You have to imagine what is going on as time passes. Perhaps the hiring manager is simply very busy and is not working on this at all. Or perhaps things are moving along without you. Statistics prove that the person who is interviewed last has the best chance of being hired. That's because the last person benefits from all the thinking the manager has done. The manager is able to discuss all of the issues of concern with this final applicant.

He had made a fortune in business and owed it to being able to see the truth in any situation.

ETHAN CANIN, *EMPEROR OF THE AIR*

Dear Harvey:

Now that you are in the final stage of your search, I wanted to summarize my feelings about the position and address what I see as some of the major issues affecting your decision.

Long-term commitment

My almost 20 year career at Gotham unequivocally attests to my loyalty and commitment to my employer and my job. It is only because this opportunity is so exceptional that, for the very first time, I am seriously considering leaving Gotham. You can be assured that this sense of loyalty will remain with me at the Foundation.

Profit-making background

I feel strongly that my experience in the for-profit sector represents value added to the Foundation. I base this on the following:

- My experience in securities accounting, clearance, and custody, where virtually 100% of your assets and revenues reside, is critical to your organization.
- My review of the Marwick Report on its review of the Comptroller's Office very interestingly included recommendations identical to the initial conclusions I drew from some of the specifics we discussed.
- The cultural changes you are introducing represent concepts ingrained in me. My experience in the for-profit sector would nicely complement, support, and help expedite your initiatives to become more businesslike in your operations.
- My research on foundation accounting, primarily at the Foundation Center, illustrated the striking similarity in the Statements on Financial Accounting Standards and the Statements on Financial Accounting Concepts between the two sectors.
- My in-depth study of your annual report assured me that the differences in accounting and financial reporting between the two sectors are insignificant. My conversation with Mark Klein, senior manager at Ernst & Young, confirmed my conclusion.

I have a very positive feel for the Foundation, its philanthropic work, its infrastructure, and its human resources practices, both in general terms and as it would affect me directly.

Harvey, I believe that the Foundation and I are ideally suited for each other. My broad managerial and technical expertise is needed for the immediate tasks at hand but will also be of value in your other areas of responsibility. My experience in operating in a decentralized environment has honed my decision-making skills and my ability to interface with others at all levels.

I am looking forward to your favorable decision.

Very truly yours,

What You Can Do during the Interview

If you go into an interview with the goal of getting a job, you are putting too much pressure on yourself to come to closure. When you walk away without an offer, you feel discouraged. When you walk away without even knowing what the job is, you feel confused and lost.

Boone smiled and nodded. The muscles in his jaw hurt. "What I meant was did you ever shoot anybody but your own self. Not that that don't count."

PETE DEXTER, *DEADWOOD*

Instead of criticizing managers who don't know what they want, try to understand them: "It seems that there are a number of ways you can structure this position. Let's talk about your problems and your needs. Perhaps I can help."

Your goal is not to get an offer but to build a relationship with the manager. You are on the manager's side, assessing the situation and figuring out how to move the process along so you can continue to help define the job.

Pay Attention to Your Competition

Most job hunters think only about themselves and the hiring manager. They don't think about the others being considered for the position. But you are different. You are acutely aware at all times that you have competition. Your goal is to get rid of them.

As you move the process along, you can see your competitors dropping away because you are doing a better job of addressing the hiring manager's needs, coming up with solutions to her problems, and showing more interest and more competence than they are.

You are in a problem-solving mode. Here's the way you think: "My goal isn't to get a job immediately but to build a relationship. How can I build a relationship so that someday when this person decides what he or she wants, it'll be me?" You have hung in there. You have eliminated your competition. You have helped define the job in a way that suits both you and the hiring manager. You have the option of saying, "Do I want this job or don't I?"

He who knows only his own side of the case, knows little of that.

JOHN STUART MILL, *ON LIBERTY*

The Five O'Clock Club®

Follow-Up Checklist: Turning Job Interviews into Offers

Biblical waiting, the kind of waiting Abram and Sarai did, and which you and I must learn to do, is a very active kind of waiting. It's a faith-journey; the waiting of a pilgrimage. We can only wait for God to give us what we cannot do ourselves; but, paradoxically, we must move toward it in faith as we wait, asking, seeking and knocking....

BEN PATTERSON, *WAITING*

Do you want a job? Follow-up is the only technique that influences the person who interviewed you. You may think you can get a job through a search firm, answering an ad, networking, or directly contacting a company. But what you are getting is *interviews* in your target area. You are not job hunting yet. You prove your mettle by seeing how—over the long run—you can turn each interview into a job. *Now* you're job hunting. And that's where follow-up comes in. Remember, you generally don't want a job offer at that first meeting. An easy hire decision may mean an easy fire decision later. Instead, establish a long-term relationship. It is not unusual to be brought in for three to nine or more interviews.

In the last chapter, you read a few examples of job hunters turning job interviews into offers. They had to think hard about what to do next. They objectively and methodically analyzed *all* the interviews they had and developed strategies for addressing every issue for *each* person with whom they met. They thought about who their likely competitors were and what the hiring managers probably preferred. Who are your likely competitors? How do you stack up against them? Prove you're better than they are, or you won't get the job.

Follow-up will dramatically increase the number of job offers you get. It is one of the most powerful tools you have to influence the situation.

Why Bother with Follow-Up?

Follow-up can be used:

- to influence both the decision makers and the influencers
- to move things along
- to show interest and competence
- to knock out your competition
- to reassure the hiring manager
- to turn a losing situation into a winning one
- to make it difficult for them to reject you
- to set the right tone/buy yourself time after you are hired

In a tight market, follow-up helps. But still *strive to have 6 to 10 contacts in the works at all times.* The job you are interviewing for may vanish: The manager may decide not to hire at all or hire a finance instead of a marketing person. There may be a hiring freeze or a major reorganization. Follow-up techniques will generally not help in these situations. If you are in a competitive market, put extra effort into those job possibilities that are still alive.

Nothing is more dangerous than an idea when it is the only one you have.

EMILE CHARTIER

And if you have lots of other contacts in the works, you will be less likely to allow yourself to be abused by hiring managers trying to take advantage of *desperate* job hunters. You can assess ridiculous requests and be more willing to walk away.

The Interview Record is a checklist of items to consider in assessing your interviews and planning your follow-up. Try to remember everything that happened at each of your meetings. Many job hunters take notes during the interviews so they will do a better follow-up. After all, wouldn't a consultant take notes during a meeting? How else can you remember all the important issues that come up? At the very least, take notes immediately after the meeting. Some job hunters keep track of every person with whom they meet by using the Interview Record. Make plenty of copies of the form for your job search. Keep them in a folder or a three-ring binder, in alphabetical order within target area.

Waiting is not just the thing we have to do until we get what we hoped for. Waiting is part of the process of becoming what we hope for.

BEN PATTERSON, *WAITING*

Assess the Interview(s)

Effective follow-up depends on knowing what happened in the interview. In fact, you will begin to interview very differently now. You now know you are there to gather enough information so you can follow up, and to give enough information back so the interviewer will be willing to meet with you again. As your coach, I'd want the following background information:

- How did it go? What did they say? What did you say?
- How many people did you see?
- How much time did you spend with each?
- What role does each of them play?
- Who is important?
- Who is the hiring manager?
- Who is the decision maker?
- Who most *influences* the decision?
- Who else did you meet (administrative assistants, receptionists, bosses from other areas)? How influential might they be? (Do not dismiss them too readily. They may be more influential than you think. A trusted assistant, for example, has a lot of influence. She had better want you there.)
- How quickly do they want to decide? A year? Months? Next week?
- What do you have to offer that your competition doesn't?
- What problems did the interviewer have? Do you have any solutions to those problems?
- How badly do you want this job? (If you want it a lot, you will be more likely to do what you need to do to get it. Or perhaps someone wants it more than you. *That* person will do the things he or she needs to do to get the job.)

The key to being a strategic player is to be in play, working on a significant level.

THOMAS KRENS, DIRECTOR, THE GUGGENHEIM MUSEUM, *THE NEW YORK TIMES*

Anyone who fears effort, anyone who backs off from frustration and possibly even pain will never get anywhere.

ERICH FROMM

Anyone who listens well takes notes.

DANTE

"Why yes, we are interviewing. But we now charge the applicant $18 an hour for the interview."

Courtesy of Jerry King, Cartoons, Inc.

Follow Up with Each Person

For *each* person with whom you interviewed, analyze and craft a follow-up note that takes into account:

- **The tone of the conversation**. Was it friendly? Formal? Familylike? Follow up with a similar tone.

- **The positives about you**. Why would this person want you there? If you interviewed with peers, why would they want you on the team? In the interview, it is *your* job to make sure each person you meet can see the benefit of having you on board.

- **The objections to you**—for *each* person you met, whether or not these objections were expressed. For example, you may know that the company typically hires someone with a background that is different from yours, or you may not

have certain experience it is looking for, or your past salary may be too high, or it may see you as overqualified. A future peer may see you as a threat (let that peer know you are not) or think you will not fit in. You may be seen as too old or too young or too something else. If you think the company is worried about having you on board for some reason, address that reason. For example, if someone sees you as too old, think of the benefits that come with age. Then you might say, "I hope you are interested in hiring someone with maturity and a broad base of experience."

Even in a highly controlled meeting, there is a lot... going on. The real process of making decisions, of gathering support, of developing opinions, happens before the meeting—or after.

TERRENCE E. DEAL AND ALLAN A. KENNEDY, *CORPORATE CULTURES*

Many job hunters want to ignore or gloss over the objections; instead, pay attention to why each person may not want you there. Joel DeLuca, author of *Political Savvy*, noted that if you are observant, you should come out of a meeting with a good sense of how hard a sell this is going to be, as well as some idea of the political lay of the land.

If [a man] is brusque in his manner, others will not cooperate. If he is agitated in his words, they will awaken no echo in others. If he asks for something without having first established a proper relationship, it will not be given to him.

I CHING

- **The key issues**. Was the interviewer concerned about interdepartmental relationships? Work overload? The political situation with a key vendor? How you will support people in other areas? How you can make his or her job easier? What makes you different from your competition? Identify those issues that are key to the interviewer(s).

- **Your feelings about the job**. If this is the one place you really want to work, say so. If you would enjoy working with your prospective manager and peers, say so. At the executive level, most decisions are based on fit. In addition to competence, people want someone they'd *like* to work with and someone who *wants* to work with them. Write with enthusiasm. Let your personality come through.

- **The next steps**. Regardless of *who* should take the next steps, what exactly are the next logical steps? What will move the process along?

The average sale is made after the prospect has said "no" six times.

Jeffrey P. Davidson, marketing consultant, The Washington Post

For example, the next step could be:

- ✓ another meeting to discuss something in greater detail
- ✓ meeting(s) with other people
- ✓ another meeting after the other candidates have been interviewed
- ✓ an in-depth review of documents
- ✓ discussing a few of your ideas with them
- ✓ drafting a proposal about how you would handle a certain area

---

Let him who wants to move and convince others be first moved and convinced himself.

Thomas Carlyle

State the "next steps" in your follow-up note. For example, "I'd like to get together with you to discuss my ideas on..." or "If I don't hear from

George in a week or so, I'll give you a call."

If you were the first person interviewed, try to be interviewed again. "As you interview others, you may more clearly define what you want. I would appreciate the opportunity to address the new issues that may arise."

There is a tide in the affairs of men,
Which, taken at the flood, leads on to fortune;
Omitted, all the voyage of their life
Is bound in shallows and in miseries.

William Shakespeare, Julius Caesar, IV, III

Influence the Influencers

Most job hunters pay attention to the hiring manager and ignore everyone else. However, most hiring managers want the input of others. You may be rejected if a future peer or subordinate says that you seem difficult to work with or the receptionist complains that you were rude. Remember that everyone is an influencer. *Follow up with everyone you met formally.* Cultivate as many advocates as you can. Have people inside rooting for you. It's better if your future peers, for example, say that you would be great to have on the team. You can influence the influencers with a letter or phone call.

Who might influence the hiring decision? **If they are future coworkers, follow the analysis in the preceding section "Follow Up with *Each* Person."** Tell outside influencers the position in which you are interested, why, and how they can help you.

Joe, a well-known top-level executive, felt one of his interviews went very well, but he was afraid the interviewer would tap into the corporate pipeline and hear untrue negative rumors about him. Joe has two choices: He can hope the interviewer doesn't hear the rumors, or he can fight for the job he deserves.

Joe has to try to control the pipeline—the key influencers in this situation. First, Joe called some influential people who thought well of him and would be respected by the hiring manager. He stated why he wanted this job and asked them to put in a good word for him. Second, Joe thought of the people the hiring manager was most likely to run into or call for information. Joe called them next and did his best to influence them to support him. Joe successfully fended off bad reports and landed the job he wanted.

Progress always involves risk. You can't steal second base and keep your foot on first.

FREDERICK B. WILCOX

Success seems to be largely a matter of hanging on after others have let go.

WILLIAM FEATHER

Be in Sync with Their Timing

Move the process along to the next step, but *at the interviewer's* pace, not yours. The timing depends on the personality of the interviewer and his or her sense of urgency.

If the situation is urgent, write your letter overnight and hand-deliver it in the morning. If the manager is laid back, an urgent delivery is inappropriate.

Use your judgment. If things are going along at a good clip, and you are being brought in every other day, you may want to let it ride *if* you think you have no competition.

Also be aware that if things are *not* moving along quickly, it may have nothing to do with you. It may well be that the interviewer is not doing *anything* about filling the position—he or she may be busy with other business. If you were the hiring manager, you would find that you can't work on the hire every minute, because you have your regular job to do, and emergencies come up as well.

If you have no idea what is going on, it would help if you've formed a good relationship with the hiring manager's assistant. Then you could call and say, "Hi, Jane. This is Joe. I was wondering if you could help me with something. I haven't heard from Ellis [her boss] for two weeks and I had expected to hear something by now. I was going to drop him a note, but I didn't want to bother him if he's really busy. I was wondering if he's still interviewing other people or if he's just been tied up, or what." Who knows what she'll say? But if she says he had a death in the family and has been out of town, that gives you some idea of what is happening. He is not sitting around talking about you all day long. He is doing other things, and the hiring process often moves more slowly than you think.

Understanding is a wellspring of life to him that hath it.

PROVERBS 16:22

Even if you're on the right track, you'll get run over if you just sit there.

WILL ROGERS

How Can You Tell If a Follow-Up Letter Is a Good One?

A good letter is tailored to the situation. It would be impossible to send it to someone other than the addressee. It sells you, separates you from your competition, addresses all issues and objections, and states a next step. Finally, its tone replicates the tone of the interview (or creates a good tone if the interview wasn't so good). For example, John's various follow-up notes to those he met at the Kennedy Foundation addressed each manager's issues.

Your letters to some people will be very detailed and meticulous. These may take you half a day to write. For others, you will write a simple letter saying that you thought they would be great to work with and addressing the issues they brought up.

Most job hunters err, however, when they assume someone at a lower level has no influence. Be careful about whom you dismiss. During the interview, try to pick up on the relationships between people. In brief, remember to influence the influencers. Write notes to prospective peers you have met. They have some say in the hiring decision—maybe a lot of say. If they don't want you, you might not get hired. For each person you met, think of why he or she would want you there. What do you bring to the party? Make sure you are not a threat. Overcome his or her objections. Address any issues raised. Use the tone set in the interview.

A job hunter, Philip, put a lot of thought into his follow-up with a *prospective peer*, Jonathan. Philip considered Jonathan an important influencer and had noted the following from their meeting:

- Philip sensed that Jonathan was worried about losing his standing as the second in command to George, the hiring manager, when the new person came in.
- He was also concerned that the new person might not be a team player or a hard worker or might not be willing to help out with his special projects, which involved computer simulations.
- He was concerned about losing the camaraderie in the department and hoped the new person would have a good sense of humor to offset the stress of working under deadline.
- He was obviously trying to conduct a very professional interview and asked Philip a number of times what he thought of the questions.
- He was relieved when Philip said he would enjoy developing materials for the department, although it was not central to the job. This is a project none of

the other competitors would be able to handle.

- He wondered about the department's reputation outside the company.

The conversation had been light and friendly. Philip considered Jonathan to be the key influencer, and thought George, the hiring manager, would be making the decision with Jonathan. Philip wrote to each of his prospective peers and also to George. This is the letter he wrote to Jonathan:

Dear Jonathan:

I was glad finally to have a chance to meet you. George had spoken of you so proudly, I knew you had earned everything you've gotten at Bluekill and have worked very hard. I, too, am a hard worker, and I know we would complement each other.

I liked your professional approach to the interview and found your questions and direction quite interesting. I hope I "did okay." I believe I could work out a schedule to accommodate your many projects—and one thing you can count on is that I'm good at developing computer simulations. In my last position, I was considered the best, and would enjoy doing the same for you. I work very hard at it, and it pays off.

My impression is that George depends on you a lot, and perhaps I could help out also. I think I could develop materials that could be used both inside and with customers, and I will be glad to hear your ideas on the matter. I've developed a great deal of material in the past that I will be happy to show you.

All things considered, I think I would make a good addition to the group, and I believe you and I would enjoy working together. As I said to you when we met, I've worked in a few companies, and I do my best to make every place I work as enjoyable as it can be. Your sense of humor surely helps, and I'm sure mine will also.

Cordially,
Philip Johnson

Time passed. Philip met again with George and with other peers. But he was concerned about whether Jonathan would still be in favor of him in light of the number of additional applicants Jonathan had met by then. Philip decided to contact Jonathan again, this time more informally. In reviewing his notes, he fixed on what Jonathan had said about the reputation of the department. Philip then arranged a networking meeting with an important person in the industry so he would have something to contact Jonathan about. The information would also help him make up his mind in case he received a job offer. Then he wrote on informal stationery:

Dear Jonathan,

In our meeting, you wondered about the reputation of your department. I'm sure you will be happy to hear, as I was, that your department is thought of as the best in the industry. I met with Cheryl Jenkins yesterday, and she raved about each person in your group—including you. You should be proud of her commendation, and I admit that I was proud as well because I sincerely hope I wind up working with you.

I mentioned to you that I would be happy to show you the computer simulation materials I have developed in the past. I have finally put them together and will call you to see if you still want to look at them. It shouldn't take more than 15 minutes of your time.

> Hope all is well.
> Best regards,
> *Philip*

Sometimes an important influencer is the best way to sway the hiring manager. Philip got the job, but he got much more: He started the job with a very good relationship with each of the people with whom he would be working. When you analyze what is important to each person, you not only increase your chances of getting the job but also increase your chances of having the new job go smoothly.

We are what we repeatedly do. Excellence, then, is not an act, but a habit.

ARISTOTLE

Discuss your follow-up problems with your private Five O'Clock Club coach or at Five O'Clock Club meetings. Make the effort required to develop strategies for your follow-up moves. It's worth the trouble. As one Five O'Clock Clubber advised, "Make sure the follow-up letter you write is absolutely the best the company will see—or don't write it." Be sure to read the follow-up case studies in this book.

There is no such thing as "soft sell" or "hard sell." There is only "smart sell" and "stupid sell."

CHARLES BOWER, PRESIDENT, BBD&O, *EDITOR & PUBLISHER*

Job Interview Follow-Up: Sample Letters

The Five O'Clock Club

Influence belongs to men of action, and for purposes of action nothing is more useful than narrowness of thought combined with energy of will.

HENRI FRÉDÉRIC AMIEL, *JOURNAL INTIME*

Motivation will almost always beat mere talent.

NORMAN R. AUGUSTINE, *AUGUSTINE'S LAWS*

Method is much, technique is much, but inspiration is even more.

BENJAMIN NATHAN CARDOZO, U.S. SUPREME COURT JUSTICE, *LAW AND INSTITUTE*

The fearful Unbelief is unbelief in yourself.

THOMAS CARLYLE, *SARTOR RESARTUS*

We are perplexed but not in despair.

NEW TESTAMENT, II CORINTHIANS 4:8

It is better to wear out than to rust out.

RICHARD CUMBERLAND, 1632-1718 BISHOP OF PETERBOROUGH, ATTRIBUTED

To him that will, ways are not wanting.

GEORGE HERBERT, *JACULA PRUDENTUM*

It is fatal to enter any war without the will to win it.

DOUGLAS MACARTHUR, SPEECH TO THE REPUBLICAN NATIONAL CONVENTION, JULY 7, 1952

> **Job follow-ups are not merely *thank you* notes. Your primary goal is not to *thank* the interviewer but to *influence* him or her.**

How Can You Tell Whether a Follow-Up Letter Is a Good One?

A good letter is **tailored** to the situation. It would be impossible to send it to someone other than the addressee. It **sells the writer, separates the writer from the competition, addresses all issues and objections, and states a next step.** Finally, its **tone replicates the tone of the interview** (or creates a good tone if the interview wasn't so good).

Look at the follow-up letter on the next page.

Paragraph 1
- talks about the next steps
- separates me from the competition: They're talking about coaching, but I'm trying to offer something additional—the development of program materials

Paragraph 2
- handles an objection: Would I enjoy working with this kind of client?

Paragraphs 3 & 4
- another objection: Would I be too independent in the job (or would I listen to my boss)?

Paragraph 5
- another objection: Why hire a strong, older person when someone with less experience would do?

Paragraph 6
- recalls the camaraderie of the interview
  Note: Most objections are unstated. You have to notice them for yourself based on the questions at the interview or your assessment of who your competition is likely to be. Also be aware of tone, facial expression, and body language.

Follow-Up after a Job Interview

M. Catherine Wendleton
163 York Avenue—12B
New York, New York 10000
(212) 555-2231 (day)
(212) 555-1674 (message)

July 18, 1988

Ms. Damona Sain
Director of Outplacement
RightBank
100 Madison Avenue
New York, NY 10000

Dear Damona:

Now I've met everyone in your group, and I'll be glad to get together with you again. I can see how carefully you have parceled out your assignments to each person. I can also see where I would fit in—something we can discuss in more detail when we get together. I certainly am expert in developing program materials and will be happy to show you things I have done in that area.

In general, I enjoy the type of client you get at RightBank because a good deal of my approach is business oriented and based on business systems and logic. That is essentially the way I operate with people from other banks, as well as from the big accounting firms. These people tend to be self-motivated and direct, and I like that. They tend to not want to be psychoanalyzed too much, and that's fine with me. I'm all for getting on with it.

On the other hand, I believe I can learn a lot from you, and am looking forward to the opportunity to do so. I am even planning to join the Jung Foundation, and visited there for the first time today.

I know you are in a delicate position dealing with the RightBank corporate problems, and I do understand the difficulties of your job. For most of my career, I have worked for senior management. All of my bosses have been able to count on me to see what needs to be done, to do it, and to work smoothly with the rest of the organization. I have a lot of ideas, but I also follow through on them and know how to get the willing cooperation of others.

I hope you are looking to hire a strong person—one you can depend on to carry out your vision as well as add to it—a person with maturity and strong corporate experience as well as one who is a solid coach and good at running a small business—which is what you are trying to do. I look forward to helping you and will do more than my share to support you.

I hope you have a wonderful vacation, and I can't tell you how jealous I am. I've never had two weeks together in my life. I'll see you when you get back. Don't think about all of this.

Cheers,

Follow-Up after a Job Interview

Influence the Influencers

These are *notes to prospective peers* for the job on the preceding page. They have some say in the hiring decision, maybe a lot of say. Make sure your follow-up letters influence them. If they don't want you, you might not get hired. Write to *each* person with whom you interviewed. For each, think of <u>why they would want you there</u>.

What's in it for them?

- What do you bring to the party? Make sure you are not a threat to them. Overcome their objections.
- Address any issues raised.
- Use the tone set in the interview.

M. Catherine Wendleton

Dear Carolyn:

I was glad to finally have a chance to meet you. Damona had spoken of you so proudly, she made me proud too. I can see that you've earned everything you've gotten at RightBank and have worked very hard. I too am a hard worker, and I know we would complement each other.

I liked your professional approach to the interview, and your questions and direction were quite interesting to me as a professional. I hope I "did OK." I believe I could work out a schedule to accommodate your needs in the group training area—and one thing you can count on is that I'm good at it. I believe I was the favorite coach at JC Penney—which was essentially all group work. I put a lot of effort into it, and I got rave reviews.

My impression is that Damona depends on you a lot, and perhaps I could help out also. I could develop materials that could be used in the group as well as in the individual program, and I will be glad to hear your ideas on the matter. I've developed a great deal of material in the past that I will be happy to show you.

All things considered, I think I would make a happy addition to the group, and I believe you and I would enjoy working together. As I said to you when we met, I've been around, and I certainly do my best to make every place I work as enjoyable as it can be. Your sense of humor surely helps, and I'm sure mine will also.

Cordially,
Kate Wendleton

M. Catherine Wendleton

July 18, 1988

Dear Peter:

It certainly was a pleasure meeting you. You add a lot of humor and a lot of ability to the place. All things considered, I think I would make a happy addition to the group, and I believe you and I would enjoy working together. I believe you are a person I would turn to to broaden my expertise in the area of evaluation. I would also help you out with the reception area, as I can see that is one of your major duties. (Just kidding.)

Damona said she would like me to concentrate on the area of materials development—something I have some experience in and would enjoy doing.

I hope you and I will have the opportunity to work together.

Cordially,
Kate

M. Catherine Wendleton

Dear Alan:

I'm glad to have met you. Your smile seems to soften things in the office, and I'm sure we would enjoy working together. I believe I could learn from each person in the group, and I also think I bring a lot to the party. My special assignment from Damona would be in developing program materials—something that is right up my alley.

All things considered, I think I would make a happy addition to the group. As I said to you when we met, I certainly do my best to make every place I work as enjoyable as possible. Your attitude surely helps in that area, and I'm sure mine will also.

Cordially,
Kate Wendleton

Follow-Up after a Job Interview

The most overlooked part of job follow-up is the statement of next steps. It is *your* responsibility to make sure the process is moved along to the next step.

For example, if they say they'll call you in a week, you can say: "If I don't hear from you in a week or so, I'll give you a call."

Don't be surprised if they don't call: Everyone is very busy, and you are probably not at the top of their list. Gently move them along—within their time frame—in your follow-up note.

Psalm 23

The Lord is my shepherd, I shall not want.
He makes me lie down in green pastures;
He leads me beside quiet waters.
He restores my soul;
He guides me in the paths of righteousness
For His name's sake.
Even though I walk through the valley of the
shadow of death, I fear no evil; for Thou art with me;
Thy rod and Thy staff, they comfort me.
Thou dost prepare a table before me
in the presence of my enemies;
Thou hast anointed my head with oil;
My cup overflows.
Surely goodness and lovingkindness will follow me
all the days of my life,
And I will dwell in the house of the Lord forever.

Although this note is short, it still contains a strategy for moving this process along to the next step.

Penelope Webb

To: Barbara Kassabian

I enjoyed our conversation last week. Your need to modernize and integrate existing systems, and to make them flexible enough to accommodate future opportunities such as the repeal of Act 27, certainly sounds like an intriguing challenge.

I appreciate your suggestion that I meet with some of the people in your group and would like very much to talk with you further. I'll call you in a few days to set something up.

Best regards,
Penny

Follow-Up after a Job Interview

Renée Rosenberg

Street Address
City, State, Zip
(555) 555-2231
Rrosenberg451@yahoo.com

July 18, 2015

Mr. Win Sheffield
General Counsel and Senior Vice President
Valentino
100 Madison Avenue
New York, NY 10000

> **Applying to be assistant general counsel. The hiring manager considers the "family environment" crucial.**

Dear Win:

The opportunity to meet and speak with you last week was a real pleasure. It is clear to me that Valentino offers the close, family environment and real team feeling that I so much enjoyed at Campeau. Since we were great friends there, we were very supportive of each other as colleagues, and the experience was one of the most rewarding I have had. I know that I would feel equally at home at Valentino, as the chemistry seems right for me.

It also seems that my 20 years' experience with Fortune 20 companies in the fashion/retail industry, both as a merchant and as a legal executive, could not be more ideally suited for heading up your new leather division.

In addition, after talking with you, I can't imagine a legal background that's a better fit:

- Extensive marketing law experience (and Valentino is a "marketing-driven" company)
- Litigation (both actual practice and complex management)
- Environmental compliance (set up a $40 million program)
- Commercial contracts (UCC Article 2)
- Antitrust compliance
- Responsibility for a worldwide trademark program (with 200 domestic and 70 foreign registrations in 35 countries)
- Licensing arrangements
- Legislative matters (we do need to do something about gray market matters).

> **During the interview, she convinced him to hire a legal generalist. But just in case he wants a specialist, she's covered.**

> **Can you handle these young, unmanageable clients? Yes, I can. And I also work well with the top brass.**

Finally, I enjoy working with the type of client you have: young, innovative, creative people who have an enthusiasm and eagerness to get the job done quickly. I appreciate their creativity because I am a creative person myself. Since I have a business background (which most attorneys do not have), I also empathize with their desire to get on with things—but in their eagerness important issues may be overlooked. I'm able to bring to bear on those issues (business as well as legal), yet encourage their initiative and still protect the company from any unwarranted liability or exposure.

Of course, I'm also experienced in working with senior management. At Campeau I advised them on a daily basis and understand the type of advice appropriate at that level.

I'm very excited about being part of the team you are building. I just know that it would prove to be a mutually rewarding experience. I look forward to getting together with you again. As you meet other candidates, other issues may arise, and I would appreciate the opportunity to address them. In the meantime, I will keep you apprised of any new developments in my search.

Cordially,

Follow-Up after a Job Interview

In the realm of ideas, everything depends on enthusiasm; in the real world, all rests on perseverance.

GOETHE

All right, I hated the job. You're right: I admit it. I'm glad to be done with it—all right!

PETER SCHAFFER, *LETTICE & LOVAGE*

The mode by which the inevitable is reached is effort.

FELIX FRANKFURTER

A Few Hints

1. This note and the one on the following page were written after a job interview. This one is to human resources, while the other is to the hiring manager.

The strategy is to keep human resources informed (and perhaps have them as an advocate), but to <u>**"do the deal" with the hiring manager.**</u>

2. It's rare that a job offer is made after the first interview. In fact, you don't want an offer that early in the process. Therefore, think of what would be required next to move the process along so it *could* turn into a job offer.

What logically do you think should happen next? For example, should you meet with another department or division head to get more information? Should you come up with a few ideas and meet again with this manager? Think it through. Take a look at the other letters in this section to see how other job hunters handled the follow up.

<u>**It's your responsibility to think of what is needed next and to make it happen.**</u>

Deborah Sweeney

March 24, 2014

Dear Kim:

I enjoyed the chance to meet with you and discuss American Express. I also found John to be a very dynamic and stimulating individual.

The position we discussed requires a combination of creative, strategic thinking and hard-nosed, practical, get-it-done skills. I think it would be a very good fit for my abilities and experience, and would be the most stimulating and exciting thing that I have ever done.

Thus I would like to meet with John again. I suggested to him that we discuss one region's business in depth, to better understand the key business issues and opportunities, and give him a clearer sense of how I would approach them.

I look forward to hearing from you.

Sincerely,

Deborah

Follow-Up after a Job Interview

Deborah Sweeney
March 24, 2014

Dear Bob:

I greatly enjoyed the chance to meet with you and learn about the structure and needs of your business.

It became increasingly clear to me that the position we discussed would be a good fit for my skills and interests. You are confronted with a complex mosaic of regional businesses, with very different profit dynamics, competitive situations, and broker/customer relationships. Major variations in regional economic trends and industry structures make this situation even more complex.

Thus you clearly need someone who can quickly develop an understanding of each regional business, and of the needs and goals of the profit centers, and then **visualize** opportunities that this creates. These could take the form of improved marketing or product development programs against current businesses, or innovative plans for the new industries and market segments that will emerge as the regional economies develop.

I think that this is consistent with my strongest skills. I am a quick study and a good strategic thinker who can digest a lot of complex information and build a coherent, actionable structure from it. I am also very good at sensing marketing opportunities and creating unique ways to capitalize on them. My broad-based marketing background provides a wide range of ideas and experience to draw from. At the same time, line management assignments in the branches have tempered my "visionary" thinking with a hard-nosed, practical approach and an appreciation for the day-to-day realities of running a business.

For these reasons, I think the assignment we discussed would be more exciting and intellectually stimulating than anything I have ever done. I would like very much to talk more about it.

As a next step, it might be valuable to discuss one region in some depth, reviewing World American Express's current business, broker, and customer relations, competitive factors, and economic trends in the market. This would allow me to give you a clearer sense of how I would actually identify opportunities and develop programs to make the most of against them, and would give me a more detailed understanding of the key opportunities and problems faced by your business.

I think this discussion could be of value to both of us, and I look forward to meeting with you again.

Sincerely,
Deborah

Follow-Up after a Job Interview

David Pandozzi
Street Address City, State
(212) 555-2231
Pandozzi213@hotmail.com

May 10, 2014

Mr. David Yegerlehner
Senior Vice President
United Way of Tristate Street
Address
City, State, Zip

Dear David:

First of all, thank you for giving me the opportunity to speak with you last week. It was really a pleasure to meet you, and I appreciated learning about the goals and needs of the United Way of Tristate from your perspective and experience.

Because of our discussion I am even more eager to find a place for myself in the planning, management, and support of human-care services. I am encouraged that there might be such an opportunity for me within the United Way of Tristate.

I spent some time reading the materials you gave me and am especially impressed with the strategic plan. I believe that I have skills, experience, and motivations that would be instrumental in the successful implementation of the plan, for example:

- strong quantitative skills: conducting research, financial, and technical information analyses

- experience in developing and assessing marketing plans and strategies for diverse target markets

- problem-solving ability that is challenged by new and continually varied situations

- excellent oral and written communication skills, with experience in delivering presentations to top-level corporate executives

- enthusiasm for the mission of United Way

I welcome and appreciate the effort you are making to explore the possibilities for me within your organization. I would like to stay in touch with you during this time, and would be pleased to meet again for additional discussions.

Thank you for your support. I'm looking forward to hearing from you when you have more information about your situation and its potential for me.

Sincerely,

David Pandozzi

Follow-Up after a Job Interview

Robert Riscica
Glen Ridge Cove
San Francisco, CA 66666
RiscicaRobert6@mindspring.com

April 15, 2014

Ms. Sara Lohaus
Technology Planning Division
Bank of America
One Pickalilly Square, 40th Floor
San Francisco, CA 66620

> **This is a logical format to follow. Each issue identified in the interview process becomes a paragraph heading.**

Dear Sara,

Your department is an impressive one. I remain very interested in the position we discussed and think that the following elements of my skills and relevant experience would serve me well in accomplishing your objectives:

Project Management

My responsibilities as **Project Director** at General Dynamics included collecting data from a project team comprised of accounting and technology professionals and **writing comprehensive functional specifications** for a new front-end interface to the general ledger system. I also prepared and gave periodic progress presentations to a steering committee of senior bank executives.

Computer Systems/Technology Exposure

Throughout my career, I have had close involvement with technology professionals, most significantly:

- at **Bank of America**, particularly in my most recent position as project manager, where I was involved in the conversion of the community banks to B of A's "utility" systems

- at **General Dynamics**, as mentioned above and as an **accounting systems liaison**, during which time I was responsible for ensuring adherence to bankwide accounting standards in the development of new application systems

- at **Wells Fargo**, where I was directly involved in the detailed evaluation of new general ledger software versus Wells' older, in-house developed package

- at **Walt Disney Co**., where I reviewed and approved new application systems for inclusion of effective audit controls

(continues)

Finance

My experience as Regional Financial Controller for B of A's West Region corporate business units and that as a Business Manager within the former National Corporate Division required a thorough understanding of global finance products and services.

Training

In my most recent position at Bank of America (Project Manager), I provided extensive training via "hands-on" workshops in the use of automated proof collection/clearance to employees in retail business units nationally. I also prepared training materials and developed test procedures for use in connection with training exercises.

PC Skills/Lotus Notes

I have extensive PC skills and experience at developing PC-based applications for general use:
- As controller for B of A in San Francisco, I developed a **PFS database application** that tracked premises receivable and billed all tenants for rent and other costs.
- As business manager for corporate finance analysis, I developed comprehensive **paradox databases** to control human resources/staffing, as well as accounts payable.

I have a high level of technical proficiency in Lotus Notes based on my intensive self-training efforts over the last few months and, as I mentioned, have a Notes Server and two workstations set up on the computer network I maintain in my home.

As we discussed, should you select another candidate for the position, I would greatly appreciate consideration for a temporary position involved with Lotus Notes. The benefit of such an arrangement, besides the obvious one of extending my severance period, is that it would provide me the opportunity to contribute to B of A's Notes environment and thereby establish myself as a viable candidate for future Notes-related positions within the bank.

Again, thank you for your interest. I look forward to hearing from you.

Sincerely,

Robert Riscica

In business, willingness is just as important as ability.
PAUL C. HOFFMAN

Follow-Up after a Job Interview

Anne Marie Power
444 Pound Ridge Road
Dallas, Texas 44444
PowerTrust@simplex.com

April 4, 2014

Charles Conlin
Kendall Guaranty Trust Company
666 Brick Wall West
Dallas, Texas 44444-0060

> **Here's another approach to organizing your follow-up around the important issues. Of course, Anne Marie wrote a customized follow-up to every person with whom she met.**

Dear Chip,

It was an exciting and eventful day. Thank you for giving me the opportunity. I learned even more about Kendall and training's mission there.

In my view, three issues about me came up during the day's meeting. I wanted to tell you about them.

1. There was some concern about my lack of experience with Fortune 500 clients. But I think my experience with a wide range of underwriting and advisory work is more to the point. I know firsthand what it takes to develop a corporate finance opportunity, compete for a mandate, and take an issuer to market. I can bring that practical perspective to my work in training, even if I've had relatively few Fortune 500 clients in my recent banking career.

2. My job changes understandably drew comments. I realize Kendall is a company where long service is the norm. As you know, I've put a lot of time, thought, and effort into this career change, and I'm committed to it and to Kendall as well. You have the kind of challenging standards and defining principles that I found compelling in the Navy and have missed in my work life ever since.

3. There may have been some concern about whether I bring to the job a larger vision of training's strategic role. I know from the Navy how crucial corporate values can be to success and how training at all levels can be used to reinforce values. In business, I've been very interested in how General Electric is using values to improve its competitiveness and performance. Aside from that, I've been more focused on corporate finance practice than strategic issues in training.

I hope you had a good time in New Orleans and Natchez. If you have any questions or other concerns I can address, please don't hesitate to call.

Sincerely,
Anne Marie Power

Follow-Up after a Job Interview

JEANNETTE LEWIS
10 Park Terrace East
Chicago, IL 00007
Jeannette.Lewis.Chicago@gmail.com

December 1, 2014

Ms. Ruth Robbins
Vice President, Manager Asset Securitization
Bank of Germany
1211 Bird-in-Cage Way
Chicago, IL 00007

Dear Ruth:

I admired greatly your thoroughness and enthusiasm, and I came away with a good understanding of Bank of Germany's strategies for growing the business in North America. I believe that given Bank of Germany's size and reach worldwide, you could become a major bank in the U.S., and I would like to help you to do that. I have given it a great deal of thought, and I have decided that I'd love to work for you and for Bank of Germany.

I believe I could add value to Bank of Germany's asset securitization business in the following ways:

Ability to immediately close deals and also address critical tax accounting issues

Because of my in-depth knowledge of the market, I am able to immediately contribute to closing existing transactions and make necessary marketing calls jointly and separately to build a profile of active deals for first quarter closure. I have structured and closed asset securitization deals in the past, and I am willing to do the detailed, unexciting, plodding work that it takes to execute the transactions.

Moreover, I am intimately aware of the complicated tax issues facing Bank of Germany as a U.S. branch of a foreign bank.

Superb contacts

Having worked with Fortune 500 companies and foreign banks for over 16 years in project finance, tax leasing, debt and equity placement, lending, and structuring corporate finance solutions for multinationals, I am confident that Bank of Germany could become a niche player in several product lines, including lead manager for asset-secured deals for a select number of corporations. In the past 6 months, I have had numerous discussions with several companies and institutional investors, and I have already done the target marketing. These companies place high value on competence, debt rating, and execution skills. They would relish working with us and Bank of Germany.

(continues)

Broad-based background and cross-sell opportunities

The tax law has changed in the U.S., and it is being modified in Germany. These changes will create tax arbitrage opportunities for German subsidiaries operating in the U.S., since they will be able to avoid loss of interest deductibility.

Given the current legislative environment in both countries, cross-sell opportunities exist for tax leasing, project and trade finance, and product enhancements involving derivatives. I believe that my experience in these product areas will be very useful in creating new opportunities for Bank of Germany.

Teamwork

As a small branch of a foreign bank, Bank of Germany seems to have a corporate culture that encourages teamwork and rewards cooperation and results. I have managed groups of people in the U.S. and abroad. I have also worked in the U.S. and overseas, and I am confident that I would fit quite comfortably in your organization.

I would like to continue our discussions, and I look forward to meeting the other members of your organization. I will call you the week of December 11th to follow up for another meeting.

Sincerely,

Jeannette Lewis

*It may be that the race is not always
to the swift, nor the battle to the strong,
but that's the way to bet.*

DAMON RUNYON

The Five O'Clock Club®

Following Up When there Is No Immediate Job

Contrary to the cliche, genuinely nice guys most often finish first, or very near it.

MALCOLM FORBES

During each meeting, you have taken up the time of someone who sincerely tried to help you. Writing a note is the only polite thing to do. Since the person has gone to some effort for you, go to some effort in return. A phone call to thank a person can be an intrusion and shows little effort on your part.

In addition to being polite, there are good business reasons for writing notes and otherwise keeping in touch with people who have helped you. For one thing, few people keep in touch so you will stand out. Second, it gives you a chance to sell yourself again and to overcome any misunderstandings that may have occurred. Third, this is a promotional campaign and any good promoter knows that a message reinforced soon after a first message results in added recall.

If you meet someone through a networking meeting, for example, he or she will almost certainly forget about you the minute you leave and just go back to business. Sorry, but you were an interruption.

If you write to people almost immediately after your meeting, this will dramatically increase the chance they will remember you. If you wait two weeks before writing, they may remember meeting someone but not remember you specifically. If you wait longer than two weeks, they probably won't remember meeting anyone—let alone you.

So promptly follow the meeting with a note. It is important to remind those to whom you write who you are and when they talked to you. Give some highlight of the meeting. Contact them again within a month or two. It is just like an advertising campaign. Advertisers will often place their ads at least every four weeks in the same publication. If they advertised less often, few people would remember the ad.

Courtesy of Jerry King, Cartoons, Inc.

"Relax, Mr. Gray, this is just a simple job interview for a sales position. So please stop pleading the 5th everytime I ask you a question."

What Michael Did

This is a classic—and it worked on me many years ago! I wanted to hire one junior accountant for a very important project and had the search narrowed down to two people. I asked my boss for his input. We made up a list of what we were seeking and we each rated the candidates on 20 criteria. The final scores came in very close, but I hired Judy instead of Michael.

In response to my rejection, Michael wrote me a note telling me how much he still wanted to work for our organization and how he hoped I would keep him in mind if something else should come up. He turned the rejection into a positive contact. Notes are so unusual and this one was so personable, that I showed it to my boss.

A few months later, Michael wrote again saying he had taken a position with another firm. He was still very much interested in us and he hoped to work for us someday. He promised to keep in touch, which he did. Each time he wrote, I showed the note to my boss. Each time, we were sorry we couldn't hire him.

After about seven months, I needed another helping hand. Whom do you think I called? Do you think I interviewed other people? Do you think I had to sell Michael to my boss? Michael came to work for us and we never regretted it. Persistence pays off.

We make a living by what we get, but we make a life by what we give.

WINSTON CHURCHILL

What to Say in Your Follow-Up Note

Depending on the content of your note, you may type or write it. Generally use standard business-size stationery, but sometimes Monarch or other note-size stationery, ivory or white, will do. A job interview follow-up should almost always be typed on standard business-size ivory or white stationery.

After an information-gathering meeting, play back some of the advice you received, any you intend to follow, and so on. Simply be sincere. What did you appreciate about the time the person spent with you? Did you get good advice that you intend to follow? Say so. Were you inspired? Encouraged? Awakened? Say so.

If you think there were sparks between you and the person with whom you met, be sure to say you will keep in touch. Then do it. Follow-up letters don't have to be long, but they do have to be personal. Make sure the letters you write could not be sent to someone else on your list.

Sample Follow-Up to a Networking Meeting

PETER SCHAEFER

To: Laura Labovich

Thanks again for contacting Brendan for me and for providing all those excellent contact names.

There's such a wealth of good ideas in that list that it will take me a while to follow up on all of them, but I'm working hard at it and will let you know what develops.

Again, thanks for your extraordinary effort. (By the way, should you ever want to "review your career options," I would be delighted to share a few names, or more than a few, with you.)

Stay tuned!

Peter

To keep in touch, simply let interviewers/ network contacts know how you are doing. Tell them whom you are seeing and what your plans are. Some people, seeing your sincerity, will keep sending you leads or other information.

It's never too late to follow up. For example: "I met you a year ago and am still impressed by... Since then I have... and would be interested in getting together with you again to discuss these new developments." Make new contacts. Recontact old ones by writing a "status report" every two months telling them how well you are doing in your search. **Keeping up with old networking contacts is as important as making new ones.**

Some job hunters use this as an opportunity to write a proposal. During the meeting, you may have learned something about the organization's problems. Writing a proposal to solve them may create a job for you. Patricia had a networking meeting with a small company where she learned that it wanted to expand the business from $5 million to $50 million. She came up with lots of

ideas about how that could be done—with her help, of course—and called to set up a meeting to review her ideas. She went over the proposal with them and they created a position for her.

However, you are not trying to turn every networking meeting into a job possibility. You are trying to form lifelong relationships with people. Experts say most successful employees form solid relationships with lots of people and keep in touch regularly throughout their careers. These people will keep you up-to-date in a changing economy, tell you about changes or openings in your field, and generally be your long-term ally. And you will do the same for them.

Has a man gained anything who has received a hundred favors and rendered none? He is great who confers the most benefits.

RALPH WALDO EMERSON, *"ESSAY ON COMPENSATION"*

The Five O'Clock Club®

Accepting the Wrong Job Offer

by Jim Hinthorn, certified Five O'Clock Club Master Career Coach

Most of the articles written about the consequences of making "bad hiring decisions" have been from the employer's perspective. As a senior HR professional responsible for recruiting, I can attest to the problems a company faces when the person they hired turns out to be a disaster—it's costly in both time and money. But what if you, as a job hunter, make a bad decision in pursuing a company that turns out not to be a good fit. Are there consequences for you? You bet there are and I'm going to share a personal story about what can happen when you make a bad decision, so you can avoid this ever happening to you. I'll let you in on a little secret up front—**if I had followed the Five O'Clock Club methodology in my job search, I could have probably prevented this disaster. Pay attention!**

Background

A few years back, I found myself in a position where I was recommending the elimination of my own job as Senior VP of HR. My current company was not doing well financially, we were considering licensing out one of our major brands, had frozen our pension plan, and had significantly reduced staff in all parts of the organization. Over the course of several months, I was able to negotiate a lucrative severance package. I had also started to explore new job opportunities by networking. At 56 years old, my plan was to obtain another top HR position, and eventually, retire into part time HR consulting.

Everything was falling into place when I got a serendipitous lead from a headhunter about a top HR job with a premier company in its industry.

So, after a very limited search and only three interviews, I accepted the top HR position with this company.

I felt like I'd won the lottery because I had landed a good job with a premier company and also walked away from my former employer with a good severance package. Could life get any better? Well, fast forward to two years later when I awoke at 6:00 AM on a Monday morning in and could not make the curtain call. By curtain call, I mean I looked at my wife and said, "I can't go to work today, I can't stand to work in that place anymore."

Running on "Empty"

I was emotionally and physically drained, the consequences of working for two years in an environment that was at odds with my personal and professional values and beliefs. What seemed like a major coup two years prior, had turned into a personal hell that lasted for the better part of the next 12 months. I am fully recovered and was able to return to meaningful work (an interesting story for yet another time). Could my descent into hell have been avoided? Yes, if I had done a better job of interviewing, done some of the Five O'Clock Club assessment exercises, and paid attention to the red flags that appeared during my discussions with this company. Let's look at some of those red flags.

The Flags

<u>First Flag</u>— I'm interviewing with the chief financial officer who is responding to my question

about a typical work day. He tells me he arrives at the office around 6:30 AM and leaves at about 6:00 PM, Monday through Friday, works 4 to 6 hours on Saturday, and occasionally comes in on Sunday morning, but only for a few hours. He is younger than I am but looks about 10 years older. I'd always had long work days because I commuted 3 hours to and from work. So my typical workweek was 55 to 60 hours at a minimum. This person only had about a 30-minute drive to work and worked 65 to 70 hours a week. I just chalked this up to the guy being a workaholic, never thinking it might be a requirement in this company. I should have questioned all those who interviewed me about their typical workday.

Second Flag— I asked about my predecessor. I knew from the headhunter he lasted only about 9 months in the job before he accepted an international job with an old business acquaintance. Those I interviewed, including the CEO, to whom I would report, told me they were very pleased with my predecessor but he had gotten a job offer that was "just too good to pass up." I actually spoke to this person who was overseas. My predecessor noted that the CEO was very demanding and told me I must be a pretty special person if the CEO wanted to hire me. I viewed his comment as a personal compliment and I thought that being demanding was normal behavior for a CEO. I should have probed more about the "demanding" statement.

Third Flag— The CEO, the person I'd be reporting to, seemed to rely more on his other direct reports for input as to whether I would be a good hire rather than determining that himself. I was supposed to have an interview with the CEO on my first visit to the company but got word shortly after I arrived that he would not have time to see me that day. On a return visit, I did get to talk to him, but it turned out to be over lunch with some of his other direct reports. It did dawn on me that the CEO knew little about me other than the feedback he was getting from his direct reports. I knew I was having good interviews so the feedback would be positive. If the CEO was

going to hire me based on his direct reports' feelings, that was alright with me. I failed to realize it was a two-way street; he knew little about me but, more importantly, I knew too little about him.

Fourth Flag— When I met with the HR staff, they were very forthright about the top HR job and how challenging it could be, given the management style and expectations of the CEO. They told me that the VP of HR who left after 9 months was very good but had left when he was offered a better opportunity, a story consistent with what others had told me. However, they did tell me that the VP of HR who preceded him just could not stand up to the CEO and that the CEO intimidated him. It was an interesting selection of words used by the HR staff but the ego part of me thought that, given my years of HR experience, I could hold my own.

In retrospect, these flags should have caused me to stop and consider seriously if this was a place I really would want to work. However, I was so excited about pocketing the severance money from my previous employer and landing the top HR job with a premier company, that I pretty much ignored the red flags. Looking back on it some years later, the sign that really turned out to be my undoing was the third flag. To take the top HR position reporting to CEO **and to have so little knowledge of the CEO's values relative to employees, was a major mistake on my part**. Had I followed more of the Five O'Clock Club principles in this interviewing process, I probably could have avoided what turned out to be a really bad career move.

What I Did Correctly

I had accurately assessed that the "influencers" in the hiring decision were the CEO's direct reports. I knew I had done a great job impressing them with my ability to help them resolve their functional needs whether it be in finance, sales, marketing, or manufacturing— I was truly "acting like a consultant" as our Five O'Clock methodology suggests. I also knew from the Five O'Clock

Club literature that, at the executive level, most decisions are based on "fit"— I knew that I had convinced the CEO's direct reports that I was a good fit. I also knew I'd be working for a company that was well known for its brands. I had researched the company and knew it was considered a premier company in its industry. I had previously worked for a company that produced brand named products and that was important to my values— a good fit for me. I thought I had done a good job in "assessing the interviews." I thought I had gathered enough information about the company and had given enough information to those I had interviewed— these are all consistent with Five O'Clock Club methodology. I played the interview game very well. I had given this company enough information about me to separate me from my competition and make me the candidate of choice. But sometimes it is better *not* to be the candidate of choice!

Where I Messed Up

I failed to do due diligence on my end. I did not get the information needed to understand the values and methods of my future boss. If I had just spent some time in assessing my interviews, as the Five O'Clock Club recommends, I would have realized an obvious and glaring error. The amount of time I spent talking to my future boss was simply not sufficient to make a good decision about the job. As I reflect back on the discussions I had with this company, I only spent about 15 minutes in actual conversation with the CEO out of a total of 10 plus hours of interviews with this company.

Although the senior managers with whom I interviewed were open about the realities of their corporate culture, **I chose to ignore what I didn't want to hear**. I failed to ask questions about corporate values and practices. I did not explore statements that suggested a working environment that might be at odds with my values. **I was looking for a quick and seamless move from my old job into a new job. I wasn't honest with myself and never asked myself** if this was really a good

move for me. As a result, I spent two years—of what should have been prime time in my career— working in an environment where human capital was expendable, mistakes were not tolerated and, if made, needed to be punished, senior managers were humiliated in front of their peers, vacations were really not to be taken, and loyalty was equated to the length of your workday. This environment might appeal to some but I found it to be abusive and toxic.

It would be easy to blame this company for the workplace injustices I had to endure, but really, I can only blame myself for taking the job. I put myself in an environment that was not a good fit. If I had followed the Five O'Clock Club's advice and analyzed my interviews with this company, I would have either not taken the job, realizing it would not be a good fit; or, at least, realized I was going to have to compromise my beliefs and values about how employees should be treated.

My advice to you is to **spend whatever amount of time it takes getting to know the person you will be working for**. I did myself a disservice by not doing that and it is a very avoidable mistake. If you assess your interviews in terms of the amount of time you spent interviewing with you future boss versus other individuals in the organization, the answer will be evident.

Last Thought

It's probably appropriate that the parting words of the CEO to me were something to the effect that "your next job should be one where you can help people." And you know, I think he was correct.

So here we are today. I am a coach for the Five O'Clock Club where our motto is to always "put the needs of the job hunter first." Guess I ended up right where I was supposed to be.

Before You Say "Yes" to a Job Offer, Check Out the New Boss and the New Culture

by Bill Belknap, certified Five O'Clock Club Master Career Coach and author of The Five O'Clock book, *For Executives Only*

Over the last two years in my private practice as a Five O'Clock Club coach, I have had the pleasure of working with more than two hundred talented managers and executives who are looking for new jobs. I have noticed an alarming theme in their stories about how their jobs ended—or are about to end. About 60 percent of these individuals have told me that, *had they known more* about their future bosses and the corporate culture, they would have *never* accepted the last job. What was missing in the process of checking out a new position—*before* accepting the offer? There were big gaps in the due diligence.

> **Managers and executives looking for a job are not spending enough time talking with the boss's boss, peers, subordinates and others.**

As I work with clients who are *considering* offers—hoping to move on to the next great position—here are some of the questions that come to mind, to help improve the due diligence:

- How much time did you actually spend with your future boss?
- Did you spend any time with your boss's boss?

- Did you meet with your some or all of your peers?
- Did you interview or meet with your potential subordinates?
- Did you speak with the key players *outside* your area, people who would be critical to your success?
- Did you talk to anyone who *used to* work for the company?
- Did you talk to anyone who had worked for your future boss within the last few years?
- If the position involves sales or marketing, did you talk to any customers?

The answers to these questions from the 60-percent-unhappy crowd were unsettling. The average time spent with the boss was less than three hours. Most had not spent any quality time with the boss's boss, a few had met one or two peers, a few had talked to their subordinates, almost no one had talked to anyone outside their functional area, no one had reached out to former employees of the company. Nobody had bothered to talk to customers.

Based on my work with executives during the last few years, I can identify three primary reasons why jobs deteriorate to the point of resignation or termination:

- **Number one issue: the boss.** The bosses have turned out to have serious shortcomings. Comments about the boss have included: world class micro-manager; abusive; substance problem; only focused on what went wrong; never complimented the staff even when things were going well; and not a coach or mentor to anyone. Or the boss resigned or moved to another area of the company in fewer than 60 days after the new executive came on board. Or the boss accepted substandard performance from other key players. One client reported a CEO who, from a personal relationship standpoint, was a delight to work for—but who had great difficulty terminating poor performers and training those in the pipeline. This meant that one or two key players had to carry the team and the workload became unmanageable.
- The business wasn't as financially healthy as portrayed.
- There was not a team culture at all. There was a lot of rhetoric masking ego-driven politics and a silo culture.

> **When you have 6 to 10 job possibilities in the works, you are more likely to probe and get the information you need to make a decision.**

What can you do to find out what you're getting into? After all, at the Five O'Clock Club we stress the importance of the "consultant mentality"—which means, among other things, finding out as much as you can about the company and the culture. Consultants are expected to probe. They're *paid* to probe. Of course no one is paying you to interview like a consultant. The payoff will come if you really understand what saying "yes" will get you into!

"How much do I have to probe?," you may ask? After all, sometimes we just want to jump at

offers. The key is to not be desperate and to be in control of your own destiny as much as possible. To put yourself in this position, the advice of the Five O'Clock Club is, "Have 6 to 10 things in the works." You have more power to probe appropriately when you can talk about all the *other* things you have going.

But how much do you have to probe? Maybe there's a lesson from another area of life: I want you to think about the last time you hired someone to build a deck or remodel a kitchen. Not only did you take a lot of time to check out the contractor, but you went through the project in agonizing detail to make sure the builder understood exactly what you wanted. You checked several references or even dropped by to see one or two of the kitchens the builder had completed. You acted like a consultant! I would bet serious money that you have been more methodical and cautious about hiring a contractor than you were about analyzing the last few jobs you've said "yes" to! So just remember your remodeled kitchen the next time you're coming down to the wire considering a job offer.

Doing Your Due Diligence

Remember these lines of inquiry and areas for exploration—some or all of them could apply to you:

- Try to get a grasp of your boss's management style. Not that you can change it, but it would be good to size up your chances of living with the quirks.
- Find out as much as you can about the corporate culture and how decisions are made. You have your own style for empowering employees. Will your style fit in the new setting?
- Will you be able to quickly address performance issues, and have final say, within reason, about hiring and firing?
- Will cross-functional teams work successfully?
- How will your future peers view your

arrival—and will they agree with the key goals you've been asked to achieve?

- Who, outside your department, is critical to your success; are they committed to help you succeed?
- How is your function is perceived-and why?
- How do key customers perceive the company?

> **You have probably been more methodical about hiring a kitchen remodeler than checking out job offers!**

This is a lot to find out! But having the consultant mentality, as the Five O'Clock Club recommends, means *being curious*—and trying to locate the minefields. We have found that managers and executives who make hiring decisions are impressed with candidates who have done their homework and ask tough but fair questions. All of the points above, by the way, become appropriate only when genuine interest in your candidacy has been shown by a company. This level of curiosity and inquiry is usually desirable and possible only after the first round of interviews.

To help you prepare for the consultant role—for insights on advanced interviewing techniques—be sure to review key sections of this book.

As you interview up the chain, here are some of the tough-but-fair questions to ask, and avenues of inquiries to take:

- "If I were to interview your staff, what are these folks going to say about what it's like working for you? What will they say drives them crazy?" TIP: Ask this question with a smile.
- "What is your process for keeping the team informed? How often do you communicate to the team as a group? When was the last time you communicated to the group? What is a typical agenda?"
- "How will you measure my success?

What will be the metrics? What will constitute outstanding performance in the first 6 months? The first year?" You need to know if the manager is able to describe success in quantifiable outcomes.

- Who has the boss or manager successfully mentored—and how was it done?
- Here's a really tough one: ask to see the boss's résumé. Seeing the résumé will help you understand his or her track record. If you don't feel comfortable asking for the résumé, you can at least say, "Do you have a bio that I can review?"
- Check references! Obviously, most of us wince at the very thought of *asking* a future boss for references. But asking is not the only way to check references. If you've hired people, you know that you can consult the industry grapevine: you ask around, you call people who are in the know. You can track down prior direct reports and even prior board members if your boss will be the CEO. You can also try to find your predecessor. His or her opinion might have to be weighed very carefully, depending on the circumstances. But the person who left the job may be able to shed light on what awaits you.

The basic idea is to *do research* on your potential new boss or bosses. The Internet is right there at your fingertips, *e.g.,* Google and www. zoominfo.com are good places to start. Search trade and industry publications for articles by or about the people you might be working for; these days the Internet is your primary tool for this.

- Find out *what the turnover is*—by area, especially sales, leadership positions, and IT.
- Check to see if there is a blog on the company. There are often real pearls in blogs.
- The easiest way to do this is type the company name and the word 'blog' in Google or use Google's Blog search.

When you've determined that you really want a position, or to work for a particular company, Five O'Clock Club coaches recommend that you "surround the hiring manager"—which means winning friends among the influencers. Don't forget that there are usually a lot of people who surround the hiring managers, at various levels and in various functions. And these can be sources of information and insight. They can play key advocacy roles, of course, but they can also help to provide information to help make an informed decision.

Don't Forget All the Other People to Interview

Here are some of the people who can help you with thorough due diligence:

1. **Talk to your potential peers**. These are possible questions—depending on your sense of what is appropriate:
   - ✓ "What are the boss's strengths and weaknesses?"
   - ✓ "How do you deal with his or her quirks?"
   - ✓ "How does the team deal with crisis or short-term performance failures?"
   - ✓ "What do you see as the top three priorities for the person who's going to be hired?"
   - ✓ "What do you see as the company's biggest challenges?"

2. **Interview the boss's boss**. After having heard so many horror stories, I would be tempted to say that this is a *must*. Whether it will always be *possible...well*, do your best to try to make it happen. You need to know if everyone is on the same page; so ask the boss's boss:
   - ✓ "What does he or she see as your major challenges and priorities?"
   - ✓ "What are the company's top three priorities?"

   - ✓ "What will constitute outstanding performance in your first six months? First year?" Again, performance should be described in terms of quantifiable outcomes.

3. **Interview your key *internal* customers**. A few examples:
   - ✓ If you're in marketing, you need to interview some of the people on the sales team.
   - ✓ If you're in sales, interview some folks in marketing.
   - ✓ If your role is in HR or Finance, meet with the heads of key departments.

4. **Interview several major customers of the company**. This can be invaluable on two fronts: it gives you some real world business perspectives, and, if you accept the position, you have already begun to build important relationships.

As I look forward to coaching hundreds more executives in the years ahead, I hope I won't see as many who've gotten burned. I don't like to hear: "I wish I hadn't taken that job. I wish I'd known." Even if you can carry out only some of the due diligence I've suggested, the odds of making a poor decision drop considerably. Even if you've uncovered enough to make you nervous—and your back is against the wall ("an offer is an offer!")—you'll know where the skeletons are. You'll be going in fully aware of the biggest challenges.

By the way, interviewing like a consultant—asking all the right people all the right questions—will put you head and shoulders above the competition. Very few candidates are this thorough, and high-performing organizations truly appreciate potential employees who know what it means to do due diligence.

PART FIVE

The Five O'Clock Club Approach to Salary Negotiation

A FOUR-STEP STRATEGY

Four-Step Salary Negotiation Strategy

Dear Five O'Clock Clubber,

Think strategically. From the very first meeting, set the stage for compensation discussions later. If a job pays $20,000 less than you want, that's okay for now. Postpone salary discussions, and remember that you are there _not_ for this specific job, but for a position that has not yet been completely defined—and in which you have some say.

A skilled negotiator has a completely different approach—and much more power—than someone who does not know these techniques. A skilled negotiator knows that he or she is not "chasing jobs, but chasing companies."

This position may not be right, but you want to make a good impression anyway because there may be other places in the organization that are better.

The important salary negotiation issues are strategic, not tactical. Those are the issues we will cover here. Good luck.

Cordially,
Kate

_I've got all the money I'll ever need
if I die by four o'clock._

HENNY YOUNGMAN

_There arises from the hearts of busy [people]
a love of variety, a yearning for relaxation of
thought as well as of body, and a craving for
a generous and spontaneous fraternity._

J. HAMPTON MOORE, HISTORY OF THE FIVE
O'CLOCK CLUB, WRITTEN IN THE 1890s

Now you know you have to impress not only the hiring manager but also other influencers so they will want to have you on board. In addition, you have to think about your likely competitors and how you can convince everyone you meet that you are the best choice. During the interview, a job hunter may also think about salary.

When job hunters ask about salary negotiation, they usually want to know how to answer the questions, What are you making now? and What are you looking for? We'll cover these issues in detail a little later, but it is more important to first look at salary negotiation from a strategic point of view. From the very first meeting, you can set the stage for compensation discussions later.

Most job hunters think about salary—unconsciously and anxiously—during their first meeting. They think, I'm making $50,000 now (or $150,000), but I know this person won't pay more than $35,000 (or $135,000). Most job hunters try to get rid of the anxiety. They don't want to waste their time if this person isn't going to pay them fairly. So when the hiring manager mentions money, the job hunter is relieved to talk about it.

Hiring manager: How much are you making now?

Job hunter: I'm making $50,000.

Hiring manager: That's a little rich for us.

We were thinking about $35,000. Job hunter: I couldn't possibly take $35,000.

End of discussion. Another wasted interview. But there is a better way. Intend to turn every job interview into an appropriate offer. Overcome the company's objections to hiring you, and overcome your own objections to working there. If the salary or something else bothers you about the job, think about how you can change it.

Think more consciously and more strategically. Intend to negotiate. Most job hunters don't negotiate at all.

- They don't negotiate the job. They listen passively to what the job is and try to fit themselves into it—or reject it.
- They certainly don't negotiate the salary. They listen to the offer and then decide whether they want to take it.

> **Don't accept or reject a job until it is offered to you.**

Job hunters decide whether or not they want the job without negotiating to make it more appropriate—and without even getting an offer! Career coaches have a maxim: Don't accept or reject a job until it is offered to you.

We'll see how you can be more proactive rather than passive. The following guidelines will allow you to take more control and more responsibility for what happens to you. Following these steps will not guarantee you the compensation you want, but you will certainly do much better than if you do not follow them. Remember the four steps you will learn here—and pay attention to where you are in those steps.

> **If you can remember these four steps with regard to a particular company, you will do better in your salary negotiation—and in your entire *search* as well.**

Step 1: Negotiate the Job

By now, you have already negotiated the job. You have created a job that suits both you and the hiring manager. Make sure it is at an appropriate level for you. If the job is too low-level, don't ask about the salary—*upgrade the job*. Add responsibilities until the job is worth your while. Make sure the hiring manager agrees that this new job is what he or she wants. Don't negotiate the salary yet.

If your ship doesn't come in, swim out to it.

JONATHAN WINTERS

Step 2: Outshine and Outlast Your Competition

By now, you have already killed off your competition. You have kept in the running by offering to do more than your competitors. You have paid more attention to the progress made in your meetings, and you have moved the process along. You have satisfied every need and responded to every objection. For some jobs, it can take five interviews before the subject of salary is discussed. All the while, your competitors have been dropping out. It is best to postpone the discussion of salary until they are all gone.

Step 3: Get the Offer

Once a manager has decided that you are the right person, you are in a better position to negotiate a package that is appropriate for you. Until you actually get the offer, postpone the discussion of salary.

The moment you feel foolish, you look foolish. Concentrate, block it out, and relax. Of course, that's not always easy.

MICHAEL CAINE, *ACTING IN FILM*

Step 4: Negotiate Your Compensation Package

Most job hunters hear the offer and then either accept or reject it. This is not negotiating. If you have never negotiated a package for yourself, you need to practice. Why not try to get some offers that don't even interest you, just so you can practice negotiating the salary? Here are some hints to get you started:

- Know the company's and the industry's pay scales.
- Know what you want in a negotiation session, and know what you are willing to do without. Negotiate one point at a time. Negotiate base pay first and then the points the employer would easily agree to. Save for last the issues of conflict. Be prepared to back off, or not even bring up, issues that are not important to you.
- You are both on the same side. Each of you should want a deal that works now and works later—not one that will make either of you resentful.
- Care—but not too much. If you desperately want the job—at any cost—you will not do a good job of negotiating. You must convince yourself, at least for the time you are interviewing, that you have alternatives.
- Try to get them to state the first bid. If they say: "How much do you want?" You say: "How much are you offering?" If pressed about your prior salary, either say instead what you are looking for or be sure to include bonus and perks. Some include an expected bonus or increase in salary.
- If the manager makes you an unacceptable offer, *talk about the job.* Look disappointed and say how enthusiastic you are about the position, the company, and the possibility of doing great things for this manager. Say everything is great, and

you can't wait to start—but your only reservation is the compensation. Ask what can be done about this.

Be reasonable. As the saying goes: Bulls win, and bears win, but pigs never win.

It Works at All Levels

Once I did a salary-negotiation seminar for low-level corporate people. One person had been a paper-burster for 25 years: He tore the sheets of paper as they came off the computer. But because he had been at the company for 25 years, his salary was at the top of the range of paper-bursters. He had the same kind of salary problem a lot of us have.

The four steps worked for him, too. He told the hiring managers, "Not only can I burst the paper, but I can fix the machines. This will save you on machine downtime and machine repair costs. And I can train people, which will also save you money."

He was:

1. **Negotiating the job**
   And:

2. **Outshining and outlasting his competition**
   And after he:

3. **Gets the offer**
   He'll have no trouble:

4. **Negotiating the salary.**

Know where you are in the four steps. If you have not yet done steps one, two, and three, try to postpone step four.

CASE STUDY Bessie
It Can Even Work against Me

Once when I was a CFO for a small firm, I wanted to hire an accounting manager who would supervise a staff of four.

I told an excellent search firm exactly what I wanted and the salary range I was looking for: "someone in the $50,000 range."

I received lots of résumés—all of which the

search firm had marked at the top: "Asking for $50,000." I interviewed a lot of people, but Bessie stood out from the crowd. I had Bessie meet with a peer of mine and also with the company president. Everyone loved her.

Finally, I told Bessie that we were pleased to offer her the $50,000 she wanted. Bessie said, "I would love to work here, but I would not be happy with $50,000. I didn't put that there."

I was stunned, but I was also stuck. We had made an investment in Bessie. Everyone had met her and loved her, and she wisely stayed mum about the money until she received the offer. A more anxious job hunter might have said early on, "I see that it says $50,000 at the top of my résumé, but I just want you to know that I am already making more than that." That would have been admirable honesty, but the person would have been out of the running.

Bessie wound up with $55,000, which is what she was worth—and we wound up with an excellent employee. Bessie had followed the four steps exactly.

1. Negotiate the job.
2. Outshine and outlast your competition.
3. Get the offer.
4. Negotiate your package.

CASE STUDY Kate, 1980
All Four Steps in Action

I was earning, let's say, around $60,000 in 1980. A search firm called me about a job that paid $40,000. Remember, search firms are a means for getting *interviews*—not for getting jobs. Don't negotiate salary with the search firm. Simply decide whether you want the *interview*.

I asked the recruiter what the job was. "It's with an advertising agency," she said. "They're looking for a woman to supervise the secretarial staff."

I had an MBA, was making $60,000, and specialized in turning around troubled firms. The

average recruiter cannot negotiate job content but *can* give information. When she described the situation, it seemed to me that the company was in trouble and was using the wrong solutions to solve their problems. I told her I would like to meet with the president. She said, "You *would*?"

I like situations in which I know who my competition is: people who want to supervise administrative assistants for $40,000. I asked the president:

- How is your company organized?
- What are your biggest accounts?
- What is the profit margin on each?
- Do you have a cost-accounting system?
- May I see your computer system?
- Did you know that certain reports would give you better profit control?

His eyes lit up. I was headed in the right direction—and was killing off my competition while I created a job more appropriate for myself. I kept talking to him about his business and what we could do to turn it around. I was trying to move it along, move it along, move it along—and outshine and outlast off my competition.

After the offer, we got into the formal discussion of salary. At this point, I wanted:

- the title "VP of Operations"
- to chair the executive committee so we could turn the company around
- easy access to the CPA firm that would be my partners in this

The actual salary was not a problem. But you can see that it would have been if I had discussed it too early, when the president was thinking about a much lower level job. After we defined a new job and he definitely wanted me, we were in a better position to discuss a salary that was right for the new position.

Salary negotiation involves more than salary. It can involve negotiating for anything you need to do the job well, in addition to your compensation package.

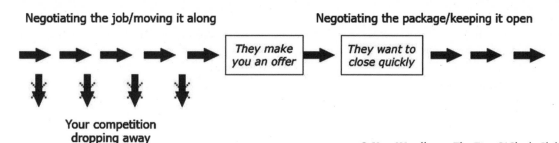

Negotiating the job/moving it along

Negotiating the package/keeping it open

They make you an offer

They want to close quickly

Your competition dropping away

© Kate Wendleton, The Five O'Clock Club®

Do the Deal Yourself

If possible, negotiate directly with the hiring manager yourself. You can see from the last example that I did all of my negotiation with the president of the firm and not through the recruiter. The recruiter was not in a position to do the kind of negotiation that I was able to do on my own. Yet the recruiter still received a fee based on the larger amount that I was offered.

By the time you receive an offer, the hiring manager has already decided that he or she wants you and is the only one who can see your true worth. He or she has an emotional stake in the outcome and is therefore usually an easier person with whom to negotiate. In addition, the negotiation is not simply about compensation but about the work you will do in return for that compensation. All of these issues are difficult to negotiate through a middleman.

If you are scared, you may actually prefer to negotiate your compensation through a search firm or through human resources. But it sometimes happens that the message you were trying to send through the middleman winds up very different from what you intended.

The recruiter feels that he or she has a stake in the outcome because, after all, it could mean the loss of a fee if you mess up. But the recruiter does not understand that you know a lot about negotiating. On the other hand, there are recruiters who do an excellent job in handling the negotiation. Simply make sure you are aware of everything they are doing so you can interject yourself back into the process if need be.

With the help of my God, I shall leap over the wall.
BOOK OF COMMON PRAYER

How to Interject Yourself Back into the Process

This is tricky. Sometimes you find yourself dealing with a middleman when you really want to speak directly to the hiring manager. Simply tell the middleman that you have come up with a few more issues related to the job that you would like to discuss with the hiring manager. Once you have gained access to the manager, discuss those job-related issues, develop rapport, and then bring up the compensation issues you would like to discuss.

Certain issues, such as benefits, are usually discussed with human resources—so don't burden the hiring manager with those. Meet directly with human resources to review the benefits package.

If you are in a complex situation, you may want to work with your career coach on this. It's very helpful to have the point of view of a trusted advisor.

> **Be sure the person with whom you are negotiating is at the right level. If you find yourself constantly bumping up against the salary level of the people with whom you are negotiating, the problem is not your salary negotiation technique. The problem is that you are talking to people who are at the wrong level.**

No modest man ever did make a fortune.

LADY MARY WORTHY MONTAGU

CASE STUDY Georgia
Using All Four Steps

I had been coaching Georgia throughout her job search. She had interviewed to head a small profit center at a hospital. She would be involved with 11 radiologists who gave cancer tests in a mobile unit and 2 administrators. She also had competition.

Georgia had met with six doctors. One particularly unpleasant one asked for a proposal on how she would handle the job. This was Wednesday—the day before Thanksgiving. He wanted it back the Monday after Thanksgiving!

Georgia and I worked at my dining room table over Thanksgiving. "You can be sure no one else is putting in this much effort," I told her.

Georgia hand-delivered not one proposal, but six, and on time. She did not want her fate in the hands of one nasty doctor. Her cover notes were different, but essentially said, "Dr. So-and-So asked for this proposal. I felt duty-bound to give you a copy as well, since the things we discussed are reflected here."

Within an hour of the delivery, Georgia got a call from her future boss (not the nasty doctor). She told me that he was elated: "We want to offer you the job. If you don't take it, we're stuck. We don't want any of the other people who interviewed, and we'll be forced to start our search over." This was music to my ears, because in effect he was telling her that *she no longer had competitors.*

Now we were in a different phase of the search. It's human nature that the person making the offer simply wants to come to closure. However, you need time to discuss things.

I said to Georgia, "You've spent plenty of time defining the job. You need an equal amount of time to define the compensation."

She went back to the doctors and repeated my words verbatim: "We've spent plenty of time defining...."

They immediately backed off. "You're right. We'll spend whatever time it takes to resolve these issues."

They didn't want to lose Georgia. She had paid her dues, and now she was in a strong position to negotiate. They made her a written offer. Then we worked up a counteroffer.

- She wanted a certain base pay.
- She would need entertainment expenses to sell this program.
- The bonus was important to her.

Take calculated risks. That is quite different from being rash.

GEORGE S. PATTON

Calculating the Bonus

We wanted a bonus based on the volume the high-tech $250,000 trucks could handle. We decided that each truck would probably need one day of maintenance a month and that each radiologist would be able to do x number of tests.

With the bonus based on truck volume, we figured what Georgia's maximum salary would be. To allow for year two, we asked the hospital to buy another truck if the volume reached a certain amount.

When Georgia delivered the counteroffer, the doctors couldn't believe it; they now had a truck operating at almost no volume, and Georgia was talking about buying another truck! It showed that she planned on making this a successful venture.

Georgia got the compensation she wanted, and something else....

Georgia Got to Keep Her Job

Because she followed up with every person with whom she met, and because she wrote such a detailed proposal, they were committed to her. Georgia had bought six months of safety in the job: She could do no wrong. The very first day, Georgia realized she'd had a misunderstanding during the interview process and needed to change something about the way the job was done. It was no problem. A job hunter who is thorough in the search process has laid the foundation for keeping her job. Unlike other new hires, the jury is not out on her. Georgia had proved herself. The doctors knew that no one knew more about this business than she did. She knew even more than *they* did!

That's why you want to follow up with *everyone*—including future peers and subordinates—during your search. You may be working with them later. And if any of them has an objection to hiring you, try to settle it during the search, rather than handling it after you are hired. Build strong relationships during the interview step.

Know where you are in the process. Take the steps in sequence. You will not get the offer until after you have negotiated the job and also killed off your competition.

If a job pays $20,000 less than you want, that's fine for now. Postpone the salary discussion. Remember that you are there not for this specific job, but for a position that has not yet been completely defined—and in which you have some say.

A skilled negotiator has a different approach—and much more power—than someone who does not know these techniques. A skilled negotiator chases companies, not jobs. A certain position may not be right, but the job hunter wants to make a good impression anyway because there may be other places in the organization that are right.

Pick battles big enough to matter, small enough to win.

JONATHAN KOZOL

Have you already received an offer? If they are *thinking* about making you an offer, that's not the same as actually *making* you an offer. It's not time to negotiate your compensation until you actually receive an offer.

Where *is* your competition, by the way? You cannot assess your negotiating leverage until you know how the hiring team sees you compared with your competition. You may have already received the offer, but could the company easily consider someone else? If so, you are not in a strong negotiating position. If the hiring team wants *nobody but you*, you are in a stronger negotiating position.

CASE STUDY Stanley
Using All Four Steps

Stanley, an executive who had been in the fashion industry his entire life, heard about a job opening that was being handled by a search firm. He met with the recruiter, who could not put him in for the job because Stanley's salary was a great deal more than what the company was willing to pay.

This is not the search firm's fault. They represent the company. They were hired by the company to fill a certain job at a certain salary level. They cannot go back to the company and say, "I know you wanted me to find someone at $100,000. I have found someone who is at $200,000, but I think you should see him."

After it was clear that the search firm would not put Stanley in for the job, he approached the firm directly.

He first wrote to the chairman (this is a targeted mailing) and followed up with a phone call. The chairman refused to see him. Then he wrote to the president, followed up with a phone call, and got a meeting.

The president said, "Not only is your base too high by $50,000, your total package would be so high that it would be out of the question." Stanley said, "I assure you that salary will not be a problem." (You will see this technique in the next chapter.) "I have always done well every place I have ever worked, and I am sure the same would happen here. May I keep in touch with you?" (He intended to *follow up* as every good Five O'Clock Clubber does.)

Stanley kept in touch by meeting with others in his industry and coming up with ideas for the president. They met a number of times. Stanley started to look better and better compared with the other candidates. This was understandable, since they were all much lower level than he was.

Eventually, Stanley got the job—at the salary that was appropriate for him. After Stanley had met with the president—and the chairman—a number of times, they tried to figure out some way to get Stanley on board.

As it happened, the chairman was planning to retire in two years, and the president was going to become chairman. Stanley was brought in to be the heir apparent to the president.

For more on this topic, read "What To Do When You Know There's a Job Opening" in our book *Shortcut Your Job Search*.

In summary, think about where you are in the four steps. It will help you concentrate on what you should be doing. If you still have competitors, for example, it is too early to negotiate salary. And practice. Salary negotiation takes a lot of skill, but by doing it right you are more likely to wind up getting paid what you are worth.

"They're Only Puttin' in a Nickel, but They Want a Dollar Song."

SONG TITLE

To do this job right is an all-encompassing proposition. I felt I wasn't doing as good a job with the kids as I wanted, and I wasn't doing as well with the business as I wanted. I needed to have a better balance between work and my family, and have some time left over for me.

JEFFREY A. STIEFLER,
RESIGNING AS PRESIDENT OF AMERICAN EXPRESS CO.,
QUOTED BY G. BRUCE KNECHT, *WALL STREET JOURNAL*

The Five O'Clock Club®

Answering the Tactical Questions

We're all in this alone.

LILY TOMLIN

By now, you know where you are in the four steps. In fact, for each company with whom you are meeting, you know exactly where you are in the process. If you are conscious of where you are, you will do much better than if you simply do what seems reasonable without regard to where you are in the process.

In addition, the more experienced you become in negotiating your compensation, the more you can assess what is appropriate for a given situation and deviate from the rules. However, until you are an experienced negotiator, it is best to play by the rules.

> **Are you presently at market rates? Below market? Above market? Knowing where you stand will help you answer the questions: "What are you making now?" and "What are you looking for?"**

What Are You Making Now? What Are You Looking For?

Now we'll look at the questions you've been waiting for. But we'll look at them strategically—so you can *plan* an appropriate answer depending on your situation. First, you need to develop some background information before you can plan your strategy for answering the questions. The strategy

will also give you hints for postponing the discussion of salary until you have an offer.

Background Information: Figure Out What You Really Make

Start with your base salary but also include your bonus and any perks, such as health insurance, a company car, a savings plan, deferred compensation, company lunches, and company contribution to insurance plans. That's what you really make—but that may not be what you will tell the prospective employer.

Background Information: Figure Out What You Are Worth in the Market

Talk to search firms, ask people at association meetings, look at ads in the paper, and—most of all—network. At networking meetings, ask, "What kind of salary could someone like me expect at your company?" A few networking meetings will give you a good idea of the market rates for someone like you.

However, you must remember that you are worth different amounts in different markets. You may be worth a certain amount in one industry, field, or geographic area, and a different amount in other industries, fields, or geographic areas.

What's more, you may be worth more to one company than you would be to another.

Research what you are worth in each of your target markets. And when you are interviewing at a specific company, find out as much as you can about the way they pay.

Background Information: Compare What You Are Making (Total Compensation) with What the Market Is Paying

You need to know if you are now at market rates, below market, or above market. This is the key to how you will answer a hiring manager or search firm that asks you, "What are you making?" or "What are you looking for?"

How to Answer: If You Are within the Market Range

Most companies want to know what you are making. If you are within the market range, they will pay you 10 to 15 percent above what you are currently making. Therefore, if you are making $40,000 and you know the market is paying $43,000 to $45,000, then you could say, "Right now I'm at $40,000, but I'm looking to move a little away from that." The only time you can safely state your current compensation is when you are at market rates.

How to Answer: If You Are Above Market Rates

A coach asked me to have a meeting with his client Sam, who was having problems finding a job because of his high salary. I did an interview role play with Sam. At one point I said, "So, Sam, what are you making now?" Sam replied, "Two hundred thousand dollars plus-plus-plus." I said, "I know you're a very competent person, but we simply cannot afford someone at your high level." Sam's salary was not hurting him, but his way of talking about it was. Even if your salary isn't $200,000-plus-plus-plus, you can easily put off the hiring manager who thinks your salary will be a problem. You have to give her a chance to find out about you, and you have to think about how you can create a job that is appropriate for your salary. You must tell her, "Salary will not be a problem"—*especially if you know it is a problem.*

You have to think to yourself that it won't be a problem when she gets to know you better and understands what you will do for her. Otherwise, you will not get anywhere.

> **Your position has to be that "salary won't be a problem." It is your job to reassure the hiring manager that you are both on the same team and can work this out. When they get to know you better—and what you have to offer—salary *won't* be a problem.**

If you are making more than the market rate, do your best to create a job that warrants the salary you want and defer the discussion of salary until you have the offer. When you're asked, "What are you making now?" use a response from the list below to reassure the hiring manager that you are both on the same team and can work this out. These responses are listed in sequence from easiest to most difficult. Try the easy response first. If the hiring manager persists, you may have to move on to one of the other responses. You are simply trying to postpone the discussion of salary until she knows you better and you have an offer.

The manager asks, "What are you making now?" You respond:

- "I'd prefer to postpone talking about the salary until I'm clearer about the job I'll be doing. When we come to some agreement on the job, I know that salary won't be a problem."
- "Salary won't be a problem. But I'm not exactly sure what the job is, so maybe we can talk more about that. I'm very flexible, and I'm sure that when we come to some agreement on the job, we can work out the salary."
- "Salary won't be a problem. I know that you do not want to bring someone in at a salary that makes you resentful, and I'm sure you do not want me to be resentful

either. I know that we'll come to a happy agreement."

- "I'm making very good money right now, and I deserve it. But I'd hate to tell you what it is because I'm afraid it will put you off. I know that salary will not be a problem. I'm a fair person and I'm sure you are, too. I know we'll come to an agreement."
- "I'm being paid very well, and I'm worth it. But I'm very interested in your company and I'm willing to make an investment in this if you are. As far as I'm concerned, salary won't be a problem."

Marie successfully postponed the discussion of salary for two years. When she came to The Five O'Clock Club, she had been unemployed for a long while. It took six months before she was on the verge of a job offer at a major fashion house, the company of her dreams. On the day she was to receive the offer, the company went *into play*. That is, another company was trying to take this one over, so all hiring was put on hold. Marie was more desperate than ever. Within a month or two, she received an offer from a major entertainment company, went to work there, and continued to keep in touch with the fashion house.

Over the next year and a half, she had meetings with the president and most of the senior executives at the fashion house. Each one asked her about her salary, and to each one she replied with one of the statements previously listed. She eventually got a tremendous offer—after having postponed the discussion of salary for two years. By the way, Marie's boss at the entertainment company told her that he hired her because she was so persistent in her follow-up. He thought she acted a little desperate, which she was after having been unemployed for so long, but he gave her the job because it seemed to mean so much to her. And, of course, she later got the job at the fashion house because she followed up with them for two years! If this desperate job hunter could postpone the discussion of salary, so can you. But you need to practice with someone. It does not come naturally.

How to Answer: If You are Making Below Market Rates

Again, you have a few options. For example, if a manager asks what you are making, you could answer instead with what you are looking for:

Manager: "What are you making right now?"

You: "I understand the market is paying in the $65,000 to $75,000 range."

Manager: "That's outrageous. We can't pay that."

You: "What range are you thinking of for this position?"

Note: You haven't revealed either what you are making or what you want—but you've still tested the hiring manager's expectations. The person who states a number first is at a negotiation disadvantage.

Or you could say, "My current salary is $32,000. I know the marketplace today is closer to $45,000. I have been willing to trade off the salary in order to build my skills [or whatever]. But now I am in a position where I don't need to trade off money, and I'm ready to take a position at market rates."

I was taught that the way of progress is neither swift nor easy.

MARIE CURIE

If You Are Pushed to Name Your Salary

Don't simply state your salary—develop a line of patter to soften it. Simply stating a number can be very confrontational, as with the $200,000-plusplus-plus job hunter. If you have exhausted all the responses, and the hiring manager throws you up against the wall and shouts, "I want to know what you are making!" you can still soften your answer by saying, for example:

- "I'm earning very good money right now—in the $90,000 to $120,000 range, depending on bonus. And I'm certainly worth it. But I'm very interested in your company, and I know we can work something out."

- "My salary is very low—only $20,000, and I know that's dramatically below market rates. But I was willing to do that as an investment in my future. Now, however, I expect to make market rates."

You should name your salary only as a last resort. Managers want to know your last salary as a way of determining your worth to them, but it is certainly not the most reasonable way to decide what you are worth. For example, you would want to be paid more if the job requires 70 hours a week and lots of travel, versus one that requires only 35 hours a week. How do you know how much you want unless you know what the job entails? You are being sensible to talk about the job first and the salary later.

Some managers cannot deal that way, so you have to be prepared in case you are forced to discuss salary prematurely. And even if you do name your salary, there are different ways you can couch it. For example:

- "My current salary is $32,500."
- "I make in the high 60s."
- "My base is around $25,000 and my bonus [commissions] is usually around $15,000, which brings my total package to $40,000."
- "I make in the range of $100,000 to $200,000, depending on my bonus." (This, of course, tells them very little.)

Remember to soften your mention of your salary with a line of patter or your response will sound too confrontational and too much like a demand: "I make... but salary won't be a problem because...."

More Complex Compensation Situations

Most people are in the position of negotiating salary, perhaps a bonus or commission, and perhaps a training program, association membership, or the timing of the first salary review.

Others have a more complex situation. For example, a senior executive may say (at the appropriate time), "You'd like to know how much I'm now making? Let me write it out for you." (Or perhaps he or she would go into the meeting with the information already filled out.) The following table contains the current year's compensation, the next year's compensation (if it is relevant) to account for bonuses, pay increases, and so on. The third column would contain a skeleton of what you are looking for or would be left blank and used as a worksheet. Be sure to write footnotes as commentary on those lines requiring it. For example, you may want to document that if you leave before April you will lose your year-end bonus. Therefore, you could not start work until after April, or the hiring company would have to make up for your loss:

	2014	**2015**	**Looking For**
Base salary	$89,000	$95,000	$95,000
Bonus	26,000	35,000	
Deferred Comp.	20,000	30,000	
Car Allowance	8,000	8,000	
Stock Options	40,000	40,000	
Addtl Medical	4,000	4,000	
TOTAL COMP.	187,000	212,000	250,000

You may leave the third column completely blank and fill it in as you are speaking. For example, you could say, "This is an exciting opportunity you are presenting, and I want to be part of it. To make it easier for you, I could imagine staying at my present base compensation level for next year, $95,000. To make the move worth my while, I could imagine a total package of $250,000, for example, and we could figure out the numbers in between."

In stating your *requirements* in a collaborative way, there is plenty of room for flexibility as well as for their comments and input. You do not run the risk of having the offer fall apart before you have actually gotten one. As you will see later, you want to hear their best offer, and *then* you can accept it or reject it.

Are you not ashamed of heaping up the greatest amount of money and honor and reputation, and caring so little about wisdom and truth and the greatest improvement of the soul, which you never regard or heed at all?

SOCRATES

> **You are trying to postpone the discussion of salary until after you have an offer, but in real life that is not always possible. Therefore, postpone it if you can. And if you can't, be sure you know how you want to answer the questions:**
> - **"What are you making now?"**
> - **"What are you looking for?"**

CASE STUDY Betsy
Simplifying the Request

Betsy went to Europe on a consulting assignment and was later offered a full-time position. She had a list of 20 or so expenses that she thought the company should cover: moving expenses, household purchases, trips home, phone calls home, gym, and so on. When we added up the entire package it exceeded $200,000, but it would have been too clumsy and too unprofessional to itemize all the things on her list.

Instead, we came up with a very neat package that included having the company pay completely for her apartments in both Prague and Dusseldorf, where housing was very expensive.

Those items alone more than made up for the extra expense of phone calls and other miscellany. The resulting package was well in excess of what she had originally wanted and gave her the comfort of knowing that unexpected expenses would not cause her great loss.

No Absolute One Way

Salary negotiation is the most nerve-racking part of the job hunting process. At the beginning of your job hunt you are at loose ends—not knowing where you are going and feeling like you will never get there. But salary negotiation is the part people fear the most. It is a surprise monster at the end of your search.

> **You're in a great negotiating position if you can walk away from the deal. Therefore, make sure you have 6 to 10 things in the works. If this deal is the only thing you have going, see how quickly you can get something else going.**

Search Firms

Search firms must know the *range* of salary you are making or the amount you are looking for. They do not need an exact amount.

Ads

In answering ads, you will rarely give your salary requirements. The trend at the moment is for many ads to read, "Please state salary requirements." Most job hunters do not, and the hiring company does *not* exclude them. Stating your salary or requirements not only puts you at a negotiating disadvantage but also allows you to be eliminated from consideration because you are too high or too low.

On the other hand, some ads state, "You will absolutely not be considered unless you state your salary requirements." Then, you should state them.

Armies of worried men in suits stormed off the Lexington Avenue subway line and marched down the crooked pavements. For rich people, they didn't look very happy.

MICHAEL LEWIS, *LIARS POKER*

What Is Negotiable?

Everything's negotiable. That doesn't mean you'll get it, but it is negotiable. First, think of what is important to you. Make a personal list of what you must have versus what you want. Decide where you can be flexible, but know the issues that are deal breakers for you.

Think of your musts versus your wants. If you get everything you *must* have, then perhaps you won't even mention items on your *want* list. Go in knowing your bottom-line requirements, what you would be willing to trade off, and what benefits/perks could compensate you if you hit a salary snag. Have your own goals in the negotiation clearly in mind.

Salary is not the only form of compensation that might be negotiated. Other items might include:

- the timing of the first review
- closing costs on a new home or a relocation package
- use of a company car
- association or club memberships
- reimbursements for education
- bonus

Which is the most meaningful or valuable to you?

The pay is good and I can walk to work.

JOHN F. KENNEDY, ON BECOMING PRESIDENT, QUOTED BY RALPH G. MARTIN, *A HERO FOR OUR TIME*

Forms of Compensation Basic Compensation

- the timing of the first review
- base salary
- deferred compensation
- incentive compensation (short and long term)
  ✓ performance bonus
  ✓ sales commission
  ✓ sales incentive plans
  ✓ stock options
- sign-on bonus
- matching investment programs
- profit sharing

Vacations

- extra vacation: vacation length is becoming tied to level or length of work experience rather than time spent with one company.

Perquisites (Perks)

- expense accounts
- company car or gas allowance
- memberships
  ✓ country club
  ✓ luncheon club
  ✓ athletic club
  ✓ professional associations
- executive dining room privileges
- extra insurance
- first-class hotels or air travel
- personal use of frequent-flyer awards

- paid travel for spouse
- executive office
- private assistant
- employee discounts
- financial-planning assistance
- C.P.A. and tax assistance
- tuition assistance
- continuing professional education
- conventions
- furlough trips for overseas assignments

Relocation Expenses

- moving expenses
- mortgage-rate differential/housing allowance
- mortgage prepayment penalty
- real estate brokerage fees
- closing costs, bridge loan
- home-buying trips
- lodging while between homes
- company purchase of your home
- mortgage funds/short-term loans
- discounted loans/mortgages
- temporary dual housing
- trips home during dual housing outplacement assistance for spouse

Related to Severance

- severance pay and outplacement
- consulting fees after termination
- insurance benefits after termination

Glossary

Deferred compensation: Ability to make deposits to a deferred salary plan from your pay on a before-tax basis so that amount of income is subject to taxation in the year you make the deposit.

Employment contract: A formal written agreement between yourself and the employer guaranteeing certain benefits, such as severance pay should you lose the job through no fault of your own. At high levels sometimes known as a golden parachute.

Letter of intent: A written confirmation of a job offer summarizing the items agreed upon (salary, benefits, perks, etc.). Not a formal contract but hard for a company to rescind. If you write it, it's called a reverse letter of intent.

Matching investment programs: Savings incentive plan in which company matches employee basic award or personal contribution toward investment.

Performance bonus: An amount of money to be paid to you contingent on your performance on the job. May be a specific amount or a percentage. Can be tied to individual, group, or corporate performance.

Perks or perquisites: Extra benefits that come with the position, such as executive dining room privileges or company car. May be negotiable or standard company policy.

Profit sharing: Cash award based on corporate earnings.

Sales commissions: Compensation directly related to sales at a predetermined percentage. Sales incentive plans: Additional compensation based on sales volume.

Signing bonus: A one-time amount of money paid as an inducement for you to join the company. Also known as a signing, or up-front, bonus.

Stock options: A grant to purchase stock at a fixed price.

Want a Signing Bonus?

Everyone's getting them, right? But those who do are often giving up something—usually base salary. Most companies give signing bonuses to keep payroll costs down!

Louis Uchitelle reports in *The New York Times*: "The hiring bonus is just the latest tool that companies have turned to in recent years to hold down wages. The others include profit sharing, flexible schedules, tuition subsidies, stock options, health club memberships and 'performance' bonuses in lieu of raises for those already on the payroll. While wages are now rising a bit faster than they have in a decade, hiring bonuses are ballooning and spreading across the work force—absorbing some of the pressure for still-greater income" (Louis Uchitelle, "Signing Bonus Now a Fixture Farther Down the Job Ladder," *New York Times*).

The bottom line for you? You've made a deal when you get a signing bonus to make up for a lost bonus if you leave your present job. Otherwise, try to get money in your base rather than in a signing or other bonus.

The Five O'Clock Club®

How to Gain Negotiating Leverage

No one can possibly achieve any real and lasting success or "get rich" in business by being a conformist.

J. PAUL GETTY, *INTERNATIONAL HERALD TRIBUNE*

Most job hunters say to themselves, "I'm so far along with this one possibility, I'll just ride it out and see what happens. If I don't get an offer from them, then I'll think of what else I should do."

Bad move. Have at least a tentative answer to the question of what you would do if this doesn't work. Having an alternative

- helps you to be more relaxed in your discussions
- increases your chances of having this possibility work out
- puts you in a better position to negotiate this position wisely
- helps you to tolerate the months that may go by before it comes to closure
- gives you something with which to compare this offer so you can make a more objective decision

> **The most important negotiating leverage you have is being in demand elsewhere. Develop other options. Be able to walk away from the deal. You can create this situation without much difficulty.**

As one Five O'Clock Clubber said during her *graduation speech* after accepting a new position, "When you are going after only one job, you think that, if it falls through, you will lose a few weeks in your search. Instead of losing a few weeks, you lose a few months. First, you have to recover from the disappointment. Then you have to gear yourself up and decide where to look next. Then you have to get your entire search going again. Take it from me, it's better to never lose that momentum at all."

CASE STUDY Gregory
Skipping a Step

When I met Gregory, he had three job possibilities in the works and wanted to bring them to closure. After all, he said, he had a family to support.

It seemed to me that Gregory's prospects were not a good match for him. After much discussion, Gregory agreed to contact additional prospective employers: This would not slow down his current negotiations and may even make things move faster.

To develop more appropriate targets, Gregory had to complete the assessment process (The Seven Stories and other exercises in our book *Targeting a Great Career*), which he had skipped. Perhaps Gregory could find work that he would enjoy doing and also meet his family responsibilities.

Gregory received six job offers. The three new companies offered him appropriate positions *before* the first three companies made him any offers at all.

Do not skip the assessment part of your search. The results help you target correctly from the start, give you something against which to compare your offers, and help you to be more objective about which job you should take next.

CASE STUDY Carolina
Self-Discipline to Do the Right Thing

Carolina had only one job prospect, and was anxious about whether she would get an offer. Her most important meeting with the company was scheduled for the following week, and she wanted to land that job. "Believe it or not," I told her, "you will do better in your upcoming round of interviews if we could first develop a strategy for getting more possibilities in the works."

That day, after Carolina prepared for the interview, she went to the library, researched 150 other companies in her target area, wrote a great cover letter, and sent it with a résumé to all of them.

By the time her important meeting came around, Carolina was so relaxed that she had almost forgotten about it. When the small things inevitably went wrong, she could say to herself, "At least I've got 150 letters in the mail working for me."

Three weeks later, Carolina got the offer she wanted. In addition, she received calls because of her mail campaign. She accepted the job with the company with whom she had been meeting, but continued to speak with the other companies just to be sure she had made the right choice. For a few weeks after starting the new job, she still kept in touch with the other companies—until she was completely sure that she had made the correct decision.

CASE STUDY Sergio
Acting Like a Consultant

In his search for only two weeks, Sergio had no trouble getting interviews. However, he was having an important first interview the day after our Five O'Clock Club meeting. He was hyped up, stressed out, and breathlessly told the group, "This job pays a lot of money. I want to go in tomorrow and get them to hire me. I think they want someone who is more technical than I am, so I have to sell myself really hard. I've prepared a handout to give them at the end of the meeting. Take a look at it, and see if she is likely to give me the job."

At first, the group was mildly confused. No one looked at the handout. They knew that was not the problem. Then people in the group commented:

"Do you really want this job, Sergio?"

"What other companies are you talking to? It's so easy for you to get interviews." "You've got to slow down." "If this job pays as much as you say it does, they're not going to make you an offer at the first meeting."

I built on the group's good comments: "Sergio, become this woman's friend. To help her, you need more information. Find out why she wants a person with strong technical experience. Find out more about her vision for the department. Help her decide what is really best for her—even if it seems, from time to time, as though you are putting yourself out of the running. Tell her that you will think about her situation and get back to her later. Then do some research. What you want from this first meeting is another meeting."

Sergio immediately calmed down. The group could hear it in his voice. In his panicky state, Sergio could not have done well in that interview. He was very grateful for the group's guidance.

Sergio met a few times with that company, kept his search going, and received four excellent offers from other companies. The one he had been so eager about faded from his interest.

If You Are Currently Working

Employed people have the same leverage as those who have other possibilities in the works. If a hiring manager says to you, "Why are you leaving?" You can say, "I don't know that I am. I may stay right where I am." You don't know for sure *what* you are going to do. To be in a strong negotiating position—and an appealing candidate—you need options.

Pretending to Have Other Offers

Why not say that you have other possibilities when, in fact, you have nothing else? Pretending you have other offers rarely works. The danger is not that you may be caught in a lie. The danger is that the company may say, "You should take the other offer," and three months later you still have no other alternatives and you have also closed off this possibility. It's so easy to get other job possibilities in the works; focus on doing that.

Human... life is a succession of choices, which every conscious human being has to make every moment. At times these choices are of decisive importance; and the very quality of these choices will often reveal that person's character and decide his fate. But that fate is by no means prescribed: for he may go beyond his inclinations, inherited as well as acquired ones. The decision and the responsibility is his: for he is a free moral agent, responsible for his actions.

JOHN LUKACS, *A HISTORY OF THE COLD WAR*

Communications Skills for Negotiating

> **It's time to negotiate. You have an offer. You and the hiring manager are no longer, figuratively speaking, on opposite sides of the table; you are now side-by-side. In this part of the process, it's up to you to set the tone of the conversation.**

Obstacles and disagreements may arise, but your intentions are in agreement: You want to work together, pending the outcome of the negotiations.

Ideally, you will both use a collaborative, problem-solving approach—perhaps with some compliments thrown in because you value each other. You will each resolve the details calmly, and try to understand the ideas and the situations faced by the other person. The goal of any negotiation is to reach an agreement.

It may take some time to hear the various aspects of the offer, respond to them, and discuss a compromise that will be acceptable to both of you. After all is said and done, you may decide to accept or reject the offer, once you hear all of the details.

However, you bear the larger part of the burden in the compensation discussion. After the hiring manager has spent so much time interviewing prospects and has made a decision about whom to hire, he or she wants to come to closure. It is your job to keep the conversation open until all of the items you want to discuss have been discussed. It is your responsibility to manage the conversation, keep it flowing, and thank the hiring manager for discussing these details when all

he or she wants to do is get someone into the job and get on with it.

There can be no greater reward than goodness to your fellow man.

CHARLES DICKENS, *A CHRISTMAS CAROL*

Most Job Hunters Try to Close Too Soon

If you were a consultant trying to land a contract, you would not expect to land that contract after just one meeting. You would not leave the meeting and say, "I think they liked me," expecting to get the contract based on that alone. You would know that the purpose of that meeting was to get information so you could better understand their issues and needs and who the players are, go back and think things through, and figure out how you could help the company. Then you would figure out what else you would need to know. Perhaps you would have to do some outside research, meet with additional people inside or outside the company, find out what other consulting firms they are considering so you would know how you stack up, or call a friend who could put in a good word for you.

Yet many job hunters come out of their very first meeting hoping they will get the job; they actually expect to get that job based on just that one meeting. There's a lot more work to be done. Be sure to read the chapter "Follow Up after a Job Interview: Consider Your Competition." Otherwise, you may try to close too soon.

Express Enthusiasm

Some job hunters think that showing enthusiasm for the job will negatively affect their negotiating position. Quite the contrary. I have seen many an offer retracted because the job hunter did not seem enthusiastic about the position during the negotiating stage. I cannot imagine a consultant or freelancer feigning lack of interest, thinking it would help to negotiate a higher rate. Instead, be sure to show enthusiasm for the position throughout the negotiation process. You can always turn the offer down later—after you have heard the entire package.

A Few Hints

Here are a few things to remember:

- Aim for a win-win situation.
- Go in knowing what you want and what you would settle for.
- Keep the business discussion going.
- Do not be rigid or demanding.
- When the hiring manager says that he or she is faced with a problem, such as other employees who would make less than you, acknowledge the problem, and try to show why it is not relevant in your case. Perhaps, for example, the job you will be doing is somewhat different from what the others are doing.
- Do not get ruffled, upset, confrontational, or sarcastic.
- Maintain a tone of speech that is businesslike, positive, and calm.

If the hiring manager will not budge on the offer, you may still decide to ask for the offer in writing so you can think about it—and to make sure you have at least one offer in your pocket. You would also still say that you want to work there. You are "Playing the End Game" (see that chapter in this book).

Money is a good servant, but a bad master.

BACON

Preparing Your Response to the Offer

To keep things simple, let's assume you are negotiating salary alone, although your compensation discussion may have many more elements. Some experts say that you should listen to the offer and say that you'll get back to the manager in a few days. In real life, that often does not work.

For example, if you are currently making $80,000 and you are offered $40,000, you can't say, "Thank you for the offer. I'll think it over and get back to you in a few days." Whatever you say in a few days will seem idiotic. With an offer so out of line, it seems that you could have had some response, such as: "I just want to be sure we're talking about the same job. As I understand it, you would like me to [describe the job]." This lets the manager know that you are disappointed with the offer.

Low Offers

One time I received an extremely low offer. Let's say that I was making $80,000. The manager offered me $40,000—obviously trying to see what he could get away with.

I said:"I was thinking more like $160,000."
He said: "$160,000!"
I said: "I was just kidding. I thought you were too."

And then he became more realistic. You should probably not try this, but I don't like to get too serious when I know someone is playing with me.

I actually wound up with a very good offer and went to work for that company. The position fit perfectly with my Forty-Year Vision. I stayed there 3 years while I continued to build The Five O'Clock Club.

If the offer is $60,000 and you want $80,000, perhaps you could express a little disappointment, such as: "Well, I'm thrilled to receive an offer. I really want to work here and I especially want to work for you. That salary is a bit low compared to what I had been thinking. Let's keep talking about it."

If you have the manager put the offer in writing, then you can hustle around to the other companies with whom you have been meeting, and see how much better you can do (see the chapter, *Playing the End Game*). At the very least, it will give you time to think. Then you could say to them, for example, "I've been giving it a lot of thought" (or "My wife and I have been talking about this" or "I've talked this over with my accountant and we can't figure out how I could manage on the amount you've offered me. I was wondering how far you could move away from this amount. What are the possibilities of [name something for the manager to consider]?").

A man is great not because he hasn't failed; a man is great because failure hasn't stopped him.

Confucius

High Offers

Let's say, for example, that you would like an offer of $90,000, and you think that is an appropriate amount.

What if you are offered $120,000? (Remember, you don't want to be greedy. Can you live up to that amount?) If you decide it is a fair figure, then you can say, "I'm very pleased with your offer, and I'm not one to quibble, so let's call it a deal."

If you are offered $110,000, $100,000 or even $90,000, your response may well be exactly the same.

Once, when I had decided to take a straight career-coaching position—after having worked for many years as a CFO—I went through the entire negotiation process but postponed discussing salary for four months while I met a dozen or so people. I went in for the offer meeting, and the manager asked me what I had been making

before. She was astonished to find out that we had not already discussed salary. After some consultation with her boss, she said that she was happy to offer me what I had been paid previously. It was a salary that was way out of line (too high) for the responsibilities we were talking about. After all, I was not going to have a staff or any of the other responsibilities I had previously had. I wanted this job so I could have virtually no responsibilities and simply concentrate on growing The Five O'Clock Club.

I told her that the amount she offered was very generous but seemed too high for what I expected I would be doing there. I named a number that was fair—but much lower. She said, "Okay. How about if we split the difference?" And I was still paid handsomely.

It doesn't pay to be greedy. If I had come in at a salary level that was too high, I might have lost my job the first time they needed to cut expenses, or my boss might have given me assignments to justify my high salary, such as a lot of overseas travel, coaching foreign executives. I wanted to coach executives only in the city where I lived because I had to run The Five O'Clock Club at night. You are always aiming for a fair compensation.

The Middle Ground

In the middle ground, that is, an offer that is just below or just above your goal, you may want to think it over, develop your lines, and then get back to the manager.

It is usually best to do all compensation negotiations in person so you can get a feel for the manager's response. Work with him or her to come up with something that is acceptable to both of you.

Other Negotiation Communications Hints

Ask open-ended questions such as, "Can you think of anything else we can do to bring our positions closer together?"

Offer ideas or information. One Five O'Clock Clubber was thrilled to get an offer to work for a certain major company, but their hands were tied. She wanted $90,000. They wanted to give it to her, but could only manage $80,000. Then she realized that two association memberships would have cost her $500 each. Would they pay for them? And what if she went to two conferences a year? Those conferences usually cost around $3,000 each, including room and transportation and conference fees.

The company was very happy with this suggestion. It was much easier for them to give her the conferences and memberships than it would have been to give her extra pay. (Managers have to be conscious of keeping the salaries equitable among employees but may have more flexibility in other budget categories.)

Build on what you have already agreed upon. "Your suggestion that you pay for my trips back home once a month helps a lot. I was wondering if you would also pay if my husband were to visit me some of those times instead of my going home."

When you are negotiating, use a collaborative tone. You are both on the same side of the table now.

The more a man lays stress on possessions, and the less sensitivity he has for what is essential, the less satisfying is his life.

CARL JUNG

Negotiating Items That Are Nonnegotiable

Peter received a written offer from a major corporation. He liked it, all except the job title: He'd been offered the title of vice president, but he wanted senior vice president. The company policy was that no one could be hired from outside with a title higher than vice president.

I said to Peter, "Are you willing to walk away from the job if you don't get the title you want?" I needed to know that so I could help him plan his strategy. Peter said he would walk away from it. Then I needed to know why. Peter said he had had the title of vice president 15 years ago, and it was too much of a blow to his ego to go back to that title. Furthermore, he felt he would not be able to do a good job if he had the lower level title, because everyone would know his title and therefore would not respond to his requests. He felt he would fail in the job if he had the title of vice president.

The rule here may surprise you. If you are at an impasse because the hiring manager wants to give you one thing and you want another, you have only one recourse: *Talk about the job!* If Peter had directly addressed the title issue, they probably would not have come to an agreement. He would have quoted company policy. In fact when job hunters are negotiating, hiring managers sometimes get the impression that the job hunter does not care about the job, but only about the salary and the benefits. Therefore, be different. Talk about the job to reassure him that that is what is most important to you. A shortened, paraphrased version of the letter Peter sent to the hiring manager appears below. Please note the italicized part, which is an important strategy for you to use.

Dear Mr. Williams:

I was thrilled to receive your offer to head up the Rickety Division and am eager to work with you to move it in a new direction. I know we will hit all of the targets you and I spoke about.

I was pleased with the compensation package you offered, and am also glad about the car situation. However, *I find it difficult to accept the offer with the title of vice president*. I had that title 15 years ago, so I feel I'd be going backward in my career. But I am also concerned that the lower title will affect my credibility and effectiveness.

I am sure we can come to some agreement. I am very eager to dig in and am looking forward to hearing from you.

Peter did not reject the offer; he said he really wanted to work there but would find it difficult to accept. It took three weeks for the company to get back to him and give Peter the title he wanted. But that was not necessarily the only result that would have been positive. For example, the company could have said, "Come in and get started, Peter. We can give you the title after three months." Or it could have said, "Peter, I'm sorry, our hands are tied on this one. But I assure you that you will not experience the problems you are dreading. Our employees will know you are division head, and that will matter to them more than the vice president title. Beth Segal came in as vice president only two years ago, and look at her now."

Peter kept the process open until he heard their best offer. That allowed him to either accept that offer if they gave him the higher title or to change his mind and take the job with the lower title and the reassurances from the company that it would be okay.

> **If you are at an impasse because the hiring manager wants to give you one thing and you want another, you have only one recourse: *Talk about the job!***

That's what you want to do also. Hear the entire offer before you decide. *Do not accept or reject any job until it is offered to you.* Before their first interview with a company, some job hunters say, "I really want this job" or "I don't want this job." They don't even know what the job is, and they have already made up their minds. This is the wrong attitude. Go into each interview intending to make it into the best job for you and for the company. This means you will probably have to negotiate—both the job and the compensation.

How to Talk about the Items You Want

Here's the rule to follow when you want to ask for something.

- Talk about the job (if you haven't been doing so already).
- Describe the situation as you see it.
- Venture a solution.

You can imagine what it feels like when you are making an offer to someone who talks incessantly about all the things he or she wants. In the back of your mind, you say to yourself, "I don't believe this person cares about the job at all. All they care about is the benefits." Sometimes job hunters even find that the offer is retracted for this reason. So make sure you mention how excited you are about the job.

> **Talk first about the job. Then explain why you want something.**

Let's say that you want a company car. Don't say, "I want a car." Instead, say, for example, "I appreciate your offer, and cannot wait to get started. I know we will really turn that place around. I am looking forward to starting on the 23rd and am pleased with the package you have offered. However, I was wondering what we might do about a car. I was thinking that I would have to do a lot of traveling between these three cities, and wonder what we might do about that. I have no car at present, and I think that renting a car might be a big expense. Is there any possibility that we could lease a car? It would be much cheaper."

Compensation negotiation is a problem-solving session. Don't be rigid. Hear them out and see what they come up with, but also come up with suggestions yourself.

You must establish your dreams and quietly move in the direction of attaining them.

Dr. Hugh Gloster, past president, Morehouse College

How to Negotiate Severance

After you have negotiated everything else, you may bring up the issue of severance. Here is one scenario.

You have settled on everything, including the start date. The deal is in the bag—but perhaps not in writing.

Set the stage by telling them how happy you are to be joining their firm. Then further set the stage by expressing your concern that you may be at risk through no fault of your own. For example:

You: "I am thrilled to be joining your firm. I know this is a good match, and I believe in what you are trying to accomplish."

Hiring manager: "We're glad you will be joining us."

You: "My only hesitation is that I am leaving a firm where I felt very secure. I'm afraid that there is the chance that your company may be taken over, or that you may wind up leaving the firm, and I wonder what would happen to me. I was wondering if there was any way you could give me some comfort about that."

Hiring manager: "Well, that's always the chance you take in today's market."

You: "Yes, you're right. But I was wondering if I could receive, for example, six months' notice if my job [or assignment] were to go away for any reason."

Notice that you are asking for payment if you are dismissed for *any* reason, but when you set the stage, you named situations that have nothing to do with you. This way, you will not appear worried about whether you can do a good job.

Asking for six months' notice is the same as asking for six months' severance. When your offer letter gets written up, it will usually be written up as severance. That will give you the cushion you could need for your next search.

These days, 6 months is common. One executive had to move across the country to take a job. He got 3 years' severance during the first 2 years, and then 2 years' severance if something happened during years 2 to 4, and 18 months'

severance after that. That severance was unusual but would alleviate the trauma of losing his job shortly after a major move.

Overcome Their Objections—and Also Your Own

Throughout this chapter, we have focused on the company, what their objections might be, and how you can overcome those objections. You also need to be aware of your own objections and handle those during the negotiations. Many job hunters think that the negotiation is strictly about salary, but it is also about whatever else worries you and whatever else you may need to do well in your job. You may want to discuss some of those things before you come on board, and other things after you are in the saddle.

What if, for example, the company expects you to travel 60 percent of the time? You could negotiate for 40 percent travel. People have negotiated to work out of their homes two days a week, have a budget for a special project, and so on. Think these things over, and be sure they are included.

Things which matter most must never be at the mercy of things which matter least.

GOETHE

Win-Win

You want a win-win situation—one with which you can both live. After you have received a job offer, the situation is no longer adversarial. You and the company are both on the same side of the table, trying to make this deal work.

Actually, it is up to you to control this part of the process. You have the most at stake. The fact is, once a hiring manager has made an offer, he or she usually wants to close quickly. His or her job is done. Now your job begins.

Therefore, you must make sure you bring up

everything you want in a way that is collaborative. Set a tone that reassures the hiring manager that you are thrilled to have the job, cannot wait to get started, but have just a few details to work out. You can say, for example, "I really appreciate your spending this time. Some of these things may not mean much to you, but they mean a lot to me."

Look at the Entire Package

Look at the entire compensation package. Do your homework so that you know the typical compensation for a similar position in the industry, and make allowances—especially in the area of benefits—as you move from one industry to another. The benefits may differ, but they should be on a par. Find out which items are automatic benefits and which are negotiable; every company's plan is different.

Be reasonable. In the past, it has almost been a given that job seekers would move only for a salary increase of 20 percent or more. In these economic times, lateral moves are much more common. Know your market worth.

> **Do not be swayed by the possibility of making $2,000 or $10,000 more. Select the job or assignment that positions you best for the long term. That is the most important criterion.**

Job Seekers Are Too Eager to Take Pay Cuts

An estimated 40 percent of all job seekers may start new jobs for less money than they should be getting because they do not know how to handle salary negotiations.

When people call to attend The Five O'Clock Club, we need to know their salary range and field so we can assign them to the right coach. No matter what their salary is, they often say, "Right now I'm making x dollars, but I'm willing to take a pay cut." I usually say back to them, "Isn't it a little early to negotiate?" They haven't even started their searches, and they are willing to settle for less.

Many job hunters think that a willingness to take a pay cut will make them more marketable, but this may not be true. For one thing, there are plenty of job hunters at that lower salary, and so there will be plenty of competition at that level, too. What's more, employers may be reluctant to hire someone they think may leave when a more appropriate offer comes along.

Instead, learn to play the game, and find out what you are worth on the market. Use that as your gauge. If you were overpaid before, then you may have to take a pay cut. But if you were underpaid, you are likely to get what you are worth.

Are You Negotiating to Be a Permanent Employee? Or a Temporary Consultant?

The Answer May Surprise You

Jim landed a great job with a large financial services company. They were starting a new technology effort and wanted him to be a key player. The base pay of $100,000 a year was more than he had made before, and he would learn things that fit in ideally with his long-range career goals as developed in his Forty-Year Vision. It would mean a major company-paid relocation for him and his family. But the prospects were enticing, so he accepted it. Two months after he had joined the company and his family had relocated, the project was canceled. He was out of a job, far from home—with only two weeks' severance.

Marcia landed a four-year consulting assignment working for a major management consulting firm at the rate of $70,000 a year. She would be paid through an intermediary (a temporary services firm) from which she would also get benefits such as health insurance and paid time off. In addition, if the project ended early, she would get four months' pay.

Given these two examples, which seems more secure: to land a full-time *permanent* position on payroll with only a few weeks' severance if you should lose your job or to take on a *temporary* assignment with a four-month guarantee? Which company has made a greater commitment to its workers? Which workers are more at risk; which have more security? Let's take a look at some other cases to learn more.

CASE STUDY Ellen
A New Way of Thinking about Herself

After an active search and more than 15 meetings with one prospective employer, Ellen received an offer from them for a high-level position in the banking industry. She had developed excellent relationships with everyone she met, and her follow-up notes were right on target. She even talked with the vice chairman of this large company.

The first compensation package offered her was mediocre, so she put a lot of thought into planning the conversation she would have to get the package increased. When she presented her ideas, the hiring manager actually told her that he would have been disappointed if she had not come back asking for more. They agreed to her request for an increase in the base, the bonus, and various perks. But they balked at her request for a fair severance package. As a new employee, she would get a mere two weeks' severance, despite coming in at a package of almost $200,000.

She discussed with them how banking was slated to continue going through downsizings. What would happen to her if the company or her division were acquired (not an unlikely scenario)? What kind of reassurance could they give her about that? None, they told her.

Ellen would have no cushion or support from the company if she lost her job. The annual salary and bonus they offered sounded great but would be almost irrelevant if she did not get to stay there awhile. For how long would she be at a salary of $200,000?

For their part, the company was taking virtually no risk at all. If she lost her job, they would be out $5,000 (two weeks' severance on her base pay). She had interviewed with a lot of people there, which represented a certain investment on the bank's part. In the old days, when a company made that kind of investment, it usually indicated that they intended to keep you. Once you had found a job, you had found a home. But the old rules are gone. If a company does not grant you a reasonable severance package, they are taking hardly any risk in having you come on board. It's almost as if they are saying, "What the heck! We did our best in selecting you. If it works, that's great. If it doesn't, it won't hurt us."

Even if you are placed on payroll, a lack of severance represents a lack of commitment on their part. Payroll is merely the way they are choosing to pay you and has no relevance to how long they will keep you. If Ellen didn't work out or if the company's circumstances changed, it would be easy to let her go.

Ellen was aware of this large imbalance and was discouraged. She had planned to cut off her discussions with other companies (which were in the early stages anyway) to commit herself to this one. She had been thinking like a true-blue, loyal employee—putting all of her eggs in one basket. As her career coach, I discussed this with her. She felt better when she realized why there was no reason to do that. Her new employer was making a very small commitment to her. Why should she make a big commitment to them?

She decided to continue talking to the other companies and hoped they would "hurry up with their decisions." "What's the hurry?" I asked her. "If you accept this job, you can't afford to view it as permanent. Rather, tell yourself and others that you've landed a very nice assignment, and that you don't know exactly how long it will last. It does fit in with your Forty-Year Vision, and it actually makes you more marketable. When

these other firms ask what you are doing these days, you can tell them about this wonderful 'assignment,' which may or may not go on for a long while." This thinking made her feel more in control.

I continued: "Perhaps you will start working with this bank, and four months later something will jell with one of the other companies. Then you can decide whether to stay or leave. You do not have a job in the old-fashioned sense. The company that hired you is acting more as if this is a short-term assignment than a permanent job, and that's how you must also see it. You're simply playing by the rules that they have set up."

Ellen decided to speak with even more companies before she started the job. She reasoned that soon she would be working long hours, and it would be easier to keep up contacts she had established than to start from scratch to make new contacts later. Ellen now sees herself as a consultant who happens to be on payroll.

It is indispensable to have a habit of observation and reflection.

Abraham Lincoln

How's the New Person Working Out?

When you are new in a job, the jury is still out on you. "How's Ellen doing?" someone may ask. "We'll have to see," another person may reply. "It's too soon to tell." When a company makes so little investment in whether or not you stay, they are less likely to keep you if something goes awry. The company should be allowed to get rid of you when they want to, but they should have to pay for this privilege. If they have to part with a substantial amount, they will think twice about letting you go.

If you have no severance, you have no breathing room—no time to feel safe and get your bearings. If Ellen had gotten a six-month severance agreement, she would have had the comfort of a six-month window to settle in and devote herself to the job and the comfort of feeling that the company was truly committed to her. The company, in turn, would have been motivated to try harder to make things work out.

In fact, this is becoming more the norm. In the last few years, many companies have realized that the traditional policy of giving two weeks' severance for one year of work is completely out of date for mid-level people.

Today, everyone knows that employees are unlikely to last 10 or 20 years and accumulate better severance arrangements, as they would have in the past. Therefore, companies are tending to grant severance packages based on the level of the person they are hiring. At present, a 6-month severance arrangement is becoming more common for those earning over, say, $80,000 a year. After all, a person earning a large amount is likely to have a longer search than someone earning a small amount.

CASE STUDY Stephen
Could He Get a Real Commitment?

Stephen was making a huge career change—from telecommunications development to the energy industry. He and his family were also making a major geographical change: from New Jersey to the Midwest. The company offered him $90,000 base plus bonus. It was a great company, and he got along well with everyone. The move fit in perfectly with his Forty-Year Vision because he had wanted to work in the energy industry on development projects. This was a dream come true. Or was it a nightmare waiting to happen?

Before the negotiations were over, Stephen asked for severance the way we suggest doing it at The Five O'Clock Club. The company asked, "What kind of severance would it take to make you comfortable so you could concentrate on your job and not worry about having moved your family here?" He answered with a smile: "The longer the severance, the better I'll feel."

The company offered Stephen an astounding two years' severance if he lost his job for any reason during the first two years, one year's sever-

ance if he lost his job during the following two years, and the normal company policy after that.

Now Stephen can concentrate on his job. The company is taking some risk on his move and making a commitment that is at least equal to his own.

Protect Yourself by Hedging Your Bets

Stacy moved from her native Philadelphia to Boston to take a job as a senior litigator with a not-for-profit. Three months later, the organization faced serious budgetary problems that were unknown to the board at the time she was hired. They had to cut back, so Stacy's job was eliminated. Here she was in a new city, with no job and only four weeks' severance.

But Stacy had planned ahead and protected herself. Though the company had paid for the move, they had not agreed to a severance package that was adequate. So she sublet her apartment in Philadelphia and rented one in Boston, rather than purchasing another residence. The company was making little commitment, so why should she take unnecessary risks?

Stacy devoted herself to the job. But she had been warned by plenty of fellow Five O'Clock Clubbers to keep up her contacts while in the new job. She had wisely heeded their advice. Thus when her position was eliminated, she was shaken but not totally unprepared. At the time of termination, she even negotiated an additional month's severance—arguing that the company had upset her life. She could not move back to her own home for the next few months because she could not kick out her tenant. Her search was back to full steam in no time at all, and she was able to move back to her old apartment within a matter of months when the sublet lease was up.

Stanley received an offer to work for a company in Pittsburgh. The pay was less than he had made in Chicago, but the cost of living was lower. He had a wife and three kids. Though the company would pay to relocate the whole family, they refused to offer him more than two weeks' severance. Stanley accepted the position anyway because he needed to work. He told the company how excited his family was about moving to Pittsburgh. However, he said that they needed to stay in Chicago until the end of the school year. Then Stanley continued to interview with other companies he had met during his search. He has seven months (until the end of the school year) to find a job that would be better for himself and his family, or to decide that it would be worth it to take the Pittsburgh job, despite the risk. In either case, he has bought himself time—time that the company would not give him.

A tough lesson in life that one has to learn is that not everybody wishes you well.

DAN RATHER

We Are All Consultants and Temporaries —No Matter How We Are Paid

Jim, Ellen, Stacy, Stanley—each has what amounts to a temporary job. So do you and I. We can consider that we are all on consulting assignments. It's just a question of terminology. And in today's market, this is a healthier attitude to have. It doesn't matter whether we are on payroll or are paid as consultants, through the company, or through an intermediary firm. In effect, we are all temporaries when we do not have a reasonable severance agreement that forces a company to pause before getting rid of us.

Hiring companies may decide the rules of the game, but workers still have the ability to respond appropriately. We can take better care of ourselves by planning our career paths and by treating companies the same way they treat us: We'll stay there as long as it suits our plans, and move on when it makes sense.

At The Five O'Clock Club, job hunters report to the group when they have landed a full-time job or consulting assignment. They give advice to those who are still looking to make a move. Sometimes those *graduates* who made the mistake

of not keeping their options open end their talks by saying: "I will never again be caught off-guard. I resolve to keep up my contacts by having a networking meeting every week or two so I know what's happening in the outside world." They are right to do this: It is a fact that those who have a base of contacts in their targeted fields have a much shorter job search than those who have to start from scratch.

Be like these Five O'Clock Clubbers who learned their lesson. Hedge your bets. Maintain your contacts with other companies. Stay active in your industry or professional associations. Read the trade journals. Continue to improve your skills. Develop a new attitude to be in sync with the realities of the world of work in the 21st century.

The Length of Unemployment Has No Effect on a Person's Future Pay

The Five O'Clock Club is a research-based organization. Therefore, we study such things as the length of people's unemployment in relation to the pay at which they are hired. Most of those Five O'Clock Clubbers who had been unemployed a year and a half to two years were able to get jobs at their old pay or more.

Most of these participants had had trouble landing a new job because of the techniques they had been using—not because of a lack of competence or because of their pay rates. When they started using the right search techniques, they quickly got jobs at the level they were worth in the market. For most people, this was at—or greater than—their old salaries.

Many noticed that their searches took a turn for the better after only two or three sessions at The Five O'Clock Club. Here, they were encouraged to:

- Develop a positive attitude and refresh themselves after a period of discouragement.
- Consider this a new search and be will-

ing to use our methodology in their search from this day forward.

- Make sure they were positioned properly for the areas they were targeting.
- Recontact those with whom they had already met *who were in an appropriate target area.*
- **Get 6 to 10 things in the works**. Then the issue became "Who else are you talking to?" rather than "How long have you been looking?" (See the chapter, *Playing the End Game.*)

Most of the searchers found appropriate positions with appropriate salaries within 10 weekly small-group strategy sessions.

History records the successes of men with objectives and a sense of direction. Oblivion is the position of small men overwhelmed by obstacles.

WILLIAM H. DANFORTH

CASE STUDY Jane
Abused in Her Present Position

Jane had earned good money in the financial services industry. She lost her job and took something with a major retailer out of desperation. She earned only one-third of her former salary.

By the time we met her at The Five O'Clock Club, she had been working there for over two years and spending 80 hours a week with no end in sight and no hope.

After only six weeks at The Five O'Clock Club, she landed a terrific position related to the financial services industry at more than she had previously been making. Her present compensation never came up. It was not an issue.

Job-Hunting Hint

It's a good idea to have a calendar that you use only for job hunting. That way, you will clearly see how much effort you have (or have not) put in, as well as the amount of follow-up you plan to do.

Note the following:

- all interviews (networking, job, and search firm)
- mailings
- networking notes written
- follow-up notes written
- follow-up calls made
- the dates when you plan to make future calls

You can also list ads answered.

Negotiating a Consulting or Freelance Assignment

Hey, no matter what—it's better than working at the post office.

JERRY STERNER, *OTHER PEOPLE'S MONEY*

Being a Consultant or Freelancer

All positions are temporary. You may receive a W-2 form at year-end, or you may receive a 1099—but no work you do is permanent. However you are paid, make sure you are paid fairly. And make sure you are gaining experience that will help you get your next assignment—inside or outside your present company. Have a backup plan. What would you do if your current assignment or situation ends?

If you happen to be looking for full-time work on payroll, you still may be offered consulting assignments. So you should learn how to negotiate them.

Today, more and more companies are bringing in workers on a contract, consulting, or freelance basis. Such workers usually get no benefits (health insurance, paid time off, training, memberships, company-paid contribution to Social Security, etc.). Other contract or temp workers are hired through an intermediary company that may or may not put the workers on payroll and pay for their benefits.

Even very senior managers find themselves serving as full-time consultants. Some companies are actually doing this illegally. If you are working full-time for a company that decides your

hours and the content of your work, you are not a consultant but an employee. This means that the company must put you on payroll and pay the extra costs associated with that.

At one very large company where I was consulting, there was a person at a relatively low level who worked on computers, kept the same hours as everyone else on staff, but who was paid a flat $15 an hour as a *consultant*—no benefits, no insurance, no paid time off. Large companies are sometimes even more likely than smaller companies to get away with this because they have so many employees. A manager may hire *consultants* because the company has *a freeze on head-counts*—he or she is not allowed to put more people on payroll because that would count as a *head*. Yet the manager is allowed to hire consultants, temps, and freelancers.

The worker is stuck. The company has all of the power. The worker who wants to work is not going to complain about unfair treatment.

To counteract this trend, workers are sometimes opting to have *a job and a dream*—a job that pays them regular wages, and other work done on the side to build a future that may be more secure than working for one company. Some workers are able to grow what was once a sideline into a stable source of income. That work may include consulting or selling part-time or trying to build a business.

Regardless of how you are paid, develop your skills and your marketability to the point where you are less likely to be taken advantage of.

CYRUS (*trying to be friendly*): *I'll tell you what. You want to work, I'll give you a job. Nothing permanent, mind you, but that upstairs room over there—the one above the office—is a hell of a mess. It looks like they've been throwing junk in there for twenty years, and it's time it got cleaned up.*

RASHID (*Playing it cool*): *What's your offer?*

CYRUS: *Five bucks an hour. That's the going rate, isn't it?... If you can't finish today, you can do the rest tomorrow.*

RASHID (*Getting to his feet*): *Is there a benefits package, or are you hiring me on a freelance basis?*

CYRUS: *Benefits?*

RASHID: *You know, health insurance, dental plan, paid vacation. It's not fun being exploited. Workers have to stand up for their rights.*

CYRUS: *I'm afraid we'll be working on a strictly freelance basis.*

RASHID (*Long pause. Pretending to think it over*): *I'll take it.*

PAUL AUSTER, SMOKE

The Search for Consulting or Freelance Work

The search for consulting or freelance assignments is exactly the same as the search for full-time work *on payroll*. Target the areas in which you are interested—following the system we use at The Five O'Clock Club. At your meeting with your prospective employer—or perhaps even in your cover letter—you can mention that you would be open to either full- or part-time work. Sometimes a consulting assignment turns into an on-payroll assignment. Sometimes the reverse is true.

Those who have successfully made the transition to consulting or freelance work often say they would never go back to working for someone full-time. Some feel and indeed may be much more secure in having a number of sources of income rather than just one.

The downside to consulting is that you must both market and deliver your services. Some consultants get so involved in delivery that they don't allow time to market. They suffer having intense periods of work, with periods of no work in between. Consultants don't get unemployment benefits during those down times. Some consultants may tend to take no time off: If you don't work, you don't get paid.

Therefore, you must set your consulting rates high enough to allow for time off. You also need time for marketing. A rule of thumb is to allow half of your time for marketing and administration, and half for the actual delivery of your services. "Marketing" includes everything you do to make yourself known, such as writing articles and then reprinting them as handouts to build your credibility, delivering speeches, building a database of possible targets and mailing to them regularly, and calling on companies.

Decide if you want to start a consulting business or if you would simply like to take a few consulting assignments while you are searching for full-time employment. This will influence what you decide to do in marketing yourself. At some point—but not now—you may need a brochure, business cards, and even an office. If you are truly trying to build a consulting business, think through how big you would like your practice to be, how many others you would eventually like to work with you, and everything else you need to develop a rudimentary business plan.

In any case, you must be positioned properly (see *Two-Minute Pitch*). Decide what your target market is, what you have that would be of interest to this market, the services you want to offer, and how you can position yourself to seem worthwhile. Whether you are looking for on-payroll or consulting work, you must learn how to differentiate yourself from your likely competitors. Then you must call on prospects.

Follow the stages of the search and pay attention to the stage you are in (Stage 1, 2, or 3). Be sure to have 6 to 10 things in the works at all times. Next, figure out how to price your services.

Here comes the future, rolling towards us like a meteorite, a satellite, a giant iron snowball, a two-ton truck in the wrong lane, careening downhill with broken brakes, and whose fault is it? No time to think about that. Blink and it's here.

<small>MARGARET ATWOOD, *GOOD BONES AND SIMPLE MURDERS*</small>

Pricing Your Services

There are two numbers you need to start with to determine your consulting fee. One is what you are now making—or have been making most recently or what others are making—in the field you are targeting.

We are assuming your consulting will be in the field where you are now considered an expert. If you want to consult in a new field (perhaps as a way to learn that field), instead of your present base plus bonus, use the rate of those at your level in the new field.

The second number to consider is what the market will bear.

The amount of money you receive will always be in direct proportion to the demand for what you do, your ability to do it, and the difficulty of replacing you.

<small>NAPOLEON HILL, PARAPHRASED BY DENNIS KIMBRO, *THINK AND GROW RICH: A BLACK CHOICE*</small>

Calculating Your Cost Rate

Take your present base plus bonus. Let's say it's $50,000 a year. Add a factor for benefits, such as health insurance. Let's say 20 percent (this includes health insurance, company-paid Social Security, and so on, but does not include paid time off).

So that's $50,000 X 1.20 = $60,000

Divide that number by the number of hours the average person is available to work in a year. We'll use 2,000 hours, just to keep the calculation simple. (You may want to use 1,600 hours, which allows for 10 holidays and 4 weeks of vacation and sick time.)

$60,000 / 2,000 = $30 per hour.

Your cost is $30 per hour—which is very different from what you will bill your customer. If you were to be able to bill 2,000 hours a year at $30 per hour, you would stay even with what you are now making. However, not only are you unlikely to bill 2,000 hours a year, you still have to buy your own health insurance, put money aside for your vacations, pay your own Social Security, and arrange for your own training, subscriptions, memberships, and so on.

Calculating Your Low Billing Rate

To account for some of that expense, increase your cost rate by 20 percent—just so you will come out a little higher than your adjusted cost rate. This allows for benefits and also for paid time off. (See chart: Low Billing Rate)

$30 X 1.20 = $36 per hour (Low Billing Rate)

You would try to bill at your low billing rate if you are just starting out or if you are on a long-term consulting assignment with a guaranteed significant number of hours per week.

A rule of thumb for short-term consulting fees is twice your cost.

Calculating Your Average Billing Rate

If you need to have more than one customer, you probably won't be able to bill 2,000 hours a year because you will have to spend time marketing your services. Earlier you saw that a rule of thumb is to spend half your time marketing. So to keep even with what you made before, you would have to bill twice your cost rate.

That's $30 X 2 = $60 per hour. (See chart: Average Billing Rate)

You would try to charge the average billing rate for your salary level if you are in a specialized field and in demand. You would also try this rate if you are a serious independent consultant and want to sell your consulting services long-term.

You will need to make up for the time you spend marketing.

Maury had enormous admiration for Bennett's grandfather, a self-made man who had opened the store by himself in 1934, a man who always believed things would turn out in his favor and who made things turn out in his favor.

ALAN LIGHTMAN, *GOOD BENITO*

A MODEL FOR ESTIMATING YOUR BILLING RATE

Base Salary & Bonus	Adj. Base = Base x 1.20 for benefits	COST (Adj. Base/ 2000)	Low Billing Rate[1] (cost x 1.2)	Aver. Billing Rate[2] (cost x 2)	High Billing Rate[3] (cost x 3)	Aver. per diem rate (aver. billing x 7)	MARKET RATES	My Tentative Rate
$ 20,000	$ 24,000	$ 12/hr	$14.40/hr	$ 24/hr	$ 36/hr	$ 168/day		
$ 30,000	$ 36,000	$ 18/hr	$ 21.60	$ 36	$ 54	$ 252		
$ 40,000	$ 48,000	$ 24/hr	$ 28.80	$ 48	$ 72	$ 336		
$ 50,000	$ 60,000	$ 30/hr	$ 36	$ 60	$ 90	$ 420		
$ 75,000	$ 90,000	$ 45/hr	$ 54	$ 90	$135	$ 630		
$100,000	$120,000	$ 60/hr	$ 72	$120	$180	$ 840		
$125,000	$150,000	$ 75/hr	$ 90	$150	$225	$1,050		
$150,000	$180,000	$ 90/hr	$108	$180	$270	$1,260		
$200,000	$240,000	$120/hr	$144	$240	$360	$1,680		
$250,000	$300,000	$150/hr	$180	$300	$450	$2,100		
$300,000	$360,000	$180/hr	$216	$360	$540	$2,520		
$500,000	$600,000	$300/hr	$360	$600	$900	$4,200		

[1.] Low Billing Rate. Use this rate if you are just starting out, or if you are on a long-term consulting assignment with a guaranteed significant number of hours per week.

[2.] Average Billing Rate. Use this rate if you are in a specialized field and in demand. You may also use this rate if you are a serious independent consultant and want to sell your consulting services long-term. You will need to make up for the time you spend marketing and so on.

[3.] High Billing Rate. If you have or are setting up a consulting firm, the rule of thumb is to bill out at three times labor cost to cover the cost of overhead, which includes support staff who are not billable, rent, and marketing.

Calculating Your High Billing Rate

If you are well-established as a consulting firm with lots of overhead, such as office space and administrative support, two times cost will probably not be enough to cover your overhead. The standard factor for this situation is three times cost. In addition, if you are seriously starting a consulting firm (rather than being an independent consultant representing only yourself), you would most likely charge the three-times rate for every billable member of your staff, or for each person you bring in to work on a project.

Finally, if you are well-known in your field, you may also insist on three times your cost rate—or, lucky you, whatever the market will bear.

$30 X 3 = $90 per hour. (See chart: High Billing Rate)

Charge this rate if you are well-known in your field, or to cover your overhead if you have or are setting up a consulting firm. Overhead includes support staff who are not billable, rent, and marketing.

You work Saturdays? Well, you must make good money. Well, so you hate it, I'm sorry, I can't help that. What are your aspirations, in that case?

CRAIG LUCAS, *PRELUDE TO A KISS*

Your *Market Worth* Is Whatever the Market Will Bear

When I'm hiring someone as a consultant, I ask them their hourly rate, multiply it in my head by 2,000, and decide if the person would be worth that much on-staff. For example, if someone wants to charge me $25 per hour, I estimate whether that person would be worth $50,000 on staff including benefits. That way, I can quickly assess whether the person is worth it to me.

If there are plenty of people who can do the same job for less, I can simply find someone else. If, however, this person is a known expert, my friends tell me that he or she is reliable, or if there is some other reason for me to think that this person is special, I may be willing to pay more than the typical going rate.

When you think about the rates you will charge as a consultant, remember that someone will be deciding whether or not you are worth it. So decide whether you are someone who can be easily replaced or are unique and in demand. *What the market will bear* will be the most important determinant of what you can charge.

What you charge will probably change over time. At first, you simply want to get a few jobs and a few clients. Later, as you become better-known in your field, the amount and the way you charge will change.

You must test the waters. Talk to others in your field and find out what they are charging; network in to see prospective hiring managers and see what they would pay. When all else fails, start negotiating with the hiring manager and observe his or her reaction. Follow exactly the rules in the *Four-Step Salary Negotiation Strategy*.

After you are well established and have a name in the market, there is a lot of flexibility. I have coached clients who have ended up working two days a week for one company and two days a week for another company—getting a flat $100,000 a year from each company! These clients had paid their dues in their respective fields and deserved what they got. They each worked only four days a week, and if they lost an assignment at one company, they still had the other one to keep them going while they looked for a replacement. Not a bad way to earn a living.

In playing baseball, or in life, a person occasionally gets the opportunity to do something great. When that time comes, only two things matter: being prepared to seize the moment and having the courage to take your best swing.

HANK AARON, FORMER BASEBALL PLAYER, COMMENCEMENT ADDRESS TO EMORY UNIVERSITY SCHOOL OF LAW, MAY 1995

Corporate Rates

Although the three-times rate is standard for organizations with overhead, companies use different numbers of hours as the base. That is, instead of using 2,000, they may use 1,600 or even as low as 1,300 to 1,400 hours. This increases the hourly rate. Or they may hike up the direct labor rates by including not only base plus bonus but also all benefits, payroll taxes, estimated raises, car allowances, and so on.

Then they come up with a rate card, which may contain inflated rates. When it's time to negotiate, they may come down quite a bit from their rate card.

For example, one company's *rates to use in pricing projects* are listed below. Use a billing rate of $225/hr. or $1,800/day for:

- Employees with salaries in the $65,000 to $80,000 range
- Outside consultants who cost us more than $500 per day

Use a billing rate of $190/hr. or $1,500/day for:

- Employees with salaries in the $50,000 to $64,000 range
- Anyone not on staff who costs us $300 to $500 per day

Use a billing rate of $150/hr. or $1,200/day for:

- Professional staff with salaries less than $50,000
- Anyone not on staff who costs us $150 to $275 per day

Use a billing rate of $50/hr. or $400/day for:
- Administrative support staff
- All temps assigned to this project

You, too, may want to create a rate card for your consulting firm. But be sure to be realistic about your worth in the market.

Setting Your Rates

When you are starting out, you will probably use just one system for charging your clients, such as an hourly rate.

When you are experienced, you may still wind up charging every client the same rate or each client a different rate. For example, you may have one or two clients who form a stable core for you, and you may have gotten far enough in your career that you are on a monthly retainer with them. You may charge other clients an hourly fee. You may charge one client per project, one a low hourly fee, and another a high hourly fee. You may charge a large corporation a higher rate than a small company, a for-profit organization more than you charge a not-for-profit (although not necessarily).

Your rates may differ by geographic area. You may charge a certain rate in the big urban areas and a lower rate in the countryside, or one rate for one part of the country and another rate for a different part.

If you are offering your services to individuals, you may use a sliding scale depending on the person's ability to pay, the way that many therapists do.

Finally, you may charge different rates for different kinds of work. When I am hiring a public relations person, to name one example, I may hire someone who is already working full-time for someone else and wants to earn extra money on the side. That person may charge me a certain hourly fee for the brainy work, such as developing strategy or writing press releases, and a lower hourly rate for the *mindless* work, such as sending emails.

> **Find out the standard fee arrangements for the industries or fields that you are targeting. The variety is endless.**

Fee Structures

Therapists and attorneys charge per hour. Workshop leaders usually charge per diem. Determine how people in your field charge, and do the same—at least when you are starting out.

The two basic structures are per time (such as per hour or per diem) and per project. There are almost infinite variations on charging structures, from a per-head rate for running a seminar, to a percent of gross billing (as in the old days of advertising). There are certain fields in which a success fee rules (that is, if the project works, you make lots of money; if it doesn't, you don't). And then there are lots of combination fee structures, such as a success fee for completion with a guaranteed nominal base amount. If you are working with a start-up company and already have a full range of consulting assignments, you may be paid in stock. Other common arrangements are retainer, commission, percent of sales, bonus, or a combination. Find out the standard fee structures for the industries or fields you are targeting. The variety is endless.

For now, we will cover the *per time* and *per project* structures. The thought processes behind these form the core of most other billing methods.

When considering the fee structure you want to use for a certain situation, remember that some structures are low risk with a predictable reward. Others are high risk (that is, you may wind up losing money or making no money) but high reward (big bucks if things work out). All fee structures can be analyzed by using this criterion.

We are what we repeatedly do.
Excellence, then, is not an act, but a habit.

Aristotle

Project Pricing versus Time-Based Pricing

The benefit of pricing per project, rather than charging a time-based rate, is that you could make much more money that way. You could also lose money if you price incorrectly or if you do not control your costs while delivering the service.

With time-based pricing, on the other hand, you can be sure of getting paid for every hour you work. As long as you get paid, there is no risk on your part. However, you cannot make a great deal of money.

If you simply want to pick up some consulting work while you search for a full-time job, you may want to stick to time-based pricing so you are not at risk. If you want to have a consulting business, you may want to become very good at project pricing (although actually many consulting businesses charge solely by time-based pricing).

Out-of-Pocket or Pass-Along Expenses

Depending on the kind of work you are doing, certain expenses may be passed along directly to your client. Out-of-pocket expenses include items such as telephone, postage, and overnight mail expenses. Travel could also be considered an out-of-pocket expense—depending on the situation. Even entertainment sometimes falls into this category. If I hire a public relations consultant, I expect that person to keep track of out-of-pocket expenses and bill me monthly.

This is standard operating practice. However, check with others in your field or industry to be sure that this practice applies.

Pass-along expenses could include the cost of hiring an outside photographer, for example. Established consulting firms often *mark up* the cost of these pass-along expenses, say by 15 percent, to make a profit on them. In many cases, this is acceptable.

Pass-along expenses are not to be confused with the cost of outside consultants you may use as if they were part of your staff. These outside consultants would be billed the same as if they were on your staff, but you would have to think through the multiplier to use: perhaps two or three times the rate they charge you. Of course, you have to do what seems reasonable.

"How did I deal with racism?" he asked rhetorically at a speech in San Antonio, Texas." I beat it. I said, 'I am not going to destroy your stereotype. I'm proud to be black. You carry this burden of racism, because I'm not going to.'"

COLIN POWELL, FORMER CHAIRMAN OF THE JOINT CHIEFS OF STAFF, AS QUOTED IN *TIME,* JULY 10, 1995

Time-Based Pricing

If you are in a field that normally charges an hourly rate, as is the case with a therapist or attorney, you need to find out what you are worth in the field and then develop yourself to the point where you have no trouble saying with confidence, "My rate is $50 per hour."

But if you are doing project work for which you want to be paid hourly, that is another matter. As the hiring manager, I will be afraid of how much time you will spend on the project. If you tell me that your rate is $30 per hour, I will still want an estimate of how much a particular job will cost me. I cannot afford to pay you $30 an hour to do graphic design work, for example, if there is no limit. You may decide to fiddle with a design for 40 hours *just to make it perfect* when all I wanted was something that was *good enough.*

You may stay up all night working at home on your slow computer. Why should I pay you $30 an hour for that work, when you could have gotten it done in half that time if you had worked on my faster computer? You may have decided to make four different sketches for me, but if you were working out of my office instead of yours, I might have told you exactly what I wanted and saved all that extra time.

Therefore, if I am paying you per hour for a project, I want to know the limit on this project. Perhaps you will do 15 hours of work at your regular rate and then come back to me to see if everything is on track before you rack up 50 hours for which you expect me to pay.

If you are willing to do the job on-site, there is less risk that you will go off in a direction I don't want. The on-site work is safer for both of us. You will get paid for every hour you work, and I will know what you are doing for the time you are billing me.

If you are working for an hourly rate, you will charge less for per diem work and even less for a monthly rate. Of course, you must spell out the number of hours you will work for a per-diem rate. If you charge $200 per day and don't specify the number of hours in a day, your employer may expect 10- or 12-hour days. If you charge per month, you must specify that it is an 8.0-hour day (or 7.5-hour day), 20-day month (there are 4.3 weeks in an average month; 21.5 work days in an average month—not allowing for holidays or other time off). If you don't specify the number of days you will work per month, your employer will expect you to be there every day for the agreed-upon monthly rate. You will never have a day off.

If you are charging an hourly rate for on-site presentations or for other work for which you have preparation time, make sure your hourly rate includes your preparation time.

If you are required to be on-site, bear in mind that most consultants charge a 4-hour minimum to make the unbillable travel worthwhile. However, if you are doing a lot of work for a certain client, you may come in for an important meeting and charge only for the time the meeting takes, even if it is only two hours. That's called establishing good will.

If you are straight hourly, you do not charge, of course, when you and your prospective client are discussing a possible assignment or when you both are reviewing the work you did.

How Long Will the Assignment Last?

Another consideration is the length of the assignment. If you should normally get $86 per hour but the company wants to pay you per diem, you would not normally charge the company $86 x 8.0 hours = $688. If it's likely to be an 8-hour day, you would then charge them, say, $600 per diem ($86 x 7.0 hours). And if the company wants to pay you monthly, you probably would not charge them $600 x 21.5 = $12,900 (because the average month has 21.5 work days). Instead, you would say that your fee is normally about $15,000 ($688 x 21.5), but you will charge them only $10,000 per month for a 20-day month with, for example, a 6-month minimum with 60 days' (or 30 days) notice to terminate. That's still $60,000 for 6 months, with time to search if the contract is not extended.

Your rates are reduced for longer amounts of time because you will have to do less marketing than if you sold your services by the hour.

Man is born with his hands clenched, but his hands are open in death, because on entering the world he desires to grasp everything, but on leaving, he takes nothing away.

THE TALMUD

Billable versus Unbillable Time

Sometimes every hour you spend is billable, and sometimes it isn't. This can be tricky, and you should think about it with regard to the situation you are in. For many of your assignments, you may bill a straight hourly, per diem, or other kind of rate. But if you wind up at a company on a regular basis, you may attend weekly staff meetings, travel on company business, and so on. May you charge for this time at your normal rate? It depends. If you are at a large company, and being paid on a monthly basis, there is no discussion. They are paying you monthly, so that includes everything.

If, however, you are being paid hourly, you may or may not be paid for extraordinary travel time. Large companies may sometimes pay you for travel at half your normal rate (depending on the circumstances), while smaller companies may pay you nothing for travel. This is something you may want to negotiate if you think it could get out of hand.

If you are attending staff or other meetings—where you aren't really *working*—may you charge

for that time? Again, it depends. If you are on an hourly basis, you may be able to charge half-time for regular (such as weekly) staff meetings. If the staff meeting is an unusual event, you may be able to charge at your regular rate. If you are attending a training seminar just to learn a new skill, for example, it is unlikely that you will be able to charge anything. However, if you are delivering a seminar, you would, of course, charge at your full billing rate. After all, you are working to your full capacity.

To keep a good relationship, make sure you do not nickel-and-dime your client to death. Throw in extra time for free sometimes (and let them know that). Perhaps call in with an idea on days when you are not there—gratis. Give a little to an important client just to keep a good relationship going.

What Will Your Market Bear?

After all of that, consider what is reasonable and customary in the market and for the company to which you are selling yourself. Would they pay someone like you $86 an hour? Or is that unlikely? If the market tends to pay only $50 an hour, that is what you are likely to get. If you get that amount, just be sure you understand that you are not making what you used to make—unless you manage to work 2,000 hours a year (or 1,600 hours, which allows for 4 weeks' vacation and 10 paid holidays).

Project-Based Pricing

Before you can possibly know what you want to charge a customer, you must figure out how much it will cost you to deliver the project. Go through the following steps:

Step 1.

List in detail the services you will provide and who will provide them.

Step 2.

Price out these services using the billing rate for each person. This means you must be able to estimate accurately how much time you and/or every other person will spend on the project. Then you will apply your billing rate (perhaps two times cost).

Step 3.

Get it in writing.

Step 4.

Control your costs.

Now let's examine each step in detail.

Step 1: List in detail the service you will provide.

List everything you will provide—both labor and out-of-pocket expenses. Be sure to include all planning and project-management time, as well as all clerical and other support time. It is not enough to include just the time you actually spend with your client. For out-of-pocket expenses, be sure to include items such as travel and printing costs.

Then estimate how much of each service will be provided. For example, how many hours do you think this project will take overall, for each component of it, and for each person working on it? How much travel will be involved (apart from routine travel to and from their office)?

Step 2: Figure out the price of each of those services.

Note the actual person or the level of the person who will be delivering each piece. Then use the billing rate for each person to determine the price of each service.

After you have priced each piece of the project, add up all the prices. This will tell you the total amount of revenue you will need on this project. It will also give you a feel for what goes into your project.

You have no idea what a poor opinion I have of myself—and how little I deserve it.

W. S. Gilbert

Step 3: Get it in writing.

Make sure the client understands what is included in the project and what is not. In Step 1, you detailed everything that would be included in the project. Make sure the client understands this. Put it in writing. As you get into the project, both you and the client will probably think of lots more you could do. Or the client will change the specifications. All of that is fine as long as the client understands what is included in the project fee and what they must pay extra for (perhaps at your hourly billing rate) because it is outside the scope of what you originally agreed upon.

Step 4: Control your costs.

You must keep track of the number of hours you and everyone working for you spend on the project—or you most likely will lose money, perhaps a lot of money.

Many consultants are so happy to get the projects that they over-deliver to the extent that they lose money. You must track the number of hours you spend on the project. In Step 1, you detailed all of the services you would deliver. Now you must see how you did against those projections of what you thought the project would include.

I have seen everyone from fine artists to senior executives bid on jobs expecting to spend a certain amount of time on them, and wind up spending twice or three times what they had originally projected. Then they are disappointed that they cannot make money.

Starting out

When you are starting out, it may be that you have to *give away the store* to get experience.

You have to figure out what the market will

bear, perhaps take what you can get, build up your credentials, and market yourself to other companies. You may even decide to do a small assignment for free—perhaps for a not-for-profit or for a friend—just so you can say you are doing that kind of work.

On the other hand, you may think you are in a weak negotiating position when in fact you are not. I have worked with many an executive whose initial thought was to undercharge dramatically for his or her services.

Follow the rules for basic salary negotiation. If there are lots of people who can do what you do, and if you have no way to separate yourself from your competition, then you are in a weaker negotiating position. On the other hand, if you are offering a service that is somewhat unique and you cannot be easily replaced, you are in a solid negotiating position.

Life is to be lived. If you have to support yourself, you had bloody well better find some way that is going to be interesting. And you don't do that by sitting around wondering about yourself.

KATHERINE HEPBURN

The Five O'Clock Club

Salary Negotiation: Power and Positioning

The amount of money you receive will always be in direct proportion to the demand for what you do, your ability to do it, and the difficulty of replacing you.

NAPOLEON HILL PARAPHRASED BY DENNIS KIMBRO, *THINK AND GROW RICH: A BLACK CHOICE*

The cynic knows the price of everything and the value of nothing.

OSCAR WILDE

Let's assume a company is about to make you an offer, and you want to prepare for the salary negotiation. What are your chances of getting the compensation you think you deserve? How can you tell whether you are in a strong negotiating position or a weak one?

Salary negotiation is about power. The more you are in demand, the better your chances of getting what you are worth. You need to know what you are worth in the market, but you also need to know how easily employers could be satisfied with someone else. If it's easy for them to replace you, you have little room to negotiate. On the other hand, if you have convinced the hiring team that you and only you are the right person for the job, you are in a better position to get the offer and also to be paid fairly.

The earlier in the process that you differentiate yourself from your competition, the better. Establishing your worth takes time, and it rarely happens during one interview. However, it can happen over a series of meetings where people get to know you better and appreciate you more.

Starting Out: Little Room for Negotiation

A recent graduate may resemble the 10 other people applying for the same job. Each has very little room for salary negotiation. Usually the best a person can hope for is to land the job by proving that he or she is superior to the other applicants, the same way experienced people do. Just landing the job may be a major accomplishment. When people are starting out, they usually have to pay their dues. They have little power.

After you gain some experience, you have more negotiating power—providing you can differentiate yourself from others.

Occasionally I would start thinking how such dull people could make money. I should have known that money-making has more to do with emotional stability than with intellect.

J. P. MARQUAND, *WOMEN AND THOMAS HARROW*

Don't Accept or Reject a Job Until It Is Offered to You

Coaches observe that job hunters often go into the interview thinking, "I want that job" or "I don't want that job." But the job hasn't even been offered to them yet. It would be better if they had a more open mind, trying to assess the situation, and doing what they can to get an offer. As our coaches say, "*After* you have heard their best possible offer, *then* you decide to accept or reject it. Not before."

Position Yourself with Your Résumé

As you have seen in a previous chapter, *Four-Step Salary Negotiation Strategy*, you are positioning yourself for the salary discussion in the first interview. But you are doing it even before that—when you are preparing your résumé. Examine the summary statement in your résumé—especially the first three lines. Make sure that people get the right impression of your level and what you have to offer them. If your description could work for someone who is lower level than you are, rewrite it.

Take a look at all the résumé samples in *Packaging Yourself: The Targeted Résumé*. A lot of work went into the first three lines to make sure that people understand—within a few seconds—what each person has to offer and his or her level.

... [N]ow does he feel his title hang loose upon him, like a giant's robe upon a dwarfish thief.

SHAKESPEARE, *MACBETH*, V, II

Well, march we on, to give obedience where 'tis truly owed....

SHAKESPEARE, *MACBETH*, V, II

Position Yourself with Your Appearance and Demeanor

Do you look and act the level you say you are? You've heard people say, "Jane just looks like an executive." Be more conscious of how people look and act at the level where you think you should be.

Position Yourself by Being in Demand

An important way to gain power is by having 6 to 10 things in the works. Your increased self-esteem will cause you to come across differently, and you will be better positioned to play the game.

The Game: Unspoken Salary Negotiation While You Position Yourself

Much of the *salary negotiation* process is unspoken. Beginning with the very first meeting, you are thinking about the needs of the hiring team and measuring yourself against your competition. You are assessing how well you are doing without overtly discussing salary. If you think that the job is too low a level to warrant the salary you want or that the hiring team likes your competition more than they like you, there is no sense in discussing salary. First redefine the job, if you can, to make it worth more. And then outshine and outlast your competitors.

Position Yourself versus Your Competition

You outshine and outlast your competitors by doing follow-up that is better than the hiring team could ever possibly get from anyone else. To do this well, you need to know where you stand regarding your competition.

After You Get the Offer, Is Your Competition Still Close Behind?

Even after you hear their best possible offer, you need to assess how far ahead of your competition you are.

There's a very big difference between "Let's offer it to John. If it doesn't work out, we can offer it to Jane" and "If John doesn't take it, we're dead. There's no one else who even comes close to what he has to offer." Certainly, you want to get the offer, but you also want to be a clear choice— far ahead of your other competitors. Be sure to ask:

- "Where are you in the hiring process?"
- "How many others are you considering?"
- "How do I compare with them?"

Remember, you need to uncover any objections they may have to hiring you. It is wise to ask, "Is there any reason why you might be reluctant about bringing me on board?"

When you get the offer, don't think you can necessarily start playing hardball. Is your competition waiting in the wings, or have you left your competition in the dust? As you become a more experienced job hunter, you will get better at finding out how you stand versus your competition.

When God loves a creature he wants the creature to know the highest happiness and the deepest misery.... He wants him to know all that being alive can bring. That is his best gift....There is no happiness save in understanding the whole.

THORNTON WILDER, *THE EIGHTH DAY*

Aim to Be Paid Fairly

Sometimes job hunters focus on getting a higher and higher salary and lose perspective on what they are worth. Your goal is to get what you are worth. If you convince them to pay you more than that, they will expect more, and you may not be able to live up to their expectations. That's why it is so important to know what you are worth in the market and then do your best to get it.

Son, I am sorry that I am not able to bankroll you to a very large start, but not having any potatoes to give you I am now going to stake you to some very valuable advice. One of these days in your travels a guy is going to come up to you and show you a nice, brand-new deck of cards on which the seal is not yet broken, and this guy is going to offer to bet you that he can make the jack of spades jump out of the deck and squirt cider in your ear. But son, do not bet this man. For as sure as you stand there you are going to wind up with an earful of cider.

ADVICE FROM SKY MASTERSON'S FATHER TO HIS SON ON A BET THAT SOUNDS TOO GOOD TO BE TRUE, FROM DAMON RUNYON'S *GUYS AND DOLLS*

CASE STUDY Judy
In the Best Negotiations, You May Never Have to Say a Word

Judy, a retail manager earning $50,000, uncovered three job possibilities. One company in particular, Apex—a large retail chain—interested her. Apex had two openings—one higher level and one lower level.

Her first goal was to get the hiring team at Apex to see her as appropriate for the higher-level position. She spent some time doing library research about the company, and she talked to people she already knew who were Apex customers. She learned a lot about what the company could be doing better.

The next time she had a meeting with the prospective employer, she mentioned her findings and proposed changes that Apex could make to remedy these problems. The hiring team was very interested in her advice and also admired her initiative. They knew she would be just as proactive on the job. Her future employer began to imagine her in the higher-level job and told her that. They also told her that she had a number of competitors for that higher-level job.

Judy Positions Herself for the Higher-Level Salary

Judy did *more* work—to position herself against her competitors. She visited various store locations and assessed what the store personnel seemed to be doing right or wrong. She asked more people what they thought of Apex and came up with more ideas about what the company could do.

At her next meeting, she told them what she had done, and they were amazed. They wanted her for the higher-level job and told her that. They also told her the salary range for that job, and it was very broad—anywhere from $50,000 to $75,000.

But remember, other companies were interested in Judy, and some spoke of offering her more money than Apex would pay her. She told the hiring manager that although she was talking to other companies, she wanted to work for Apex.

When they made her the offer, they did not want to risk losing her to *their* competitors—the other companies with whom Judy was talking. The hiring manager said, "We don't want to quibble, so we're going to offer you the very top salary to start, as well as a few other perks. We really want you here."

Judy never had to formally negotiate her salary. She positioned herself so well that their best offer came first.

Does this always work? No. But it is important for you to follow the same strategy that Judy did. You increase your chances of getting the best the company can offer when you:

- think about and outshine your competition
- have other potential offers
- show the company what it would be like to have you in the job you want

However, be sure you are qualified for that higher-level position, or your tenure in the job may be short-lived.

Storybook happiness involves every form of pleasant thumb-twiddling; true happiness involves the full use of one's powers and talents.

JOHN W. GARDNER, *SELF-RENEWAL: THE INDIVIDUAL AND THE INNOVATIVE SOCIETY*

CASE STUDY Rick
Bargaining for What He Wants

This is an advanced technique that you may skip if you like. Sometimes a company may want you very much but may be afraid to bring you in at the appropriate level. It may be too big a decision for them. You can help make that decision easier.

Rick, an architect, saw himself at the partnership level of a prestigious architectural firm. Although the company wanted to hire him, they were afraid to bring him in as a partner. Job hunters think they are the only ones who are scared. But often companies are scared, too— afraid of doing the wrong thing.

Rick said to them: "I believe this is the right place for me, and I believe that partnership is the right level for me. I'm so convinced of that, I'm willing to make an investment in this if you are. Bring me in at the level just below partner. But starting with my first day on the job, give me assignments at the partner level. At the end of three months, I'd like a salary and level review, and you decide."

The company felt very comfortable with this approach. If Rick could not perform at the level of partner, he would still be a good hire at the next-lower level.

At the *two*-month mark, Rick became a partner.

It's a Career-Management Issue

Job hunters say that they are often promised something in a new job, but it never materializes. And they are correct. Companies soon forget what they thought of you during the hiring process, and you are stereotyped by the new job. Everyone is soon back to business as usual.

The trick is to make sure they agree to do something *starting with your first day on the job* that reminds them of their promise to you. In Rick's case, for example, he asked for assignments at the partner level—starting with his very first day on the job. The following is another example.

CASE STUDY Charlie
Negotiating a Career Change

Charlie is a great administrator. Department heads always succeed with him at their side. But he wanted to move into product management.

He interviewed for a product-management position, but the hiring manager realized what an asset Charlie would be as an administrative manager and wanted him in that job instead.

Charlie said: "As your chief administrator, I would be able to help you greatly. But I want to move into product management. Perhaps we can negotiate something that will satisfy us both.

"Your department will take a while to straighten out. I'm afraid that if I come in and kill myself working as your administrator, you will soon forget what I had really wanted.

"So let's make a deal. I'll come in as your administrator providing that, day one, you put me on a product-management task force or do something that gets me involved in product management. In the beginning, I'll spend 90 percent of my time on administration and 10 percent on product management. At the end of the first year, I want to be spending 90 percent of my time on product management and 10 percent of my time on administration. I'll even find and train my successor."

The boss liked that idea. To prove his commitment, he allowed Charlie to spend the first week on the job working as part of a product-management team. That way, he got to know everyone in that group. When Charlie started working in the administrative area, he continued to go to the product-management staff meetings. It was clear to everyone what Charlie was promised, and he was able to make the transition.

It is unreasonable to expect people to remember the career promises they make to you during the interview. Even getting those promises in writing is not much help. With the press of everyday business—and because you are good at what you do—there is never a good time to make the transition, and you find yourself negotiating all over again while you are doing work you do not want to do. Over time, your resentment will build, and your only conclusion will be that people don't keep their promises.

Instead, your conclusion should be that you gave away too much. You should have negotiated something that reminded them on a daily basis what they had promised you. When a company wants what you have to offer, you are in a very strong position to negotiate a career change.

One can never consent to creep when one feels an impulse to soar.

HELEN KELLER

Playing the End Game

Of all the traps and pitfalls in life, self-disesteem is the deadliest, and the hardest to overcome, for it is a pit designed and dug by our own hands, summed up in the phrase, "It's no use—I can't do it."

MAXWELL MALTZ, "YOU CAN DO THE IMPOSSIBLE," *THIS WEEK*

This is the fun part—the part you've worked so hard to get to. You have had successful interviews and done thorough follow-ups. Now the offers are about to come in. Let's suppose you have a number of job possibilities. The game is to have them all come to closure within the same general time frame. It is not as effective to get an offer, turn it down, and a few months later, get another offer. Instead, try to have them happen at the same time. Then you'll seem more valuable in the marketplace, increase your chances of getting fair offers, and be able to select the one that positions you best for the long run.

To do that, first get a lot of Stage 1 and Stage 2 contacts going all at once. When a company is interested in you, don't wait to see what they offer you. Instead, rush out and get more things going.

Success is a process, a quality of mind and way of being, an outgoing affirmation of life.

ALEX NOBLE, "IN TOUCH WITH THE PRESENT," *CHRISTIAN SCIENCE MONITOR*

CASE STUDY Paul
No Longer Saw Himself As "Unemployed"

That's what Paul learned to do. He was unemployed and felt that his situation was a major handicap. He had created a self-fulfilling prophecy.

When Paul got his first offer, from Englander, Inc., it was not a good one. The job was too low level for him, and the pay was inadequate. He felt that the company was taking advantage of him because he was unemployed—and he was right.

They wanted him to drop everything and help out in an emergency by going on a sales call in another city—before putting him on payroll. They were acting as if "he's unemployed and desperate." Actually, Paul was feeling the same way about himself.

Despite his feelings of desperation, Paul declined to go on the trip. It would have made him feel worse. He told the company he was tied up with other things and simply could not make it.

It'll be a game! Imagine you are looking for employment and I'm the woman at the agency. In front of me is an enormous desk, covered with details of jobs—for none of which you are suitable. That's what they always imply anyway. (Stern voice) "Sit down, please, Miss—er, Schoen, isn't it?"

PETER SCHAFFER, *LETTICE & LOVAGE*

Paul Decides to Play the Game

Instead of deciding whether to accept or reject the offer, Paul decided to play the game. Hiding his hurt and anger, he said, "I truly believe that yours is the company I want to work for. The problem is that I'm talking to a number of other companies right now, and I think it may take me a few weeks to wrap things up. I feel I owe it to myself to see these other possibilities through. Would it be okay if I got back to you in two weeks?" They agreed.

Paul then spent all of his energy making new contacts, getting new things in the works—and getting other offers.

The two weeks came and went as he continued to stay in touch with Englander, Inc., letting them know that he was still interested in them. He said that he would probably wind up working there but that a few additional companies had expressed interest in him, and it would take a few weeks longer. Was that okay with them?

Paul wound up with 18 job possibilities and 8 job offers! He had written extensive follow-ups to every person in all 18 companies. That's how he turned his interviews into offers.

Many of the offers were excellent, and some were jobs he would consider taking only reluctantly. The other offers greatly enhanced his value in the eyes of every company with whom he was speaking—including Englander, Inc.

Paul continued to report back to them on the way he was being received in the marketplace. They started to see other roles for him in their company. His *unemployed* status was no longer relevant to them because it was no longer relevant to Paul. As he spoke to more and more hiring teams, he started feeling better about himself. The companies also sensed the difference. The issue was no longer Paul's status but the fact that so many companies valued what he had to offer.

In the end, Paul's main decision had to do with the direction he wanted his career to take: He needed to decide which job would position him best for the long run. It was not easy.

As he continued his talks with all 18 companies, a number of them increased the responsibilities of the jobs they were talking to him about. Paul was having a lot of fun, and his self-esteem was greatly improved.

No passion so effectively robs the mind of all its power of acting and reasoning as fear.

Edmund Burke, *On the Sublime and Beautiful*

Increasing His Desirability

Paul ended up taking a position with Englander, Inc., after all—but not the position about which they were originally speaking to him. They offered him a job that was two levels higher than the original one, with greatly increased pay. What's more, they were proud to have him on board and even issued a press release telling the world that he had joined their company.

By the way, you don't need eight offers to play the game. Three is a good number.

You just got to be very levelheaded and keep moving forward.

Robert DeNiro, actor

Slowing Down a Company That Is Ahead of the Others

What can you do to slow down an offer while waiting for others to come through? If you are paying attention, you will most likely see an offer edging toward the finish line way ahead of the others. The time to slow it down is earlier on. When a company asks you back for another interview, and you feel it is getting too far ahead of the others, say, "I'm really eager to come back and meet with you again, but my schedule is pretty full next week. Could we schedule it for the week after that?" Use your judgment, of course. It may be that putting them off for a week would be inappropriate. If you feel you would just irritate them by postponing a meeting, then don't do it.

But what if Paul was not able to get so many other possibilities going? What if he had been made a terrible offer and felt he was forced to accept or reject it with no assurance that others would come his way? This could well have been the case because, after all, offers are more likely to come your way when you have momentum—a lot of things going all at once. If Paul had really been in need of money, he might have decided to take that first offer and do well at it while he was there but continue to search for a job that was more appropriate for his experience.

Some people may consider it unethical to take a job knowing that they will continue to search for another one. But if you were a career coach, you would see many cases in which a company hired someone—perhaps even moving his or her family—and then fired that person after a very short while for reasons having nothing to do with the employee. "Oh, I'm sorry we moved you here to Chicago. The project you were assigned to has been canceled. We'll give you some severance, but you are out of a job."

Companies are no longer dependable. Job hunters must fend for themselves and protect themselves. They didn't start this. Company executives did when they decided to cut people rather than retrain them or find another place for them inside the same company. In self-defense, employees must learn how to play the game—the new game of having a job in today's market.

You will give the company a full day's work for a full day's pay. What you are not giving them is your loyalty—until companies decide to be loyal back.

Because everyone is doing it, a manager who isn't (downsizing) wonders why he's not and looks around at his staff to see who he can do without.

ERIC ROLFE GREENBERG, AMERICAN MANAGEMENT ASSOCIATION, *THE NEW YORK TIMES*

CASE STUDY Charlie and Brad
The Numbers You Need

The company Charlie and Brad worked for decided it no longer wanted to be in the insurance business and closed that business down.

Charlie and Brad had always wanted their own business and—with some severance pay in hand—they saw this as an opportunity to explore

their dream. Perhaps they could sell their original business idea to a financial services company—yet keep part of the equity. That way they could essentially have their own business but with the backing of a large organization.

The search Charlie and Brad conducted is exactly like a job search, and the numbers are the same. So see what you can learn from their experience.

Initial Contacts from Networking

At the time I met Charlie and Brad, they had already spoken to 20 large companies. They had actually known for some time that the business they were in would close, so as soon as they learned this, they had gotten to work. Four of the companies were somewhat interested in their idea. Charlie and Brad wanted me to help them make those four companies more interested.

Although they did not want to hear it, I told Brad that the problem was not with the four companies. Their numbers were too small, and they needed to drum up more interest in their idea. That would make their reluctant suitors more interested in doing a deal with them. When a company sees that others are pursuing you, they feel more secure about considering you for themselves. That's the way the game is played.

Here are the numbers that Charlie and Brad were working with:

Companies Contacted	Companies Interested	Offers to Date
20	4	0

After all Charlie and Brad had done, it would be difficult to get offers by working and reworking their contacts with those same four companies. The number that first had to change is the number of companies contacted. Then the other numbers would also be likely to increase.

But human nature being what it is, Charlie and Brad did not feel like taking their eyes off the companies that were already interested. It took a number of weeks before they agreed to think about how to contact additional companies.

Once you fully apprehend the vacuity of a life without struggle, you are equipped with the basic means of salvation.

TENNESSEE WILLIAMS

Networking, by Definition, Is Serendipitous; Direct Mail Can Fill in the Gaps

Charlie and Brad had networked into those 20 companies. They both agreed that there were hundreds of companies that could possibly be excited about their idea, but most of those companies did not even know that there was an idea to be had.

Charlie and Brad had no certain way to network into any companies besides the ones with which they had already met. And even if they could network in, that method would take too much time to uncover even one additional interested company.

They were willing to do a direct-mail campaign to 60 more companies. After all, they already knew how to express their idea in an appealing way.

Charlie and Brad quickly did research to find the names and addresses of the 60 companies, as well as the appropriate people to contact. They sent out a well-written one-page letter to each of them. In the letter, they asked the companies to call them if they were interested. (If they had decided to follow up each letter with a phone call, that would have been a targeted mailing rather than a direct-mail campaign.)

Within one day, an important company called. Within the next two weeks, three more called—including two highly prestigious companies they were very excited about. They met with

those companies. Now they had a good reason to recontact the companies with which they had originally met. Within a short time, they received three offers. The numbers in their campaign were now as follows:

Companies Contacted	Companies Interested	Offers to Date
80	8	3

This was a lot of work, but it increased their chances of having something happen. Of the three offers they finally received, they accepted one that offered them the best of both worlds. They got 51 percent equity, a base pay higher than what either of them had been making in their previous jobs, plus full benefits.

Formerly when great fortunes were only made in war, war was a business; but now when great fortunes are only made by business, business is war.

CHRISTIAN N. BOVEE, 1820-1904

> **The next time you want a company to make you an offer, instead of focusing on that, contact additional companies and try to get them interested in you. It actually shortens your search.**

You can get a job at any point in the process. You may not have to go to the lengths that Charlie and Brad and Paul went to. Luck can always be a factor. It is something you should allow for, but it is certainly not something you want to count on—and even if you're lucky once, it probably won't happen again in your next search.

The approach these job hunters used is the most dependable way to get a number of genuinely good offers in the shortest period of time.

Success, it may surprise some to hear, comes from doing, not negotiating, not counting lines, not weighing credits. Do it, do it, don't wait for it. Some very good actors sit out their entire lives while waiting for the right part. Make every part the one you've been waiting for. Learn the confidence you can only gain under fire. The confidence lends relaxation. Relaxation opens all your resources for the demands of your role. And when the big role does come along you'll need all 100 percent of what you've got to give. Don't be caught 25 percent short; don't be caught one percent short. Be completely available to whatever challenge comes your way, by being totally in charge of your craft, your material, yourself.

MICHAEL CAINE, *ACTING IN FILM*

The
Five
O'Clock
Club®

PART SIX

Keeping It Going

AFTER YOU'VE GOTTEN THE JOB YOU WANT

The
Five
O'Clock
Club

Starting Out on the Right Foot in Your New Job

. . . be patient toward all that is unsolved in your heart and try to love the questions themselves like locked rooms and like books that are written in a foreign tongue.

RAINER MARIA RILKE, POET

Starting out can be tricky: You are *on board* but *the jury is still out* on you. It is a time of trial. You are often being watched to see if you will work out. Here are some things you need to do to start out on the right foot and keep moving in the right direction.

"Welcome aboard, Johnson! Bruno, your acting supervisor, will get you started."

Courtesy of Jerry King, Cartoons, Inc.

Before You Start

- **Say thank you**. Contact all the people who helped you get the new position. Often people don't make this effort because they feel they'll be in the new job for a long time. But today, when the average American changes jobs every four years, the odds say you're going to change jobs again soon. You need to keep up those contacts. Then think about ways to keep in touch with these contacts—if you read something that someone on your list would appreciate, clip it and send it.

- **Don't cut off other job prospects**. The new job might not work out, so hedge your bets. Don't cut off all of the people with whom you have been exploring positions. Don't take yourself off the market. Instead, tell people that you are "doing work for" a certain type of company, but want to stay in touch with them. You never know. Three months into the job, you may find out that it is not a good fit or that the hiring manager misled you. Protect yourself by staying in the market until you feel you understand the situation there and are somewhat secure.

- **Cultivate your relationship with your boss**. If your peers, subordinates and clients all wind up loving you, but your boss does not, you will not survive. If you are senior level, you must take extra care because more will be expected of you. Between the time you accept the offer and actually start the job, work closely with your boss to develop your onboarding plan. Make sure you know what your boss expects you to get done during the first three months and beyond.

The price one pays for pursuing any profession or calling is an intimate knowledge of its ugly side.

JAMES BALDWIN, *NOBODY KNOWS MY NAME*

José, an executive and Five O'Clock Club member, could not start at his new job for a number of months. He would have to sell his present home, find another one a thousand miles away, and he and his wife would have to find new schools for his children. José flew to the new organization once every few weeks. During that time:

- José worked with his new boss to develop an onboarding plan (of how he would learn and become integrated into the organization) and a work plan (of goals and objectives to be accomplished after he arrived). He also confirmed that he would have the resources he would need to do his job well.
- He intentionally forged a strong relationship with his boss.
- José scheduled individual as well as group meetings with his soon-to-be staff members to get feedback, iron out expectations and to make sure they were on-board with the work plan. He also led the discussions on major projects that they were tackling.
- He made sure he formed relationships with his peers.
- To make sure he thoroughly understood who was likely to play key roles in his success, he attempted to complete the exercise in the next section, "Circles of Influence."

By the time he actually started in the new job, it felt as if he had been there quite a while and all went smoothly.

It is not the critic who counts; not the man who points out how the strong man stumbled or where the doer of deeds could have done better. The credit belongs to the man who is actually in the arena, whose face

is marred by dust and sweat and blood; who strives valiantly; who errs and comes up short again and again; who knows the great enthusiasms, the great devotions; who spends himself in a worthy cause; who, at best, knows in the end the triumph of achievement, and who, at worst, if he fails, at least fails while daring greatly, so that his place shall never be with those timid souls who knew neither victory nor defeat.

THEODORE ROOSEVELT

Right Away

- **Don't fix things or do anything *big* for the first three months**. That is one of the biggest mistakes people make. Take time to learn the system, the people, and the culture.

  You cannot possibly understand, in those first months, the implications of certain decisions you may make. You may be criticizing a project that was done by someone really important. Or you could be changing something that will affect someone on the staff in ways of which you aren't aware.

  Change agents, beware. If you were hired to make major changes, take it slowly. I worked as the Chief Operating Officer for a small company and was brought in to make major changes. When I was pressed to do things quickly, I asked: "How long has this been broken?" The CEO said, "Four years." "Then," I said, "it can wait another three months while I study the situation."

- **Make yourself productive immediately**. This does not contradict the point I just made. Do things that are safe. For example, install a new system where there has been none. This is *safe* because you aren't getting rid of some other system. What isn't safe? Firing half your staff the first week!

- **Introduce yourself to everybody**. Be visible—walk around and meet people as soon as possible, including those who work for you. Meet everybody. Too many managers meet only the *important* people while ignoring those who will actually do the day-to-day work. It may be that your best source of information — the person who will tell you the hidden landmines — is a lower-level professional or an administrative assistant. These are people who watch everything but are not caught up in the day-to-day politics. Figure out who your best sources are.

- **Don't make friends too fast**. Someone who befriends you right away could also be on the way out. That doesn't mean you shouldn't be friendly, however. Go to lunch with several people rather than becoming known as someone who associates only with so-and-so. Get to know everybody, and then decide with whom to get closer.
- **Take over compensation of your subordinates immediately**. Look at review and raise dates, and make sure no one is overlooked. You can't afford to wait three months to get settled while one of your people is stewing about an overdue salary review.
- **Get your budget—quickly**. If it isn't good, build a better one. If you spend some time at the beginning trying to understand the budget, the things you hear over the next few weeks will mean more to you.
- **Consider hiring an Executive Coach**. Even before you smell trouble—and especially when you do, you need someone outside the organization to give you some perspective and advice. Otherwise, you are in danger of getting way off course. For 12 years, I worked with Cecilia, starting when she became the new head of marketing in a fast-growing organization. As the organization grew, she grew. We met a number of times in the

very beginning of our relationship, and then once or twice a year for the next twelve years! The "Circles of Influence" exercise in the Members Only section of our website made it easy for her to tell me the changing situation she faced and helped me to understand and help her figure out what to do next. I became her trusted advisor whom she could turn to whenever she wanted to discuss a situation. I believe that having an Executive Coach helped her keep that important job as that turbulent organization grew. The Five O'Clock Club has an executive coach who is right for you and will help to steer you through the troubled waters that lie ahead.

Try not to do anything too daring for the first three months. Take time to learn the system.

Destiny is not a matter of chance, it is a matter of choice; it is not a thing to be waited for, it is a thing to be achieved.

WILLIAM JENNINGS BRYAN, AMERICAN POLITICIAN

In the First Three Months

- **Learn the corporate culture**. People new to jobs lose those jobs often because of personality conflicts rather than a lack of competence. Keep your head low until you learn how the company operates. Some companies have certain writing styles. Some expect you to speak a certain way. In certain companies, it's the way they hold parties. Do people work with their doors open or their doors shut?

All those things are part of the culture, and they are unwritten. To learn them, you have to pay attention.

Tom, for example, lost his job because his management style rubbed everyone the wrong way. Tom was a *touchy-feely* manager who, when he wanted his employees to do things, schmoozed with them, saying things such as, "You know, I was kind of thinking about this and...." But the corporate culture was such that the employees liked and expected to be asked straight out. Tom's style made them feel patronized and manipulated. And his own staff did him in.

Pay your dues before doing things at a variance with the corporate culture. After you build up some credits, you have more leeway. Let your personality emerge when you understand the company and after you have made some contribution.

What we anticipate seldom occurs; what we least expect generally happens.

BENJAMIN DISRAELI, 19TH CENTURY BRITISH PRIME MINISTER

- **Learn the organizational structure— the real structure**, not the one that is drawn on the charts. (See the Circles of Influence exercise.) Ask your assistant to tell you who relates how with whom, who knows what, who thought of this project, who is important. You could be surprised.
- **As far as subordinates are concerned, find out other people's opinions and then form your own.** Consider that you may have a different perception because you have different values.
- **Find out what is important in your job**. For example, when I coach people for a corporation, coaching is not the only important thing in my job. The people who come to me are sent by human resources, and I must manage my relationship with these people. It doesn't matter how good

a coach I am if I don't maintain a good relationship with human resources.

- **Pay attention to your peers**. Your peers can prove as valuable to you as your boss and subordinates. Do not try to impress them with your brilliance. That would be the kiss of death because you'd cause envy and have a very large reputation to live up to. Instead, encourage them to talk to you. They know more than you do. They also know your boss. Look to them to teach you and, in some cases, protect you.

Sharon, an executive, found out that her last three predecessors had been fired. She knew from talking to people that her boss was the type whose ego was bruised when someone had ideas. He had a talent for getting rid of these people.

> **Pay attention to your peers. Look to them to teach you and, in some cases, protect you.**

Know how to ask. There is nothing more difficult for some people. Nor for others, easier.

BALTASAR GRACIAN, THE ART OF WORLDLY WISDOM

To protect herself, Sharon built relationships with her peers, the heads of offices around the country. After a year and a half, her boss' brother took her to breakfast and told her that, unlike her predecessors, she could not be fired: It would have been such an unpopular decision that it would have backfired on her boss.

- **Don't set up competition**. Everyone brings something to the party and should be respected for his or her talent, no matter what their level. Find ways to show your respect by asking for their input on projects that require their expertise.
- **Set precedents you want to keep**. If you

start out working 12-hour days, people will come to expect it of you—even if no one else is doing it. When you stop, people will wonder what's wrong.

- **Set modest goals for your own personal achievement and high goals for your department.** Make your people look good, and you will, too.

The character of a person is formed as well as revealed by his own concept of self-interest.

JOHN LUKACS, *A HISTORY OF THE COLD WAR*

> **You'll be busy in your new job and may not keep up your outside contacts. In today's economy, that's a big mistake.**

Three Months and Beyond . . .

- **Continue to develop contacts outside the company.** If you need information for your job, sometimes the worst people to ask are your boss and the people around you. A network is also a tremendous resource to fall back on when your boss is busy—and you will seem resourceful, smart, and connected.

- **Keep a hero file for yourself**, a hanging file where you place written descriptions of all your successes. If you have to job hunt in a hurry, you'll be able to recall what you've done. You will also use it if you stay. If you want anything, whether it be a raise or a promotion or the responsibility for a particular project, you can use the file to build a case for yourself.

- **Keep managing your career**. Don't think, "I'll just take this job and do what they tell me," because you might get off on some tangent. Remember where you were heading and make sure your career keeps going that way. Be proactive in moving toward your goal.

- **Take on lots of assignments**. If a project comes up that fits into your long-term plan, do it. If one doesn't fit into your plan, you can do it or you can say, "Oh, I'd love to do that, but I'm really busy." Make those kinds of choices all the time.

To act with confidence, one must be willing to look ahead and consider uncertainties: "What challenges could the world present me? How might others respond to my actions?" Rather than asking such questions, too many people react to uncertainty with denial.

PETER SCHWARTZ, *THE ART OF THE LONG VIEW*

Thank-You Note after Getting a Job

Here's a good model to follow when you have to write one of these.

Anita Attridge
400 First Avenue
Dayton, Ohio 22090

May 8, 2013

Mr. Jerry Iannaccone
3450 Garden Place
Des Moines, Iowa 44466

Dear Jerry:

The happy news is that I have accepted a position at Ohio State Trust as Controller for their Ohio branches. I'll be responsible for financial reporting and analysis, loans administration, budgeting, and planning. I think it's a great match that will make good use of both my management skills and banking experience, and the environment is congenial and professional.

I really appreciated your interest in my job search. I very much enjoyed speaking with people like you about your career, and I appreciated your advice and encouragement. The fact that you so willingly gave of your time meant a great deal to me, and it certainly was beneficial.

If I can reciprocate in some way, please feel free to be in touch with me. I will also probably be in contact with you in the months ahead. My new office is at 75 Rockfast Corner, Dayton 22091. You can reach me at 200-555-1212.

Sincerely,
Anita Attridge

The Five O'Clock Club

Epilogue

... [T]he country demands bold, persistent experimentation. It is common sense to take a method and try it. If it fails, admit it frankly and try another. But above all, try something.

FRANKLIN DELANO ROOSEVELT, SPEECH, ATLANTA, 1932

There is no one way to job hunt; one neat solution to job hunting cannot answer it all. There are many ways.

The results of what you do in a job hunt are neither good nor bad; they are simply results to be observed and thought about. They are indicators of the correctness of the direction you are pursuing; they are not indictments. They are not personal; they are the world's feedback to what we are doing. These results can keep us on track, and if we look at them objectively, then they should not throw us off track.

Information is not good or bad; it is simply information. Things are changing so fast that we each need all the relevant information we can get. We may tend to block out information we find threatening—but that is precisely the information we need to get. Knowing the truth of what is happening around us may help us decide how to take care of ourselves. The information is not out to harm us—it is simply there.

To view your life as blessed does not require you to deny your pain. It simply demands a more complicated vision, one in which a condition or event is not either good or bad but is, rather, both good and bad, not sequentially but simultaneously.

NANCY MAIRS (WHO HAS MULTIPLE SCLEROSIS), *CARNAL ACTS*

To be what we are, and to become what we are capable of becoming is the only end of life.

ROBERT LOUIS STEVENSON

There is a place for you, and you must look for it. Do not be stopped when others seem as though they are moving ahead. You, too, have a lot to offer if you would only think about yourself and not them. You are on your own track. Put your energy into discovering what is special about you, and then hold on to it.

You will be knocked down enough during your job hunting. Don't knock yourself; push back. Push past the people who offer you discouragement. Find those nurturing souls who recognize your worth and encourage you.

... [T]here are days when the result is so bad that no fewer than five revisions are required. In contrast, when I'm greatly inspired, only four revisions are needed.

JOHN KENNETH GALBRAITH

Don't tell me the facts about yourself; tell me who you really are. When you are writing to someone, ask yourself, What am I really trying to say to this person? What would I say if this person were right here? You are writing to a real person, and when your personality comes through and you say what you mean to say, then your note is unique.

Read your work out loud. It will give you a sense of the timing, the flow. You will find out if it is readable. You will notice where it stumbles. Have someone else read it, too. Most people need an editor.

Take a few risks, but do it with some restraint. Don't be self-indulgent, but do let your personality seep through. You are not simply a *banker with 20 years' major banking experience.* You are *mature, with worldwide contacts and a sense of stability.*

Pare down your writing. Get rid of the lines that have no energy. Think about getting rid of your first paragraph completely. Perhaps you wrote it just to warm up.

Write to make an impact, to influence the reader.

It is impossible to enjoy idling thoroughly unless one has plenty of work to do.

JEROME K. JEROME

Continue to job hunt, but be easy on yourself. I worked on this book whenever I could, but some days I didn't feel like thinking, so I researched quotes, or made a chart, or organized my material. All of these things later made my writing easier—so I was always making progress.

The same can be applied to your job hunt. Some days you may research an industry or a number of companies, or you may write a proposal or a follow-up note. But you have to spend most of your time interviewing—just as I had to spend most of my time writing.

Job hunting takes practice, just as writing takes practice. I am not a professional writer, and you are not a professional job hunter. Neither of us, you or I, is perfect. But we are each trying to understand the process. This understanding will make us each less anxious and more patient about what we are doing.

Develop tricks to nudge yourself along. Find someone to report your progress to. If you cannot join a job-hunt group, then meet with a friend. Talking gives you perspective and gives you the energy to keep on going.

Set goals for yourself. For example, aim at all times to be in contact, either in person or in writing, with six people who are in a position to hire you or recommend that you be hired. Keep

in touch with these six people. Strive to add more people to your list, because others will drop off. Plan to continue to network even after you find a job. Make networking a part of your life.

Keep pushing even when you get afraid—especially when you get afraid. On the other hand, if you have been pushing nonstop for a while, take a break completely, relax, and then push again.

Get together with a friend and talk about your dreams. In talking about them, they seem possible. And in hearing yourself say them out loud, you can test how you really feel about them. Then you can discover the central dream—the one that will drive you.

Where I was born and how I have lived is unimportant. It is what I have done with where I have been that should be of interest.

GEORGIA O'KEEFFE

You will find endless resources inside yourself. Get inside yourself, find out what the dream is, and then do it. Stir yourself up. Go for it.

The fact is, if you don't try, no one will care anyway. The only reason to do it is for yourself—so you can take your rightful place in the universe. The only reason to do it is because we each have our place, and it seems a shame to be born and then to die without doing our part.

We are all controlled by the world in which we live....The question is this: are we to be controlled by accidents, by tyrants, or by ourselves?

B. F. SKINNER

The world is big. There are many options; some job hunters try to investigate them all. Instead, begin with yourself. Understand that part. Then look at some options and test them against what you are. You can hold on to that as a sure thing. You can depend on what you are for stability.

*I am larger, better than I thought, I did
not know I held so much goodness.*

WALT WHITMAN

A former client called me today. When I first met him, he had been out of work for a year. Now he was calling to say that he had been made vice president of his company. He has found his niche and has never been happier. Everyone notices it. And he keeps on networking—keeps on enjoying the process.

The world keeps changing. It won't stop. We must change, too. We are the dreamers of dreams.

*We are the music-makers,
And we are the dreamers of dreams...
Yet we are the movers and shakers
of the world for ever, it seems.*

ARTHUR O'SHAUGHNESSY, "MUSIC AND MOONLIGHT"

Far better it is to dare mighty things, to win glorious triumphs, even though checkered by failure, than to take rank with those poor spirits who neither enjoy much nor suffer much, because they live in the gray twilight that knows not victory nor defeat.

THEODORE ROOSEVELT

PART SEVEN

What Is
The Five O'Clock Club?

FIND YOUR PERSONAL PATH IN JOB SEARCH
AND CAREER SUCCESS

How to Join the Club

The Five O'Clock Club: Where Professional Success Gets Personal Attention

"One organization with a long record of success in helping people find jobs is The Five O'Clock Club."

FORTUNE

- Weekly Job-Search Strategy Groups
- Private Coaching
- Books, Audio CDs and audio downloads
- Membership Information
- When Your Employer Pays

THERE *IS* A FIVE O'CLOCK CLUB NEAR YOU!

For more information on becoming a member, please fill out the Membership Application Form in this book, sign up on the web at:
www.fiveoclockclub.com,
or call: 1-800-538-6645
(or 212-286-4500 in New York)

The Five O'Clock Club Search Process

The Five O'Clock Club process, as outlined in *The Five O'Clock Club* books, is a targeted, strategic approach to career development and job search. Five O'Clock Club members become proficient at skills that prove invaluable during their entire working lives.

Career Management

We train our members to manage their careers and always look ahead to their next job search. Research shows that an average worker spends only four years in a job—and will have 12 jobs in as many as 5 career fields—during his or her working life.

Getting Jobs . . . Faster

Five O'Clock Club members find more satisfying jobs, faster. The average professional, manager, or executive Five O'Clock Club member who regularly attends weekly sessions finds a job by his or her 10th session. Even the discouraged, long-term job searcher can find immediate help.

The keystone to The Five O'Clock Club process is teaching our members an understanding of the entire *hiring* process. A first interview is primarily a time for exchanging critical information. The real work starts *after the interview*. We teach our members how to *turn job interviews into offers* and to negotiate the best possible employment package.

Setting Targets

The Five O'Clock Club is action oriented. *We'll help you decide what you should do this very next week to move your search along.* By their third session, our members have set definite job targets by industry or company size, position, and geographic area, and are out in the field gathering information and making contacts that will lead to interviews with hiring managers.

Our approach evolves with the changing job market. We're able to synthesize information from hundreds of Five O'Clock Club members and come up with new approaches for our members. For example, we discuss temporary placement for executives, how to use voice mail and the Internet, the use of LinkedIn and other social media, and how to network when doors are slamming shut all over town.

The Five O'Clock Club's Weekly Small Group Strategy Sessions

The Five O'Clock Club weekly meeting includes you, 6 to 8 peers (people at your same salary level) and a senior Five O'Clock Club career coach who has been certified by us. The meeting is a carefully planned *job-search strategy program where participants go away with an assignment to help them get more interviews in their target markets or turn those interviews into offers*. We provide members with the tools and tricks necessary to get a good job fast—even in a tight market. Networking and emotional support are also included in the meeting.

Participate in 10 *consecutive* small-group strategy sessions to enable your group and career coach to get to know you and to develop momentum in your search.

Weekly Presentations via Audio CDs or audio Downloads

Prior to each week's teleconference, listen to the assigned audio presentation covering part of The Five O'Clock Club methodology. These are scheduled on a rotating basis so you may join the Club at any time.

Small-Group Strategy Sessions

During the first few minutes of the teleconference, your small group discusses the topic of the week and hears from people who have landed jobs. Then you have the chance to get feedback and advice on your own search strategy, listen to and learn from others, and build your network. All groups are led by trained career coaches with years of experience. The small group is generally no more than six to eight people, so everyone gets the chance to speak up.

Let us consider how we may spur one another on toward love and good deeds. Let us not give up meeting together, as some are in the habit of doing, but let us encourage one another.

Hebrews 10:24-25

Private Coaching

You may meet with your small-group coach—or another coach—for private coaching by phone or in person. A coach helps you develop a career path, solve current job problems, prepare your résumé, or guide your search.

Many members develop long-term relationships with their coaches to get advice throughout their careers. If you are paying for the coaching yourself (as opposed to having your employer pay), please pay the coach directly (charges vary from $100 to $175 per hour). **Private coaching is not included in The Five O'Clock Club seminar or membership** fee and the Club gets no portion of whatever you pay the coach. For coach matching, see our website or call 1-800-538-6645 (or 212-286-4500 in New York).

Fortune, *The New York Times, Black Enterprise, Business Week*, The TODAY Show, NPR, CNBC and ABC-TV are some of the places you've seen, heard, or read about us.

From the Club History, Written in the 1890s

At The Five O'Clock Club, [people] of all shades of political belief—as might be said of all trades and creeds—have met together.... The variety continues almost to a monotony.... [The Club's] good fellowship and geniality—not to say hospitality—has reached them all.

It has been remarked of clubs that they serve to level rank. If that were possible in this country, it would probably be true, if leveling rank means the appreciation of people of equal abilities as equals; but in The Five O'Clock Club it has been a most gratifying and noteworthy fact that no lines have ever been drawn save those which are essential to the honor and good name of any association. Strangers are invited by the club or by any members, [as gentlepeople], irrespective of aristocracy, plutocracy or occupation, and are so treated always. Nor does the thought of a [person's] social position ever enter into the meetings. People of wealth and people of moderate means sit side by side, finding in each other much to praise and admire and little to justify snarlishness or adverse criticism. People meet as people—not as the representatives of a set—and having so met, dwell not in worlds of envy or distrust, but in union and collegiality, forming kindly thoughts of each other in their heart of hearts.

In its methods, The Five O'Clock Club is plain, easy-going and unconventional. It has its "isms" and some peculiarities of procedure, but simplicity characterizes them all. The sense of propriety, rather than rules of order, governs its meetings, and that informality which carries with it sincerity of motive and spontaneity of effort, prevails within it. Its very name indicates informality, and, indeed, one of the reasons said to have induced its adoption was the fact that members or guests need not don their dress suits to attend the meetings, if they so desired. This informality, however, must be distinguished from the informality of Bohemianism. For The Five O'Clock Club, informality, above convenience, means sobriety, refinement of thought and speech, good breeding and good order. To this sort of informality much of its success is due.

The Schedule

See our website for the specific dates for each topic. All groups use a similar schedule in each time zone.

Fee: $49 for LIFETIME membership (includes Beginners Kit, a LIFETIME subscription to *The Five O'Clock News*, and LIFETIME access to the Members Only section of our website), **plus** session fees based on member's income (the price for the Insider Program includes audio-CD lectures, which retail for as much as $150).

Reservations are required for your first session. Unused sessions that you paid for (as opposed to employer-paid programs) are transferable to anyone you choose or will be donated to members attending more than 16 sessions who are having financial difficulty.

The Five O'Clock Club's programs are geared to professionals, managers, and executives from a wide variety of industries and professions, and also recent graduates. Most earn from $30,000 to $500,000 per year. Half of the members are employed; half are unemployed. **You will be in a group of your peers.**

> **To register, please fill out form on the web (at www.fiveoclockclub.com) or call 1-800-538-6645 (or 212-286-4500 in New York).**

Lecture Presentation Schedule

- History of the Five O'Clock Club
- The Five O'Clock Club Approach to Job Search
- Developing New Targets for Your Search
- Two-Minute Pitch: Keystone of Your Search
- Using Research and Internet for Your Search
- The Keys to Effective Networking
- Getting the Most Out of Your Contacts
- Getting Interviews: Direct/Targeted Mail

- Beat the Odds when Using Search Firms and Ads
- Developing New Momentum in Your Search
- The Five O'Clock Club Approach to Interviewing
- Advanced Interviewing Techniques
- How to Handle Difficult Interview Questions
- How to Turn Job Interviews into Offers
- Successful Job Hunter's Report
- Four-Step Salary-Negotiation Method

> **Audio excerpts from many of these presentations can be found on our website in the "How to Get a Job" section.**

All groups run continuously. Dates are posted on our website. The textbooks used by all members of The Five O'Clock Club may be ordered on our website or purchased at major bookstores.

> **The original Five O'Clock Club was formed in Philadelphia in 1883. It was made up of the leaders of the day who shared their experiences "in a spirit of fellowship and good humor."**

Questions You May Have about the Weekly Job-Search Strategy Group

Job hunters are not always the best judges of what they need during a search. For example, most are interested in lectures on answering ads on the Internet or working with search firms. We cover those topics, but strategically they are relatively unimportant in an effective job search.

At The Five O'Clock Club, you get the information you really need in your search—*such as how to target more effectively, how to get more interviews, and how to turn job interviews into offers.*

What's more, you will work in a small group with the best coaches in the business. In these strategy sessions, your group will help you decide what to do, this week and every week, to move your search along. You will learn by being coached and by coaching others in your group.

We find ourselves not independently of other people and institutions but through them. We never get to the bottom of our selves on our own. We discover who we are face to face and side by side with others in work, love, and learning.

ROBERT N. BELLAH, ET AL., *HABITS OF THE HEART*

Here are a few other points:

- For best results, attend on a regular basis. Your group gets to know you and will coach you to eliminate whatever you may be doing wrong—or refine what you are doing right. Our research shows that if

you attend only once a month, the group will have little or no impact on your search results.
- The Five O'Clock Club is a members-only organization. To get started in the small-group teleconference sessions, you must purchase a minimum of 10 sessions.
- The teleconference sessions include the set of 16 audio-CD presentations on Five O'Clock Club methodology. In-person groups do not include CDs.
- After that, you may purchase blocks of 5 or 10 sessions.
- We sell multiple sessions to make administration easier.
- If you miss a session, you may make it up any time. You may even transfer unused time to a friend.
- Although many people find jobs quickly (even people who have been unemployed a long time), others have more difficult searches. Plan to be in it for the long haul and you'll do better.

Carefully read all of the material in this section. It will help you decide whether or not to attend.

- The first week, pay attention to the strategies used by the others in your group. Soak up all the information you can.
- Read the books before you come in the

second week. They will help you move your search along.

To register:

1. Read this section and fill out the application.
2. After you become a member and get your Beginners Kit, call to reserve a space for the first time you attend.

To assign you to a career coach, we need to know:

- your current (or last) field or industry
- the kind of job you would like next (if you know)
- your desired salary range in general terms

For private coaching, we suggest you attend the small group and ask to see your group leader, to give you continuity.

The Five O'Clock Club is plain, easy-going and unconventional.... Members or guests need not don their dress suits to attend the meetings.
(FROM THE CLUB HISTORY, WRITTEN IN THE 1890S)

What Happens at the Meetings?

Each week, job searchers from various industries and professions meet in small groups. The groups specialize in professionals, managers, executives, or recent college graduates. Usually, half are employed and half are unemployed.

The weekly program is in two parts. First, listen to a lecture on some aspect of The Five O'Clock Club methodology. Then, job hunters meet in small groups headed by senior full-time professional career coaches.

The first week, get the textbooks, listen to the lecture, and meet with your small group and the senior coach who is leading the group. During your first session, listen to the others in your group. You learn a lot by listening to how your peers are strategizing their searches.

By the second week, you will have read the materials. Now we can start to work on your search strategy and help *you* decide what to do next to move your search along. For example, we'll help you figure out how to get more interviews in your target area or how to turn interviews into job offers.

In the third week, you will see major progress made by other members of your group and you may notice major progress in your own search as well.

By the third or fourth week, most members are conducting full and effective searches. Over the remaining weeks, you will tend to keep up a full search rather than go after only one or two leads. You will regularly aim to have 6 to 10 things *in the works at all times*. These will generally be in specific target areas you have identified, will keep your search on target, and will increase your chances of getting multiple job offers from which to choose.

Those who stick with the process find it works.

Some people prefer to just listen for a few weeks before they start their job search and that's okay, too.

How Much Does It Cost?

It is against the policy of The Five O'Clock Club to charge individuals heavy up-front fees. Our competitors charge $4,000 to $6,000 or more, up front. Our average fee is $360 for 10 sessions (which includes audio CDs (or downloads) of 16 presentations for those in the teleconference program). Those in the $100,000+ range pay an average of $540 for 10 sessions. For administrative reasons, we charge for 5 or 10 additional sessions at a time.

You must have the books so you can begin studying them before the second session. (You can purchase them on our website, at Amazon. com, or ask for them at your local library.) If you don't do the homework, you will tend to waste the time of others in the group by asking questions covered in the texts.

Is the Small Group Right for Me?

The Five O'Clock Club process is for you if:

- You are truly interested in job hunting.
- You have some idea of the kind of job you want.
- You are a professional, manager, or executive— or want to be.
- You want to participate in a group process on a regular basis.
- You realize that finding or changing jobs and careers is hard work, but you are absolutely willing and able to do it.

If you have no idea about the kind of job you want next, you may attend one or two group sessions to start. *Then see a coach privately for one or two sessions*, develop tentative job targets, and return to the group. You may work with your small-group coach or contact us through our website or by calling 1-800-538-6645 (or 212-286-4500 in New York) for referral to a private coach.

How Long Will It Take Me to Get a Job?

Although our members tend to be from fields or industries where they expect to have difficult searches, the average person who attends regularly finds a new position within 10 sessions. Some take less time and others take more. During the worst recessions, our average professional, manager and executive still found employment in an average of 16.4 weeks (as opposed to the 35 weeks that the population as a whole was taking—assuming they didn't give up on searching).

One thing we know for sure: **Research shows that those who regularly attend the small-group strategy sessions get more satisfying jobs faster and at higher rates of pay than those who search on their own, only work privately with a career coach, or simply take a course**. This makes sense. If a person comes only when they think they have a problem, they are usually wrong. They probably had a problem a few weeks ago but didn't realize it. Or the problem may be different from the one they thought they

had. Those who come regularly benefit from the observations others make about their searches. Problems are solved before they become severe or are prevented altogether.

Those who attend regularly also learn a lot by paying attention and helping others in the group. This *secondhand* learning can shorten your search by weeks. When you hear the problems of others who are ahead of you in the search, you can avoid them completely. People in your group will come to know you and will point out subtleties you may not have noticed that interviewers will never tell you.

Will I Be with Others from My Field/ Industry?

Probably not, but it's not that important. If you are a salesperson, for example, would you want to be with seven other salespeople? Probably not. You will learn a lot and have a much more creative search if you are in a group of people who are in your general salary range but not exactly like you. Our clients are from virtually every field and industry. The *process* is what will help you.

We've been doing this since 1978 and understand your needs. That's why the mix we provide is the best you can get.

Career Coaching Firms Charge $4,000-$6,000 Up Front. How Can You Charge Such a Small Fee?

1. We have no advertising costs, because 90 percent of those who attend have been referred by other members or an association you belong to. (Be sure to ask your alumni or trade association to contact us for a special rate for its members.).

   A hefty up-front fee would bind you to us, but we have been more successful by treating people ethically and having them pretty much *pay as they go*.

   We need a certain number of people to

cover expenses. When lots of people get jobs quickly and leave us, we could go into the red. But as long as members refer others, we will continue to provide this service at a fair price.

2. We focus strictly on *job-search strategy,* and encourage our clients to attend free support groups if they need emotional support. We focus on getting *jobs that fit in with your career goals,* and that reduces the time clients spend with us and the amount they pay.

3. We attract the best coaches, and our clients make more progress per session than they would elsewhere, which also reduces their costs.

4. We have expert administrators and a sophisticated computer system that reduces our overhead and increases our ability to track your progress.

May I Change Coaches?

Yes. Great care is taken in assigning you to your initial coach. However, if you want to change once for any reason, you may do it. We don't encourage group hopping: It is better for you to stick with a group so that everyone gets to know you. On the other hand, we want you to feel comfortable. So if you tell us you prefer a different group, you will be transferred immediately.

What If I Have a Quick Question Outside of the Group Session?

Some people prefer to see their group coach privately. Others prefer to meet with a different coach to get another point of view. Whatever you decide, remember that the group fee does not cover coaching time outside the group session. Therefore, if you wanted to speak with a coach between sessions—even for *quick questions*—you would normally meet with the coach first for a private session so he or she can get to know you better. *Easy, quick questions* are usually more complicated than they appear. After your first private session, some coaches will allow you to pay in advance for one hour of coaching time, which you

can then use for quick questions by phone (usually a 15-minute minimum is charged). Since each coach has an individual way of operating, find out how the coach arranges these things.

What If I Want to Start My Own Business?

The process of becoming a consultant is essentially the same as job hunting and lots of consultants attend Five O'Clock Club meetings. However, if you want to buy a franchise or existing business or start a growth business, you should see a private coach. Regardless of the kind of business you want to have, be sure to read our book: *Your Great Business Idea: The Truth About Making It Happen.*

How Can I Be Sure That The Five O'Clock Club Small-Group Sessions Will Be Right for Me?

Before you actually participate in any of the small-group sessions, you can get an idea of the quality of our service by listening to all 16 audio CDs that you purchased. If you are dissatisfied with the CDs for any reason, return the package within 30 days for a full refund.

Whatever you decide, just remember: **Research shows that those who *regularly* attend the small-group strategy sessions get more satisfying jobs faster and at higher rates of pay than those who search on their own, *only* work privately with a career coach, or simply take a course.** If you get a job just one or two weeks faster because of this program, it will have more than paid for itself. And you may transfer unused sessions to anyone you choose. However, the person you choose must be or become a member.

The Five O'Clock Club's Job-Search Buddy System

Do you wish you had someone to talk to —fairly often and informally—about the little things? "Here's what I'm planning to do today in my search? What are *you* planning to do? Let's talk tomorrow to make sure we've done it." You and your job-search buddy could keep each other positive and on track, and encourage each other to do what you told your small group you were going to do: Make that call, send out those letters, write that follow-up proposal, focus on the most important things that should be done—rather than (for example) spending endless hours responding to job postings on the Web.

With your buddy, practice your Two-Minute Pitch, get ready for interviews, bounce ideas off each other. Some job-search buddies talk every day. Some talk a few times a week. Most of the conversation is by phone and e-mail.

Sometimes, people match themselves up as buddies. Just pick someone you get along with in your small group. Sometimes, your coach can match you up. However you do it, stay away from negative people who talk about how bad it is out there. They will drag you down.

The small group changes over time: people get jobs; new people come in. If you lose one buddy who got a job, get another buddy.

Your buddy does not have to be in your field or industry. In fact, being in the same field or industry could keep you focused on the industry rather than on the *process*. But you *do* have to get along! The relationship may last only a month or two, or go on for years. Some buddies become friends.

Of course, you should see your Five O'Clock Club career coach *privately* for résumé review, target development, salary negotiation, and job interview follow-up. It's usually best to get professional coaching advice for these areas. And nothing beats the weekly small-group strategy sessions for making progress in the job search itself. Those who regularly attended the small group got jobs in half the time.

Using The Five O'Clock Club
From the Comfort of Your Home

A man who found the Five O'Clock Club books at his library near Denver calls to ask if there is a local branch. A woman in Seattle who bought the books on Amazon wants to know if she can attend our weekly seminars. A man in Phoenix who received *Targeting a Great Career* from his daughter also wants to attend. And an HR executive wants to know whether we can help her employees in an office closing in Miami.

In our early years, the reach of The Five O'Clock Club—because of the popular Club books—exceeded its presence, but systems have been in place for the past ten years to allow people anywhere to access the Club seminars and coaching by phone and computer.

The Launch of the Insider Groups

Teleconferencing has long come into its own, and for ten years we have offered weekly Club meetings on a nationwide basis. Our Insider Groups (via teleconference) were launched in February 2000, and the first teleconference group included executives from California, North Dakota and Maryland. Prior to the conference call, each person listens to the topic of the week on his or her audio CD or reads the topic in the books. They can listen to the "topic of the week" at their leisure and are then ready for the weekly teleconference.

Following the conference, participants can stay on the line and chat with each other—and most do. In addition, they can browse our LinkedIn Group and network with the almost 1,000 Five O'Clock Clubbers who participate. They can "reply all" to the emails sent to members of their small group and stay in touch with each other that way. And they can talk daily to their Job-Search Buddies, offering advice and encouragement that follow The Five O'Clock Club's

methodology. What's more, they can talk to their private coach about a specific interview coming up, get advice on turning a job interview into an offer, or get help negotiating their compensation.

Website as a Public Service

Anyone can wander through the various areas of www.FiveOClockClub.com and tap into vast amounts of useful information—without being a member! For example, click on How To Get a Job to find a menu of 13 substantive articles that represent the heart of the Five O'Clock Club methodology. These articles cover job targeting, interviewing and salary negotiations—and how to start out on the right foot on your new job. There is also a free mini-course to help you assess the **quality** of your job search. Sure, you're working hard, but are you doing the right things?

Remember, The Five O'Clock Club is the ONLY organization devoted to conducting research on behalf of job hunters. We are the only organization with a research-based methodology for you to use rather than the vanilla job-search techniques that everyone else uses. We are the ONLY organization that has books and audios that document the methodology you should use in your job search.

In the Free Articles section you can access hundreds of articles that have appeared in our monthly magazine, *The Five O'Clock News*.

The Weekly Small-Group Strategy Sessions

You are assigned to a small group of your peers (same salary level). Each session is moderated by a certified Five O'Clock Club coach, lasts for an hour, and is guided by the same principles and techniques presented in our books and audios. These are not general discussions on job-search topics; each session moves you forward in your search by helping you to identify steps to take during the coming week. You leave the session with an assignment and proactive coaching on how to do it.

"Our group coach expects us to recap what we've done and we get an assignment. The momentum you get with The Five O'Clock Club makes the big difference," reports one Clubber.

One California Insider member said, "It's really been neat. I've been involved with other job-hunting groups, but they don't have the full breadth of job-search regimen that you have with The Five O'Clock Club. Reading the books and listening to the audios ahead of time helps keep us focused. Our coach expects us to recap what we've done and we get an assignment. The momentum you get with The Five O'Clock Club makes the big difference. I've stagnated with other groups." And he finds that there is a benefit in working with a group whose members are in California, Florida, Massachusetts and New Jersey. "It gives us a different perspective on issues. We have great rapport on the phone and we email and call each other after the session is over."

Reach Out and Touch Someone

You can get assigned to a Five O'Clock Club coach for private one-on-one coaching. Most of these match-ups result in telephone sessions—the coach may be in Maryland or Chicago, the client in California or Maine. Many clients want an hour or two of private coaching to help them determine goals and targets. You can find a sampling of coach bios and photos on our website.

Our coaches are trained in The Five O'Clock Club method and are committed to our ethical standards. At other such firms, a newly hired coach with experience is up and running that day. At The Five O'Clock Club, a coach with experience must go through our four-month certification program, un-learn what they thought they knew about job search, and master the methodology.

Seasoned career coaches are attracted to our certification program. Candidates for the Guild must study our 250-page training manual and pass exams to be admitted; they must do two "before" and "after" résumés so they don't give you a cookie-cutter résumé; they must observe 10 small-group coaching sessions and write an essay on what they have learned; and they must do an audition on some aspect of The Five O'Clock Club methodology so they can again prove that they have mastered it. With some 50 coaches in training, in addition to our certified coaches, we are in a position to meet the volume of coaching requests that may come our way in the future.

Be sure to tell your friends about us, and tell your employer that you want The Five O'Clock Club as your outplacement provider!

When Your Employer Pays

Does your employer care about you and others whom they ask to leave the organization? If so, ask them to consider The Five O'Clock Club for your outplacement help. The Five O'Clock Club puts you and your job search first, offering a career-coaching program of the highest quality at the lowest possible price to your employer.

Over 25 Years of Research

The Five O'Clock Club was started in 1978 as a research-based organization. Job hunters tried various techniques and reported their results back to the group. We developed a variety of guidelines so job hunters could choose the techniques best for them.

The methodology was tested and refined on professionals, managers, and executives (and those aspiring to be) from all occupations. Annual salaries ranged from $30,000 to $400,000; 50 percent were employed and 50 percent were unemployed.

Since its beginning, The Five O'Clock Club has tracked trends. Over time, our advice has changed as the job market has changed. What worked in the past is insufficient for today's job market. Today's Five O'Clock Club promotes all our relevant original strategies—and so much more.

As an employee-advocacy organization, The Five O'Clock Club focuses on providing the services and information that the job hunter needs most.

Get the Help You Need Most: 100 Percent Coaching

There's a myth in outplacement circles that a terminated employee just needs a desk, a phone, and minimal career coaching. The new trend is to provide job hunters with databases of fake job openings and other online help and call it "outplacement." The price is ridiculously low, but then an employer can claim that it is providing outplacement to all employees.

Our experience clearly shows that down-sized workers need qualified, reliable coaching more than anything else. Most traditional outplacement packages last only 3 months. The average executive gets office space and only 5 hours of career coaching during this time. Yet the service job hunters need most is the career coaching itself—not a desk and a phone.

Most professionals, managers, and executives are right in the thick of negotiations with prospective employers at the 3-month mark. Yet that is precisely when traditional outplacement ends, leaving job hunters stranded and sometimes ruining deals.

It is astonishing how often job hunters and employers alike are impressed by the databases of job postings claimed by outplacement firms. Yet only 10 percent of all jobs are filled through ads and another 10 percent are filled through search firms. Instead, direct contact and networking—done The Five O'Clock Club way—are more effective for most searches.

For the latest information on our
outplacement services, go to our
website, www.fiveoclockclub.com, and
look in both the "For Employers"
and "For Employees" sections.

You Get a Safety Net

Imagine getting a package that protects you for a full year. Imagine knowing you can come back if your new job doesn't work out—even months later. Imagine trying consulting work if you like. If you later decide it's not for you, you can come back to The Five O'Clock Club.

We can offer you a safety net of one full year's career coaching because our method is so effective that few people actually need more than 10 weeks in our proven program. But you're protected for a year.

You'll Job Search with Those Who Are Employed—How Novel!

Let's face it. It can be depressing to spend your days at an outplacement firm where everyone is unemployed. At The Five O'Clock Club, half the attendees are working, and this makes the atmosphere cheerier and helps to move your search along.

What's more, you'll be in a small group of your peers, all of whom are using The Five O'Clock Club method. Our research proves that those who attend the small group regularly and use The Five O'Clock Club methods get jobs faster and at higher rates of pay than those who only work privately with a career coach throughout their searches.

So Many Poor Attempts

Nothing is sadder than meeting someone who has already been getting job-search help, but the wrong kind. They've learned the traditional techniques that are no longer effective. Most have poor résumés and inappropriate targets and don't know how to turn job interviews into offers.

You'll Get Quite a Package

You'll get up to 14 hours (or more, depending on the package) of private coaching—well in excess of what you would get at a traditional outplacement firm. You may even want to use a few hours after you start your new job.

And you get one full year of weekly small-group career coaching. In addition, you get books, audio CDs, and other helpful materials.

To Get Started

The day your human resources manager calls us authorizing Five O'Clock Club outplacement, we will immediately ship you the books, CDs, and other materials and assign you to a private coach and a small group.

Then we'll monitor your search. Frankly, we care about you more than we care about your employer. And since your employer cares about you, they're glad we feel this way—because they know we'll take care of you.

What They Say about Us

The Five O'Clock Club product is much better, far more useful than my outplacement package.
SENIOR EXECUTIVE AND FIVE O'CLOCK CLUB MEMBER

The Club kept the juices flowing. You're told what to do, what not to do. There were fresh ideas. I went through an outplacement service that, frankly, did not help. If they had done as much as the Five O'Clock Club did, I would have landed sooner.
ANOTHER MEMBER

When Your *Employer* Pays for The Five O'Clock Club, *You* Get:

- **Up to 14 hours (or more, depending on the package) of guaranteed private career coaching** to determine a career direction, develop a résumé, plan salary negotiations, etc. In fact, if you need a second opinion during your search, we can arrange that too.
- **ONE YEAR of weekly small-group strategy sessions via teleconference** (average about 5 or 6 participants in a group) headed by a senior Five O'Clock Club career consultant. That way, if you lose your next job, you can come back. Or if you want to try consulting work and then decide you don't like it, **you can come back**.
- **LIFETIME membership** in The Five O'Clock Club: Beginners Kit and two-year subscription to The Five O'Clock News.
- **The complete set of our four books** for professionals, managers, and executives who are in job search.
- **A boxed set of 16 audio CDs** of Five O'Clock Club presentations.

COMPARISON OF EMPLOYER-PAID PACKAGES

Typical Package	Traditional Outplacement	The Five O'Clock Club
Who is the client?	The organization	Job hunters. We are employee advocates. We always do what is in the best interest of job hunters.
The clintele	All are unemployed	Half of our attendees are unemployed; half are employed. There is an upbeat atmosphere; networkng is enhanced.
Length/type of service	3 months, primarily office space	1 year, exclusively career coaching
Service ends	After 3 months—or before if the client lands a job or consulting assignment.	After 1 full year, no matter what. You can return if you lose your next job, if your assignment ends, or if you need advice after starting your new job.
Small group coaching	Sporatic for 3 months Coach varies	Every week for up to 1 year; same coach
Private coaching	5 hours on average	Up to 14 hours guaranteed (depending on level of service purchased)
Support materials	Generic manual; web-based info	• 4 textbooks based on over 25 yrs. of job-search research • 16 40-minute lectures on audio CDs • Beginners Kit of search information • LIFETIME subscription to the Five)'Clock Club magazine, devoted to career-management articles
Facilities	Cubicle, phone, computer access	None; use home phone and computer

The Way We Are

*The Five O'Clock Club means sobriety, refinement
of thought and speech, good breeding
and good order. To this, much of its success is due.
The Five O'Clock Club is easy-going and
unconventional. A sense of propriety, rather
than rules of order, governs its meetings.*

J. HAMPTON MOORE, *HISTORY OF THE FIVE O'CLOCK CLUB*
(WRITTEN IN THE 1890S)

Just like the members of the original Five O'Clock Club, today's members want an ongoing relationship. George Vaillant, in his seminal work on successful people, found that "what makes or breaks our luck seems to be... our sustained relationships with other people." (George E. Vaillant, *Adaptation to Life,* Harvard University Press, 1995)

Five O'Clock Club members know that much of the program's benefit comes from simply showing up. Showing up will encourage you to do what you need to do when you are not here. And over the course of several weeks, certain things will become evident that are not evident now.

Five O'Clock Club members learn from each other: The group leader is not the only one with answers. The leader brings factual information to the meetings and keeps the discussion in line. But the answers to some problems may lie within you or with others in the group.

Five O'Clock Club members encourage each other. They listen, see similarities with their own situations, and learn from that. And they listen to see how they may help others. You may come across information or a contact that could help someone else in the group. Passing on that information is what we're all about.

If you are a new member here, listen to others to learn the process. And read the books and listen to the presentations so you will know the basics that others already know. When everyone understands the basics, this keeps the meetings on a high level, interesting, and helpful to everyone.

Five O'Clock Club members are in this together, but they know that ultimately they are each responsible for solving their own problems with God's help. Take the time to learn the process, and you will become better at analyzing your own situation, as well as the situations of others. You will be learning a method that will serve you the rest of your life, and in areas of your life apart from your career.

Five O'Clock Club members are kind to each other. They control their frustrations—because venting helps no one. Because many may be stressed, be kind and go the extra length to keep this place calm and happy. It is your respite from the world outside and a place for you to find comfort and FUN. Relax and enjoy yourself, learn what you can, and help where you can. And have a ball doing it.

---

*There arises from the hearts of busy [people] a love
of variety, a yearning for relaxation of thought
as well as of body, and a craving for a
generous and spontaneous fraternity.*

J. HAMPTON MOORE, *HISTORY OF THE FIVE O'CLOCK CLUB*

Lexicon Used at The Five O'Clock Club

The LEXICON — to help you talk about your search

The Five O'Clock Club lexicon is a shorthand — a way to quickly analyze your search and to clearly speak about your search to other Five O'Clock Clubbers. We all speak the same language so we can help each other. Our counselors across the country also speak the same language.

Whether you are in a group or working privately with a Five O'Clock Club career counselor, you can learn our language and analyze your search. After you read the summary below, study our books "as if your were in graduate school." You will learn to better express where you are in your job search, and be better able to figure out what to do next.

The average person who attends The Five O'Clock Club regularly has a new job within just ten weekly sessions–even those who have been unemployed up to two years. Follow our method and you will increase your chances of getting a better job faster.

The following questions will help you to pinpoint what is wrong with your search.

I. Overview and Assessment

How many hours a week are you spending on your search?

Only two or three hours a week, you say? The good news is that you have not yet begun to search. That's why you're making so little progress. To develop momentum in your search, spend 35 hours a week on a full-time search; if you are employed, spend 15 hours a week for a solid, part-time search.

What are your job targets?

If your job targets are wrong, everything is wrong. A target includes:

- industry or organization size,
- the position you want in that industry, and
- your targeted geographic area.

For example, let's say you want to target the health care industry. That's not a good target. It needs to be better defined. For example, perhaps you would consider hospitals. In the metropolitan New York area, for example, there are 80 hospitals. Let's say you're a marketing person, and you would consider doing marketing in a hospital in the NY area. That's one target: Hospitals is the industry, marketing is the position, and NY area is the geographic area. You could also target HMO's. Let's say there are 15 HMO's that you consider appropriate in the NY area. You could do marketing for them. That's a second target. You could also work for a consulting firm in the NY area that does health-care consulting. That's your third target.

But let's say you and your spouse have always loved Phoenix. You think you may like to investigate all three of those industries in the Phoenix area. That's three more targets. The reason you divide your search into targets is so you can have control over it, and tell what's working and what isn't. You make a list of all of the organizations in each of your targets–we call that your "Targeting Map." Then you find out the names of the people you need to contact in each of those targets–the hiring managers of the departments or divisions you are interested in.

That's the start of an organized search. At the very beginning of your search, you can assess how good your targets are and whether you stand a chance getting a job within a reasonable timeframe. Take a look at "Measuring Your Job Targets" in our books.

How does your résumé position you?

The average résumé is looked at for only ten seconds–regardless of length. When someone looks at your résumé, will they pick up the most important information that you want them to know about you? The summary and body should make you look appropriate to your target. We recommend that the first line of your summary tell the reader exactly how they should see you, e.g., as an "Accounting Manager" or whatever. They will want to stereotype you anyway, so why not help them see you the way you want to be seen?

The second line should differentiate you from your competition: How are you different from all of those other Accounting Managers out there? Your second line could say, for example, "Expert in Cost Accounting."

That is followed by three or four bulleted accomplishments–the most important things you want them to know about you. That way, if they spend only 10 seconds on your résumé, they will see what you want them to see. For the complete Five O'Clock Club approach, see our Résumé book. It contains summaries related to over 100 industries and professions.

What are your back-up targets?

Decide at the beginning of the search before you start your first campaign. Then you won't get stuck later when things seem hopeless.

Have you done the Assessment?

If you have no specific targets, you cannot have a targeted search. Do the Assessment exercises in our books. You could see a counselor privately for two or three sessions to determine possible job targets. When a person joins the Club, we want them to do the exercises even if they are perfectly clear about what they want to do next. Doing the assessment helps a person to do better in interviews and helps them to have a better resume. Do not skip the assessment, especially the Seven Stories Exercise and the Forty-Year Vision.

II. Getting Interviews

How large is your target area (e.g., 30 companies)?
How many of them have you contacted?

When you know your targets, you can research them and come up with a list of all of the companies in your target areas. Figure out how large your target market is. If you have contacted only a few companies in your target area, contact the rest. If you haven't contacted any, contact them all. That's a thorough–and fast–search.

How can you get (more) leads?

You will not get a job through search firms, ads, networking or direct contact. Those are techniques for getting interviews–job leads. Use the right terminology, especially when speaking to someone who has already landed a job. Do not say: how did you get the job, if you really want to know where did you get the lead for that job. In our books, you will find cover letters and approaches for each of these techniques. A good search does not rely on just one technique. We want our members to consider all four techniques for getting interviews in your target markets.

Do you have 6 to 10 things in the works?

When a job hunter is going after only one position—and hoping they will get an offer—that is a weak search. Our research shows that a good job hunter has 6 to 10 things in the works at all times. This is because five will fall away through no fault of your own: Maybe the company decides to hire a finance person instead of a marketing person, or maybe they decide to hire their cousin!

Do not put all of your eggs in one basket. When one offer falls through, you will have lost months in your search because you have to gear up all over again. To avoid losing momentum, make sure you have 6 to 10 things in the works at all times—through search firms, ads, networking or direct contact. It's not as hard as it sounds. Just follow our approach.

If you have 6 to 10 things going at once, you are more likely to turn the job you want into an offer because you will seem more valuable. Don't go after only one job.

How's your Two-Minute Pitch? (Who shall we pretend we are?)

A Two-Minute Pitch is the answer to the question, "So, tell me about yourself." Practice a tailored Two-Minute Pitch. Tell the group—or a friend—the job title and industry of the pretend hiring manager. You will be surprised how good the group is at critiquing pitches. Do it a few weeks in a row until you have a smooth presentation.

Practice it again after you have been in search a while, or after you change targets. Make sure your pitch separates you from your competition.

You seem to be in Stage One (or Stage Two or Stage Three) of your search.

Know where you are in the process. If you are in Stage One—making initial contacts you will recontact later—make lots of contacts so at least 6 to 10 will move to Stage Two: the right people at the right levels in the right companies. You will

get the best job offers in Stage Three—talking to 6 to 10 people on an ongoing basis about real jobs or the possibility of creating a job.

Are you seen as insider or outsider?

Are people saying: "I wish I had an opening for someone like you." You are doing well in meetings. If your target is good, it's only a matter of time.

III. Turning Interviews into Offers

Want to go through the Brick Wall?

The brainiest part of the process is turning your job interview into an offer. First, make sure you want the job. If you do not want the job, perhaps you want an offer, if only for practice. If you are not willing to go for it, the group's suggestions will not work.

Who are your likely competitors and how can you kill them off?

"Outshine and outlast your competition" does not mean dirty tricks, but reminds you that you have competitors. You will not get a job simply because "they liked you". The issues are deeper. Ask: Where are you in the hiring process? What kind of person would be your ideal candidate?

What are your next steps?

The "next step" means: what are you planning to do if the hiring manager doesn't call by a certain date, or what are you planning to do to assure the hiring manager does call you.

Can you prove you can do the job?

Most job hunters take the "Trust Me" approach. Instead, prove to them that you can do the job, often by doing additional research or by writing a "proposal" of how you would handle the job.

Which job positions you best for the long run? Which job is the best fit?

Don't decide only on salary. Since the average person has been in his or her job only four years, you will have another job after this. See which job looks best on your resume, and makes you a stronger candidate next time. Take the job that positions you best for the long run.

In addition, find a fit for your personality. If you don't "fit," it is unlikely you will do well there. The group can give feedback on which job is best for you.

> "Believe me, with self-examination and a lot of hard work with our coaches, you can find the job... you can have the career... you can live the life you've always wanted!"
>
> **Sincerely,**
> **Kate Wendleton**

Membership

As a member of The Five O'Clock Club, you get:

- A LIFETIME subscription to The Five O'Clock News—10 issues a year filled with information on career development and job-search techniques, focusing on the experiences of real people.
- LIFETIME access to the Members Only section of our website containing, for example, all of our basic worksheets, our 111-page bibliography of research resources, and many other items.
- Access to reasonably priced weekly seminars featuring individualized attention to your specific needs in small groups supervised by our senior coaches.

- Access to one-on-one coaching to help you answer specific questions, solve current job problems, prepare your résumé, or take an in-depth look at your career path. You choose the coach and pay the coach directly.
- An attractive Beginners Kit containing information based on over 25 years of research on who gets jobs... and why... that will enable you to improve your job-search techniques—immediately!
- The opportunity to exchange ideas and experiences with other job searchers and career changers.

All that access, all that information, all that expertise for the one-time membership fee of only $49, plus seminar fees.

How to become a member— by mail or Email:

Send your name, address, phone number, how you heard about us, and your check for $49 (made payable to "The Five O'Clock Club") to our headquarters address: The Five O'Clock Club, 300 East 40th Street, New York, NY 10016, or sign up at www.fiveoclockclub.com. Or call us at 1-800-538-6645.

We will immediately mail you a Five O'Clock Club Membership Card, the Beginners Kit, and information on our seminars followed by our magazine. Then, call 1-800-538-6645 (or 212-286-4500 in New York) or email us (at info@ fiveoclockclub.com) to:

- reserve a space for the first time you plan to attend, or
- be matched with a Five O'Clock Club coach.

Membership Application

The Five O'Clock Club

☐ **Yes! I want to become a member!**

I want access to the most effective methods for finding jobs, as well as for developing and managing my career.

I enclose my check for $49 for a LIFETIME membership, payable to The Five O'Clock Club. I will receive a Beginners Kit, a LIFETIME subscription to *The Five O'Clock News*, LIFETIME access to the Members Only area on our website, and a network of career coaches. Reasonably priced weekly small-group strategy sessions via teleconference are held every evening across the country.

Name:_____

Street Address:_____

City:_____State:_____Zip Code:_____

Work phone: (_____)_____

Home phone: (_____)_____

Email:_____

Date:_____

How I heard about the Club:_____

MASTERING THE JOB INTERVIEW

The following *optional* information is for statistical purposes. Thanks for your help.

Salary range:

☐ under $30,000   ☐ $30,000-$49,999   ☐ $50,000-$74,999

☐ $75,000-$99,999   ☐ $100,000-$125,000   ☐ over $125,000

Age: ☐ 20-29   ☐ 30-39   ☐ 40-49   ☐ 50+

Gender: ☐ Male ☐ Female

Current or most recent position/title: _____

Please send to:
Membership Director,
The Five O'Clock Club Headquarters
300 East 40th St.,
New York, NY 10016

The original Five O'Clock Club® was formed in Philadelphia in 1893. It was made up of the leaders of the day who shared their experiences "in a setting of fellowship and good humor.

Index

About the Author

Kate Wendleton is a nationally recognized authority on career development. She founded The Five O'Clock Club in 1978 and developed its methodology to help job hunters, career changers and employees of all levels, making The Five O'Clock Club the only organization to conduct ongoing research on behalf of employees and job hunters.

Kate was a nationally syndicated columnist for eight years and a speaker on career development, having appeared on the *Today Show*, CNN, CNBC, Larry King, National Public Radio and CBS, and in *The Economist, The New York Times, The Chicago Tribune, The Wall Street Journal, Fortune* magazine, *Business Week* and other national media.

For the past two years, Kate has spent every Saturday with young adults who have aged out of foster care, trying to give them the opportunity to make the most of their lives. This organization, Remington Achievers, is a not-for-profit arm of The Five O'Clock Club.

Kate also founded Workforce America, a not-for-profit Affiliate of The Five O'Clock Club, that served adults in Harlem who were not yet in the professional or managerial ranks. For ten years, Workforce America helped each person move into better-paying, higher-level positions as each improved in educational level and work experience.

Kate founded, and directed for seven years, The Career Center at The New School for Social Research in New York. She also advises major corporations about employee career-development programs.

A former CFO of two small companies, she has twenty years of business-management experience in both manufacturing and service businesses.

Kate attended Chestnut Hill College in Philadelphia and received her MBA from Drexel University. She is a popular speaker with groups that include associations, corporations, and colleges.

While living in Philadelphia, Kate did long-term volunteer work for the Philadelphia Museum of Art, the Walnut Street Theatre Art Gallery, United Way, and the YMCA. Kate currently lives in Manhattan with her husband, and she has a number of children, including young men who have aged out of foster care.

Kate is the author of The Five O'Clock Club's five-part career-development and job-hunting series for professionals, managers and executives as well as *Your Great Business Idea: The Truth About Making It Happen, WorkSmarts* (co-editor) and The Five O'Clock Club's boxed set of sixteen lectures on audio CDs as well as via downloads.

About The Five O'Clock Club and the "Fruytagie" Canvas

Five O'Clock Club members are special. We attract upbeat, ambitious, dynamic, intelligent people—and that makes it fun for all of us. Most of our members are professionals, managers, executives, consultants, and freelancers. We also include recent college graduates and those aiming to get into the professional ranks, as well as people in their 40s, 50s, and even 60s. Most members' salaries range from $30,000 to $400,000 (one-half of our members earn in excess of $100,000 a year). In addition to attending the weekly small-group strategy sessions at the Club, The Five O'Clock Club Book Series contains all of our methodologies—and our spirit.

The Philosophy of The Five O'Clock Club

The "Fruytagie" Canvas by Patricia Kelly, depicted here, symbolizes our philosophy. The original is actually 52.5 by 69 inches. It is reminiscent of popular 16th century Dutch "fruytagie," or fruit tapestries, which depicted abundance and prosperity.

I was attracted to this piece because it seemed to fit the spirit of our people at The Five O'Clock Club. This was confirmed when the artist, who was not aware of what I did for a living, added these words to the canvas: "The garden is abundant, prosperous and magical." Later, it took me only 10 minutes to write the blank verse "The Garden of Life," because it came from my heart. The verse reflects our philosophy and describes the kind of people who are members of the Club.

I'm always inspired by Five O'Clock Clubbers. They show others the way through their quiet behavior... their kindness... their generosity... their hard work... under God's care.

We share what we have with others. We are in this lush, exciting place together—with our brothers and sisters—and reach out for harmony. The garden is abundant. The job market is exciting. And Five O'Clock Clubbers believe that there is enough for everyone.

About the Artist's Method

To create her tapestry-like art, Kelly developed a unique style of stenciling. She hand-draws and hand-cuts each stencil, both in the negative and positive for each image. Her elaborate technique also includes a lengthy multi-layering process incorporating Dutch metal leaves and gilding, numerous transparent glazes, paints, and wax pencils.

Kelly also paints the back side of the canvas using multiple washes of reds, violets, and golds. She uses this technique to create a heavy vibration of color, which in turn reflects the color onto the surface of the wall against which the canvas hangs.

The canvas is suspended by a heavy braided silk cord threaded into large brass grommets inserted along the top. Like a tapestry, the hemmed canvas is attached to a gold-gilded dowel with finials. The entire work is hung from a sculpted wall ornament.

Our staff is inspired every day by the members of The Five O'Clock Club, and our mantra, which is to "always do what is in the best interests of the job hunter." We all work hard—and have FUN! The garden is abundant—with enough for everyone.

We wish you lots of success in your career. We—and your fellow members of The Five O'Clock Club—will work with you on it.

—Kate Wendleton, President

The original Five O'Clock Club was formed in Philadelphia in 1883. It was made up of the leaders of the day, who shared their experiences "in a spirit of fellowship and good humor."

 THE GARDEN OF LIFE IS abundant, prosperous and magical. ❦ In this garden, there is enough for everyone. ❦ Share the fruit and the knowledge ❦ Our brothers and we are in this lush, exciting place together. ❦ Let's show others the way. ❦ Kindness. Generosity. ❦ Hard work. ❦ God's care.

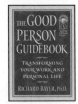